DICTIONARY OF SUBJECT TITLES

R.L.N. Shastri

KALPAZ PUBLICATIONS
DELHI–110 052

Dictionary of Subject Titles

Rs. 590

ISBN: 81-7835-258-3

Published in 2004 in India by
Kalpaz Publications
C–30, Satyawati Nagar
Delhi–110 052
E-mail: Kalpaz@hotmail.com

Lasertypesetting by: Varsha Graphics, Delhi
Printed at: Mehra Offset Printers, New Delhi

Preface

As a result of the rapid growth of knowledge in various fields particularly during the last century and its continuing exponential growth, an unprecedented diversification of subjects and emergence of new subjects are taking place before our eyes. We are all bewildered in a way by all that is happening. We are also feeling the impact of this phenomenon which is often beneficial to us. There is a need for many to know at least some of the subjects that they come across in their daily activities. It is thought that it will serve a useful purpose if as many subject names as possible are assembled in one place with their definitions and brief explanations. We are aware that this dictionary is by no means complete or exhaustive and continuing efforts will be made to compile more subject names and add them in future editions.

It is hoped that this dictionary will be useful as a reference work for students, teachers, researchers, librarians, those in public services and administration and the general reading public. Any valid suggestions for improvement of the book are welcome from the users and will be incorporated in future editions.

The author wishes to thanks all those who encouraged him in his efforts and lent a helping hand. My special thanks are due to my daughter Smt. R. Durga, M.Com., M.A., M.Ed., PGT (Commerce), Kendriya Vidyalaya, Indian Institute of Science, Bangalore for her assistance in subjects concerned with Commerce, Business Studies, Management and Education. I am particularly grateful to Shri Amit Garg, Director Publications, Gyan Books (P) Ltd. for the keen interest he has taken in the publication of this book and for his useful suggestions.

R.L.N. Shastri

Introduction

Growth of Knowledge

Primitive man gained his knowledge from the nature and object around him. Rocks, stones, plants, animals, the sky, sun, moon, stars, eclipses, clouds, hills, rivers, oceans and whatever he could see with his eyes attracted his attention. Slowly he discovered for himself how to make use of the objects around him for his needs. Hunters and gatherers were making efforts to find food, shelter and covering for the body. Some found their way into the caves to escape from the ravages of climate and weather.

Ancient scriptures like the Vedas were repositories of knowledge. The apothecaries, herbalists, alchemists and the like have made their contributions of those days. The sages and philosophers have also helped humanity to understand the nature of the universe. In the earlier eras knowledge was not divided into compartments. Philosophers and savants like Aristotle made their contributions in science as well as other areas. Science in those days was known as natural philosophy. For example, the journals like Philosophical Transactions of the Royal Society of London, contain many valuable contributions in science. The Cambridge Philosophical Society publishes Standard Science Journals like "Biological Reviews".

With the multidimensional growth of knowledge in recent centuries, it has become necessary to compartmentalise it into broad divisions and subdivisions like Arts, Humanities, Social Sciences Natural Science etc. And sciences were grouped as natural sciences and physical sciences. Further subdivisions like earth sciences, life sciences, physical sciences, environmental sciences, management sciences, behavioural sciences have emerged. Often the boundaries and demarcations of these groupings were arbitrary and not so clear cut and overlapping is also inevitable.

Explosion of Knowledge

The phenomenal explosion of knowledge in almost all fields

during the latter half of the 20th century has been unparalleled in the whole history of humanity. The advancement of concepts, techniques and technologies has led to the splitting of the traditional fields of study into branches. The growth of knowledge at an exponential rate is still continuing. Now we have many new sciences like space science, information science and technology, nuclear sciences, computer science, biotechnology, etc.

The universities and other educational and training institutions are offering many innovative courses tailored to the needs of the generation. Some are vocational courses while others are of academic interest. Sports science has become a highly sophisticated field. Many new vocations are opening up in response to the demands of the times.

In the course of my research for the present dictionary project started more than a decade ago, I came across a book entitled "Dictionary of Vocational Titles" published in U.S.A. several years ago. It is now available only in a few American Libraries and probably out of print. It contains details of about twenty thousand vocations including the educational requirements, nature of duties, scope of employment, emoluments etc. Since its publication many new vocations have come into existence. Of course, the objectives, scope and orientation, approach and content of that book are entirely different from the present dictionary and vast changes have taken place in all fields since its publication. The purpose of mentioning about the book here is only to point out the need for a book of that nature, although different in approach and content at the present juncture. The general public and the student population are really bewildered at the rapid proliferation of subjects taking place all around.

Inter Disciplinary and Multidisciplinary Approaches

While on the one hand traditional disciplines and fields of study are branching out into new vistas, leading to over specialisation particularly in the medical field, there is a growing realisation and recognition of the interaction and interdependence of disciplines and the need for interdisciplinary and multidisciplinary approaches in unravelling the secrets of nature and of human behaviour in social and economic fields. The need for conservation of natural resources and protection of ecological and environmental well-beings are receiving urgent attention.

Several fruitful and successful examples are inter and

multidisciplinary approaches can be cited. The infusion of digital technologies into the audio-visual fields, introduction of optical fibre technologies in the communication field, biomedical engineering, statistical, mathematical, quantitative and even psychological approaches in economics, biometrics and psychometrics in forensic sciences and human resources management, scientific investigations of meditation, yoga, alternative systems of medicine like Ayurveda etc., parapsychology and even some of the so-called occult sciences etc. are only a few of the many on-going studies.

Many spin-offs from space science and technology have benefitted mankind: satellites in remote sensing and communication and other applications in medical technology and other fields of everyday life. Advances in genomics, stem cell research, nano technology, material science etc. hold great promise for the future. All these developments and advances are of interest and have their direct impact on common people also apart from specialists and experts in their respective fields.

Dictionary of Subject Titles

Having this background in mind I have taken up the task of putting together the various subjects of study in one book and give their definitions and explanations. The title of the book may need some clarification because both the words subject and title have different connotations in different contexts. In the present dictionary the word subject is used in the sense of a branch of knowledge, a course of study and a discipline. Title simply means name. So the dictionary gives definitions of different fields and branches of study. Most of the subjects are offered as courses of study in educational institutions at different levels. Some are dealt with in research institutions, some are vocational courses.

Sometimes the same subject name is used in different connotation in different contexts. For example, the word law is used as a subject of study while it is generally understood as an enactment passed by the legislature. In the same way medicine is a general term comprising study of medical science as also as a specialization as opposed to surgery, there are also different usages of medicine as a branch of study like general medicine, internal medicine, tropical medicine, etc.

One of the terms most frequently used and often abused is

science. Some people refer to all subjects as sciences apart from the sciences in the strict sense, examples of such usage are political science, judicial science, etc. The word engineering is nowadays used not only in the traditional sense but also in other contexts like genetic engineering, crystal engineering, social engineering, etc. Similarly the word technology has become very handy in many contexts like medical technology, agricultural technology banking technology, etc.

Some techniques like endoscopy chromatography, tissue culture etc, have developed to such an extent that they have acquired the status of subjects in their own right. Sometimes specialization has gone to great heights. For example, paediatrics, radiology, nursing, etc. were at one time considered as single subject. Now we have paediatric oncology, paechiatric anaesthesiology, etc. Similarly, we come across neurological nursing, psychiatric nursing, home nursing, operation theatre nursing, etc. A subject like psychiatry has many specialisations like addiction psychiatry, forensic psychiatry, child psychiatry, geriatric psychiatry etc. in the fields of computer science and engineering and information technology, rapid developments are leading to the emergence of various new disciplines.

Such amazing advancements and the resulting diversification of subjects are really baffling people at all levels. Even experts and specialists in their respective fields have occasion and the need to know about other subjects. Students who are about to make career decisions would like to know which courses and subjects would interest them and suit them most. Media persons invariably face situations in which atleast a superficial acquaintance with some subjects becomes a necessity.

Questions about names of subjects and their content frequently appear in competitive examinations and quizes.

Librarians often face intriguing questions about the placement of a book in a subject-wise classification and in preparing subject indices. The task of locating a book in a large library is facilitated by a knowledge of the subject to which the particular book belongs. Researchers have many occasions to know at least the definitions of some subjects which they may come across in their search for relevant literature.

The plight of the general public is even more difficult in the present day maze of subjects all around them. They come across the names of some subjects in the media. When they go to a large multispeciality hospital they will be at a loss to know which specialist doctor to contact for their ailment; when they come across sign boards like radiation oncology, pulmonology or orthopaedics it may be intriguing for them to know what they mean. Science writers and communicators may also have occasions to know the nature of the newly emerging branches of knowledge.

Is there any one source that can possibly supply all this information needed by so many people? To the best of my knowledge I am not aware of any. General dictionaries or language dictionaries may give the names of a few better known subjects. Very large dictionaries may give the names of more subjects than the smaller versions, but one cannot expect to find the names of some of the newly emerging and less known subjects. Then there are so-called subject dictionaries. Each subject dictionary generally deals with the definitions of some of the important technical terms used in the concerned subject. Incidentally they may give the names of the main branches of that particular subject with which they are concerned about a few of the related subjects of interest to them. In this way such information about subjects is at best scattered and often not adequate enough. One may have to refer to the latest research publications to find the names and definitions of some of the newly emerging fields of knowledge. One cannot expect people to have the time, patience and competence to refer to such scattered and diverse sources in search of the name of a subject of passing interest to them. The present dictionary of subject titles aims and hopes to fulfil this need and facilitate easy reference to locate the subject of interest at one place.

A few years ago I compiled a dictionary (English to Telugu) of 2000 subject titles on my own initiative. It was published by the Telugu Academy, Hyderabad in the year 2000. Encouraged by the response to that dictionary, I continued my efforts in the direction and compiled the present dictionary containing 3600 subject titles in English. I am aware that it is by no means complete or exhaustive. I hope to continue my efforts in this direction and add more subject titles in future editions. For example, subjects like Glucobiology and psychological economics have come to my notice while the present dictionary is in the process of publication. I am sure this phenomenon will continue to impact us in future also.

A

ABACA : A hard fibre derived from *Musa textiles,* Also known as Manila hemp

ABNORMAL PSYCHOLOGY : Branch of Psychology pertaining to (1) Study of the psychological methods and behaviours of abnormal people and (2) Study of extreme psychological phenomena.

ABSOLUTE CHRONOLOGY : The process of dating an object in terms of years based on the study of gravel and other deposits wherein it is found particularly by the study of radio active minerals in igneous rocks.

ABSORPTIOMETRIC ANALYSIS : Chemical analysis of a gas or liquid by measurement of the peak electromagnetic wave lengths that are unique to a specific material or element.

ABSORPTION SPECTROSCOPY : The study of spectra obtained by the passage of radiant energy from a continuous source through a cooler, selective absorptive medium.

ABSTRACT ALEGEBRA : See pure Mathematics.

ACADEMIC LAWS : Laws pertaining to educational matters like, for example, educational institutions, conduct of examinations, admissions, conferring degrees etc.

ACARALOGY : A branch of zoology dealing with the mites and ticks.

ACCELERATOR : BASED NUCLEAR PAYSICS : Study of nuclear physics on the basis of accelerator experiments. Accelerator is one of the most complex machines and has wide range of applications.

ACCIDENT AND EMERGENCY RADIALOGY : Branch of medicine concerned with the use of radiological techniques and methods like X-rays, ECG etc., to accident victims and in emergency cases.

ACCOUNTANCY : The art of identifying, classifying, recording, summarising and interpreting business transactions of financial nature.

ACOUSTIC ENGINEERING : Branch of engineering concerned with the production, reproduction, magnification and recording of sound.

ACCOUSTIC PHONETICS : Study of the physical qualities of speech sounds.

ACOUSTICS : The science of sound including the cause, nature and phenomena of the vibrations of elastic bodies which affect the organ of hearing.

ACOUSTOOPTICS : The science that deals with the interactions between acoustic waves and light.

ACROBATICS : Art of performing spectacular gymnastic feats.

ACTING : Art of playing a character or role on the stage or in films or T.V. plays etc.

ACTINOCHEMISTRY : Branch of chemistry concerned with chemical reactions produced by light or other radiation.

ACTINOLOGY : The branch of physics dealing with electromagnetic radiation and its chemical effect.

ACTINOMETRY : Measurement of radiation in a chemical compound.

ACTIVATION ANALYSIS : A method of chemical analysis based on the detection of characteristic radionucleides following a nuclear bombardment. Also known as radio-active analysis.

ACTIVE OPTICS : Use of actuators and computers to overcome gravitational and thermal deformations of mirrors used in telescopes.

ACTUARIAL BRAND VALUATION : The methodology involves multidisciplinary approach involving skills such as actuarial, econometric, financial and marketing.

ACTUARIAL SCIENCE : The Science of making computations pertaining to insurance business.

ACUPRESSURE : Medical treatment involving pressing the body at specific points.

ACUPUNCTURE : A method of treatment with the help of needles, which unblocks and clears energy flow within the main channels or meridians located through the body.

ADAPTIVE OPTICS : The theory and design of optical systems that measure and correct wave front aberrations in real time, that is, simultaneous with the operation of the system.

ADDICTION PSYCHIATRY : Psychiatric study and treatment of addiction to smoking, drinking, drugs and such other bad habits.

ADHESIVE TECHNOLOGY : Manufacture of adhesives like glues and gums and synthetic adhesives used in paints and other industries.

ADMINISTRATIVE LAW : Study of law pertaining to problems of administration like public administration, business administration, hospital administration, school administration, hotel administration etc.

ADULT EDUCATION : A branch of education concerned with imparting education to illiterate or semiliterate adults.

ADULT NUTRITION : Study of the nutritional requirements of adults as opposed to children and adolescents.

ADULT PSYCHOLOGY : Study of psychological characteristics and problems of adults.

ADVANCED ACCOUNTANCY : Study of advanced problems in accountancy.

ADVANCED COMPUTING : Includes operating system concept, software engineering, data communication and networking. Advanced C++ using data structure, data base technologies (ORACLE, MS SQL Services), programming in Visual Basic, Windows Programming, Web technologies I (Foundations, ASP, XML), Web technologies) II (Core Java, enterprise JAVA, WAP), Component technologies (COM/DCOM, CORBA/ Microsoftnet).

ADVANCED LIFE SAVING SYSTEMS : Branch of medicine concerned with life saving methods and treatments adopted for critically ill patients.

ADVANCED MATERIALS FOR MICRO AND NANO SYSTEMS: Study of special materials suitable for and used in the manufacture of micro and nano sized objects and systems.

ADVERTISING : A means of communicating information pertaining to products, services or ideas by other than direct personal contact and on an openly paid basis with an intent to sell or otherwise obtain favourable consideration.

ADVERTISING MANAGEMENT : Management of advertising business involving procurement of advertisement assignments, making arrangements for their display and transmission through various media.

AEGEAN ARCHITECTURE : Refers to the broad classification for the buildings of the stone and bronze ages.

AERIAL MAPPING : See Aerocartography.

AERIAL PHOTOGRAPHY : See Aerophotography.

AEROACOUSTICS : Study of the aerodynamic sound produced by air flows.

AEROBALLISTICS : Study of the interaction of projectiles or high speed vehicles with the atmosphere.

AEROBICS : Exercises like brisk walking, jogging , running, swimming cycling, skipping etc.

AEROBIOLOGY : Study of microorganims, pollen and spores present in the air.

AEROCARTOGRAPHY : The making of planimetric and contoured maps and charts on the basis of photographs of the ground surface from an aircraft, spacecraft or rocket. Also known as AERIAL MAPPING.

AERODYNAMICS : The science that deals with the motion of air and other gaseous fluids and with forces acting on bodies when they move through such thuds or when such fluids move against or around the bodies.

AEROGEOGRAPHY : Geographic study of earth features by means of aerial observations and aerial photography.

AEROGEOLOGY : The geological study of earth features by means of aerial observations and aerial photography.

AEROGRAPHY : 1. The study of air or atmosphere 2. The practice of weather observation, map plotting and maintaining records.

AEROLITHOLOGY : The science of meteoric stones.

AEROLOGY : The study of free atmosphere throughout its vertical extent as distinguished from studies confined to the layer of the atmosphere near the earth's surface.

AEROMECHANICS : The science of air and other gases in motion or equilibrium.

AERONAUTICAL : CLIMATOLOGY : The application of the data and techniques of climatology to aviation meteorological problems.

AERONAUTICAL METEOROLOGY : The study of the effects of weather upon aviation.

AERONAUTICS : The science that deals with flight through the air.

AERONOMY : The study of the atmosphere of the earth or other bodies particularly the relation to composition, properties, relative motion and radiation from outer space or other bodies.

AEROPHOTOGRAPHY : Making of photographs of the ground surface from an aircraft, spacecraft or rocket. Also known as aerial photography.

AEROSOLS AND RADIATION : The study of the effect of radiation on the substances found suspended in air or other gases.

AEROSPACE DYNAMICS : Study of dynamic changes in aerospace.

AEROSPACE ENGINEERING : Engineering aspects of building and operating of spacecraft and related projects involved in space exploration.

AEROSPACE MEDICINE : Study of health and medical condition of astronauts and other space travellers before departure, during space travel and after returning to the earth.

AEROSPORTS : Sky diving, paramotoring and other sports activities conducted with aircraft.

AEROSPACE TECHNOLOGY : Applications of aerospace research findings and spinoffs in other fields and in everyday life.

AEROSTATICS : The science of the equilibrium of gases and of solid bodies immersed in them.

AEROTHERMOCHEMISTRY : The study of gases, which takes into account the effects of motion heat and chemical changes.

AEROTHERMODYNAMICS : The study of aerodynamic phenomena at sufficiently high gas velocities.

AEROTHERMOELASTICITY : The study of the response of elastic structures to the combined effects of aerodynamic heating and loading.

AFFINITY CHROMATOGRAPHY : A chromatographic technique that utilizes the ability of biological molecules to bind to certain ligands specifically and irreversibly, used in protein chemistry.

AFFINITY TECHNOLOGY AND MOLECULAR RECOGNITION: Frontier areas in modern biotechnology. Many biologically active materials exhibit close affinity to other organic and in-organic substances and bind them specifically. Attaching such a compound to a solid matrix and passing the crude extract allows the specific bonding of the biomolecule and its isolation.

AGARICOLOGY : Science pertaining to Agaricus and other mushrooms.

AGRASTOLOGY : Study of grasses which belong to the Poaccae family. Important crops like rice, wheat, sugarcane, maize belong to this family which is economically one of the most important families of plants.

AGRIBUSINESS MANGEMENT : Management of business concerned with commercially important agricultural products.

AGRICULTURAL BANKING : Branch of banking management concerned with the agricultural sector.

AGRICULTURAL BIOTECHNOLOGY: Application of biotechnology for crop improvement.

AGRICULTURAL BOTANY : Botanical study of crop plants.

AGRICULTURAL CHEMISTRY : Study of chemistry of chemical fertilizers, insecticides, herbicides, fungicides, rodenticides, soils, agricultural products etc.

AGRICULTURAL COMMUNICATION : Transmission of information to farmers about cultivation practices, crop pests, diseases, fertilizers, soils, weather, irrigation and research findings pertaining to the above aspects through the media.

AGRICULTURAL ECONOMICS : Study of the economics of agriculture including investment for cultivation and inputs, agricultural loans, subsidies, incomes, prices of agricultural commodities, land holdings, wages of agricultural labour etc.

AGRICULTURAL ENGINEERING : The study of the engineering aspects of agricultural implements and equipments, manufacture and maintenance.

AGRICULTURAL ENTOMOLOGY : Study of insects causing crop pests and methods of their prevention and control. Also includes study of beneficial insects like honey bees and other pollinating insects.

AGRICULTURAL EXTENSION : Explaining results of research pertaining to modern methods of cultivation, prevention and control of crop pests, use of fertilizers and irrigation methods to farmers and arranging demonstrations in their fields and agricultural research stations.

AGRICULTURAL FINANCE : Study of financing of agriculturists including loans, grants, subsidies and other forms of financial assistance.

AGRICULTURAL GEOGRAPHY : Study of the geographical distribution of soils, crops, pests etc.

AGRICULTURAL GEOLOGY : A branch of geology that deals with the nature and distribution of soils, the occurrence of mineral fertilizers and the behavior of underground water.

AGRICULTURAL INFORMATION MANAGEMENT: Dissemination of information about agricultural practices, pests and diseases, weather conditions, market prices of agricultural commodities etc through the media.

AGRICULTURAL MARKETING : Marketing of agricultural produce and products.

AGRICULTURAL METEOROLOGY : Branch of meteorology concerned with supplying weather information to farmers during various stages of crop growth and issuing advance warnings about impending cyclones and floods.

AGRICULTURAL MICROBIOLOGY : Branch of microbiology concerned with the study of microorganisms which are involved in agriculture like, for example, soil microorganisms, nitrogen fixing bacteria, and those concerned with dairy products, spoilage of agricultural produce and products.

AGRICULTURAL PROCESSING : Study of the various processes which are applied to agricultural products in order to prepare commercially useful substances from them.

AGRICULTURAL STATISTICS : Estimation of crop yields and calculation of annual agricultural production.

AGRICULTURAL ZOOLOGY : Study of crop pests caused by insects, rodents and birds and pollinating insects, honey bees, silk worms, dairy animals, poultry etc.

AGRIELECTRONICS : Automated bioreactor for seed/ tissue propagation, digital analyser for fruit juices and other food materials, sensors for quality assurance of food products and beverages.

AGRICULTURE : The production of plants and animals useful to man involving soil, cultivation and the breeding and management of crops and livestock.

AGROCLIMATOLOGY : Branch of climatology dealing with the climatic requirements of crops and the prevailing climatic conditions in cultivated areas.

AGROECOLOGY : The ecology of cultivated plants.

AGROECONOMY : Study of the agricultural economy of a given area or region.

AGROFORESTRY : Growing forest trees on the bunds of agricultural lands and marginal lands.

AGRONOMY : Study of economics of agriculture in a broad sense.

AIMS : Short form for advanced integrated manufacturing software. It is a Windows based integrated business management software that links a company's production, sales, materials, quality and financial operations.

AIR CONDITIONING : Branch of engineering concerned with controlling the temperature and humidity in a room or building in such a way as to make it pleasant for people to live and safe for weather sensitive equipment.

AIRCRAFT BODY AND FRAME MANUFACTURING : Branch of engineering concerned with aircraft body and frame manufacturing.

AIRCRAFT ELECTRICAL SYSTEMS : Manufacture, installation and maintenance of electrical systems in aircraft.

AIRCRAFT ENGINEERING TECHNOLOGY : Engineering and Technology involved in the manufacture and operation of aircraft.

AIRCRAFT MAINTENANCE ENGINEERING : Branch of engineering concerned with the upkeep of aircraft in good working condition and carrying out necessary repairs.

AIRCRAFT PROPULSION : Branch of aeronautical engineering concerned with the propulsion of aircraft.

AIR HOSTESS TRAINING : Training imparted to women to prepare them as air hostesses in airlines involving communication and language skills, courtesy, catering, First Aid emergency services etc.

AIR QUALITY CONTROL : Monitoring air quality to minimize pollution sources.

AIR TECKETING : Subject concerned with the issue of tickets, making reservations, confirmations, cancellations, refunds, etc., for aeroplane passengers.

AIR TRAFFIC CONTROL : Control of aeroplane flight movements and their arrival and departure at aerodromes.

AIR WARFARE : Course of study and training in air warfare.

AKTOLOGY : Study of near shore and shallow water areas, sediments, life and environments.

ALCHEMY : Study of ancient attempts to convert base metals into gold or silver.

ALGAL BIOTECHNOLOGY : Application of biotechnological techniques to algae for the benefit of man.

ALGAL PHYSIOLOGY : Study of the physiological processes of algae like respiration, photosynthesis, growth etc. Due to the unique habitats, structure and life cycles of algae, their physiology shows several special features.

ALGEBRA : Science of mathematical analysis in which letters are used to represent numbers.

ALGOL : Acronym for ALGO rithmic language. It is a problem oriented high level programming computer language for mathematical and scientific use.

ALGOLOGY : Study of algae, the primitive, primarily aquatic, photosynthetic flowerless plants having no differentiation of the plant body into root, stem and leaf. Also known as phycology.

ALLELOCHEMISTRY : The science of compounds synthesized by one organism that stimulate or inhibit other organisms.

ALLERGOLOGY : Branch of medical science concerned with allergies.

ALIMENTOLOGY : The science of nutrition.

ALLOPATHY : That method of treating diseases by which it is endeavored to produce a condition of the system either different from, opposite to or incompatible with the condition essential to the disease.

ALPHA TOXONOMY : The level of taxonomic study concerned with characterising and naming species.

ALTERNATIVE DISPUTE RESOLUTION : Alternative dispute resolution methods like arbitration, conciliation, mediation, negotiation etc., have been parliamentarily accorded recognition in the legal services authorities act, 1987 and the arbitration and conciliation Act, 1996. The international centre for alternative dispute resolution offers a diploma course in the subject which is a branch of legal studies.

ALTERNATIVE TECHNOLOGY : One of the names usually given to a type of technology which has some or all of the following attributes : minimum usage non-renewable resources, minimum interference with the environment either regional or local, self-sufficiency and the absence of exploitation or alienation of individuals.

AMERICAN STUDIES : Study of the history, culture, language and literature, political system etc., of America and its people.

ANAESTHESIOLOGY : Branch of medicine concerned with the administration of an anaesthetic to deprive the feeling of sensation of pain at the time of performing surgery or for other purpose. Generally chloroform or other substances with similar properties are used as anaesthetics.

ANALYTICAL BIOCHEMISTRY : Quantitative and qualitative analysis of biochemical compounds.

ANALYTICAL CHEMISTRY : Branch of chemistry concerned with techniques which yield any type of qualitative and quantitative information about chemical systems.

ANALYTICAL EPIDEMIOLOGY : Analytical methods of investigation of epidemic diseases.

ANALYTICAL GEOMETRY : Geometry in which location is analytically represented by co-ordinates; methods of algebra are largely used in this.

ANALYTICAL GEOMORPHOLOGY : Also known as Dynamic Geomorphology.

ANALYTICAL INSTRUMENTATION : Use of analytical instruments such as LC-MS, GC-MS, MNR, CAN Analysis, SEM, X-ray diffraction etc., in chemical analysis.

ANALYTIC MECHANICS : Application of calculus to classical MECHANICS.

ANATOMY : Study of the structure of different organs in the body. Usually treated as a branch of biology and medicine.

ANCIENT INDIAN HISTORY : Study of the history of India of ancient times.

ANDROLOGY : Branch of medicine concerned with the defects and diseases of the male reproductive system, their diagnosis and treatment. Treatment includes both medical and surgical methods. Determining reason for impotence, and lack of progeny and remedial measures also included within the purview of this science.

ANEMOLOY : Scientific investigation of winds.

ANEMOMETRY : The study of measuring and recording the direction and speed of the wind.

ANGIOGRAPHY : Branch of medicine concerned with the study of blood vessels. Also known as angiology.

ANGIOLOGY : See Angiography.

ANIMAL BIOTECHNOLOGY : Utilization of animals for the production of vaccines and drugs.

ANIMAL BREEDING : The science of evolving improved breeds of cattle and other domestic animals by means of selection, hybridization, artificial insemination and other methods. Also known as animal improvement.

ANIMAL ECOLOGY : A study of the relationships of animals to their environment.

ANIMAL EMBRYOLOGY : Study of the development of embryos in animals.

ANIMAL GENETICS : Branch of zoology and veterinary sciences concerned with the study of inheritance of genetic characters in animals.

ANIMAL GYNECOLOGY AND OBSTETRICS : Branch of veterinary science concerned with the study of female reproductive system and its diseases and delivery of young ones in cattle and other animals.

ANIMAL HUSBANDARY : Study of the principles and methods of rearing cattle and other domestic animals.

ANIMAL IMPROVEMENT : Study of methods of developing improved breeds of domestic animals. Also known as Animal Breeding.

ANIMAL NUTRITION : Study of the nutritional requirements and nutritional deficiency diseases of animals.

ANIMAL PATHOLOGY : Study of animal diseases, their diagnosis prevention and treatment.

ANIMAL PHYSIOLOGY : Study of the physiological processes of animals like digestion, respiration, excretion, circulation, hormones, reproduction etc.

ANIMAL PRODUCTION : Branch of animal husbandry concerned with large scale production of animal population.

ANIMAL PSYCHOLOGY : Studies of behaviours of various species of animals.

ANIMAL REPRDOCUTION : Study of the methods and processes of reproduction in animals. The method of artificial insemination was first successfully developed in animals. Another example of animal reproduction studies is the cloning of sheep and other animals.

ANIMAL SCIENCES : Morphology, Taxonomy, Anatomy, Physiology, Ecology, Genetics, Cytology of animals are grouped as animal sciences, which form the subject matter of zoology.

ANIMAL TISSUE AND CELL CULTURE : Branch of animal science concerned with growing animal and human tissues and cells in nutrient medium- Now widely used in medicine.

ANIMATION FILM MAKING : Technique of making films from pictures drawn by hand or with computers, using special equipment. This art form has developed enormously in recent years.

ANIMOTRONICS : A Cutting edge technology that combines animation, electronics and robotics.

ANNOUNCING AND COMPERING : A course of training for Radio and T.V. announcers and programme presenters.

ANTHROPOGENESIS : See anthropogeny.

ANTHROPOGENY : Study of the factors leading to the origin of man like the geological study of the physical conditions of the earth when man first appeared. Also known as anthropogenesis.

ANTHROPOGEOGRAPHY : Study of the inter-relations between geographical environment and man and the world wide distribution of man through the ages.

ANTHROPOLOGY : The study of the inter-relations of biological, cultural, geographical and historical aspects of mankind.

ANTHROPOMETRY : Branch of physical anthropology which deals with measurement of humans.

ANTHROPONOMY : Science of human behaviour.

ANTHROPOTOMY : See anatomy.

ANTI-AGING MEDICINE : Science and practice of longivity medicine which aims to extend the life span of humans.

APICULTURE : Rearing of honey bees. Apiculture is taken-up as a cottage industry, in fields, gardens and villages not only for harvesting the honey collected and stored by the bees but also for the pollination of crops by the bees.

APIOLOGY : The scientific study of bees, particularly of honey bees.

APPAREL DESIGN : The art of preparing newer designs for clothing is offered as a vocational course.

APPAREL MACHINE ENGINEERING : Branch of engineering concerned with the manufacture of machines used in making apparel.

APPAREL MANUFACTURING TECHNOLOGY : Newer technologies in the manufacture of apparel.

APPAREL MARKETING AND MERCHANDISING : A course of study covering the methods of marketing and merchandising apparel.

APPAREL PRODUCTION MANAGEMENT- Study of management techniques as applied to apparel production.

APPLIED ANTHROPOLOGY : Application of anthropology in medicine, forensic science, defence studies etc.

APPLIED ARTS : It includes all aspects of commercial art, visualization, illustration, press layout, photography and animation.

APPLIED BIOCOMPUTING : Application of computer methods for biological studies.

APPLIED BIOSCIENCE : Application of biology in medicine, agriculture, psychology, sociology etc., for the welfare of man.

APPLIED BIOTECHNOLOGY : Application of biotechnology mainly in medicine and agriculture.

APPLIED BOTANY : Application of plant sciences to agriculture, pharmacy, environmental sciences and utilization of plant products for various purposes.

APPLIED CHEMISTRY : Application of chemistry in industry, medicine, agriculture and other fields for the benefit of man.

APPLIED CLIMATOLOGY : The scientific analysis of climatic data in the light of useful application for an operational purpose.

APPLIED COMPUTER SCIENCE : Application of computer science in other fields and in many human activities.

APPLIED ECOLOGY : Activities involved in the management of natural resources.

APPLIED ECONOMICS : Application of economic principles and techniques for the analysis of economic problems.

APPLIED ELECTRONICS : Application of electronics in telecommunications, home appliances, space exploration and other fields.

APPLIED EPIDEMIOLOGY : Application of epidemiological methods and studies in the management of health and medical care.

APPLIED FINANCE : Application of financial principles and studies in government and corporate sectors.

APPLIED GENOMICS : Application of knowledge of genome studies in medicine, sociology, plant and animal breeding etc.

APPLIED GEOCHEMISTRY : Application of geochemistry for the exploration of minerals, oil, natural gas and other underground resources.

APPLIED GEOLOGY : Application of geology for exploration of water, minerals and natural gas resources and in agriculture and industry.

APPLIED GEOPHYSICS : Application of the techniques of geophysics for the discovery and location of economic minerals, for example, petroleum.

APPLIED HISTORY : Application of historical evidence in solving sociological, political, economic and religious problems.

APPLIED LANDSCAPE DESIGN : To design the open areas around or near buildings, offices, factories, hotels and other public and private places not only for functional purposes but also for a beautiful and compatible natural environment. Real estate development firms starting new projects, municipalities constructing airports, or parks use landscape techniques. Branch of horticulture.

APPLIED LANGUAGE STUDIES : Application of study of languages for translators, interpreters, correspondence with other countries and other purposes.

APPLIED LIFE SCIENCE : See Applied bio-science.

APPLIED LINGUISTICS : Application of linguistics in language teaching, teaching students with hearing and speech problems and for many other purposes.

APPLIED MATHEMATICS : A branch of mathematics concerned with the study of the physical, biological and sociological worlds.

APPLIED MECHANICS : Application of mechanics in engineering and other fields.

APPLIED METEOROLOGY : The application of current weather data analysis or forecast to specific practical problems.

APPLIED MICROBIOLOGY : Application of microbiological methods for the manufacture of enzymes, vitamins, antibiotics and other medicines and other industrially useful substances.

APPLIED NUTRITION : Application of nutrition theory and principles to the preparation of menu especially for sick people, athletes, and other special groups like army personnel etc.

APPLIED OPTICS : Application of principles and methods and techniques of optics to ophtholmology, microscopy, astronomy, photography and telecommunications.

APPLIED ORNITHOLOGY : Application of knowledge of birds in the control of agricultural pests, disease vectors, environmental sciences.

APPLIED PHYSICS : Application of principles, methods and techniques of physics in engineering, medicine, geology, biology, chemistry, instrumentation and other disciplines.

APPLIED PHYSIOLOGY : Application of physiology in medicine, pharmaceuticals, sports etc.

APPLIED PSYCHOLOGY : Application of the methods and results of psychology in medicine, management, sociology, and in tackling problems in practical life.

APPLIED SOCIOLOGY : Application of sociological principles to study of problems in society.

APPLIED STATISTICS : Application of statistics in various disciplines and in everyday problems.

APPRAISING AND DEVELOPING EMPLOYEE PERFORMANCE (ADEP) : It is a performance development system that aligns each individual employee's roles and responsibilities with the organisational and team mission values and strategy. ADEP provides managers and employees with role clarity, periodic performance feedback and coaching and meaningful performance reviews.

APPROPRIATE TECHNOLOGY : The application of a technology which is appropriate for the factor endowments that exist. Developing countries usually have a large labour force and relatively little spare investment capital thus making labour intensive industry the most appropriate.

AQUACULTURE : Cultivating fish and other food animals and otherwise useful plants and animals in fresh or marine waters. Also known as aquatic farming.

AQUATIC BIOLOGY : Biological and ecological study of animals and plants living in fresh water and marine environments.

AQUATIC CHEMISTRY : Branch of chemistry concerned with the analysis of chemical changes taking place in fresh water and marine environments due to various physical, chemical and biotic factors.

AQUATIC FARMING : See aquaculture.

AQUATIC MEDICINE : Treatment of diseases with the use of water.

AQUICULTURE : Cultivation of natural faunal resources of water; see aquaculture.

ARANEOLOGY : Branch of zoology concerned with the study of spiders.

ARBITRATION LAW : Branch of legal studies concerned with the resolution of disputes by means of arbitration.

ARBORICULTURE : The cultivation of ornamental trees and shrubs.

ARCHEOLOGICAL ANTHROPOLOGY : Study of man and his evolution on the basis of archeological findings.

ARCHEOLOGICAL CHEMISTRY : The application of chemical theories and experimental procedures especially of analytical chemistry to the elucidation of problems in archeology.

ARCHEOLOGY : Study of the physical, anatomical and cultural remains of ancient (mainly prehistoric) peoples.

ARCHERY : Ancient form of warfare using bows and arrows. employed for hunting wild animals and for self defence by forest tribes. Included as an item in sports competitions even to this day.

ARCHITECTURAL CONSERVATION : Preserving the structure and beauty of buildings.

ARCHITECTURAL ENGINEERING : Principles and methods of engineering used in architecture.

ARCHITECTURE : The art and science dealing with building construction including execution of the original plan. actual construction and decoration.

ARCHITECTURE OF SOFTWARE SYSTEMS : The art and science of building compute software systems.

ARCHIVAL STUDIES : Study of documents or records relating to the affairs of a family, corporation, community, city or nation kept in libraries and museums.

ARCHIVES KEEPING : The science of keeping and preserving documents or records relating to the affairs of a family, corporation, community, city or nation kept in libraries and museums.

AREAL GEOLOGY : Distribution and form of rocks or geological units of any relatively large area of the earth's surface.

AREA STUDIES : Studies of a given area's human and natural resources.

ARITHEMETIC : The science of numbers or the art of computation by figures or numerals.

ARMAMENT DESIGN : Design of weapons employed in warfare.

ARMAMENT ENGINEERING : Branch of engineering concerned with the manufacture of weapons used in warfare.

ARMAMENT TECHNOLOGY : Technology involved in developing new types of armament and their use in warfare.

ART HISTORY : History of various types of art forms like painting, sculpture etc.,

ART CRITICISM : Study and training in criticism of fine arts including aesthetic theory and analytical skills to write effectively about the arts.

ARTHROSCOPIC SURGERY : Key hole surgery on injured joints using arthroscopy.

ARTHROSCOPY : Study of joints with the help of an optical device, for medical diagnosis.

ARTIFICAL INTELLIGENCE : The development of computers to do things normally requiring human intelligence.

ASCENDING CHROMATOGRAPHY : A technique for the analysis of mixtures of two or more compounds in which the mobile phase (sample and carrier) rises through the fixed phase.

ASHLAR ARCHITECTURE : Refers to the type of architecture wherein all the walls were built by stone.

ASIAN STUDIES : Study of the history, culture, languages, literatures and politics of Asian peoples.

ASSEMBLING : Fitting the components of a machine in their proper positions in order to start the machine to function.

ASSEMBLY ENGINEERING : Includes automated engine and vehicle assembling lines, parts feeding etc.

ASSET LIABILITY MANAGEMENT : Management of assets and liabilities of a company.

ASSYRIAN ART : A branch of Mesopotomian Art which held a dominant position during 750-612 B.C.

ASTHENOLOGY : Doctrine of diseases connected with debility.

ASTHMOLOGY : Branch of medicine concerned with the study and treatment of the respiratory allergic disease known as asthma.

ASTROBALLISTICS : Study of Phenomena arising out of motion of a solid through a gas at high speeds. For example, interaction between a meteoroid and atmosphere.

ASTROBIOLOGY : The study of the probable living organisms on celestial bodies other than the earth.

ASTROLITHOLOGY : The science of aerolites.

ASTROLOGY : The pseudoscience which claims to enable man to discover effects and influences of the heavenly bodies on human and other mundane affairs and to foretell the future.

ASTROMETRY : The branch of astronomy concerned with the measurement of the positions of the celestial bodies.

ASTRONAUTICS : Branch of science concerned with space travel.

ASTRONAUTICS & SPACE ENGINEERING : Study of space systems engineering, satellite subsystems design criteria etc.

ASTRONOMICAL PHOTOGRAPHY : The use of the photographic process to record surface features of celestial objects, their positions and motions (for measurement) and their radiations (photometers) and spectra (spectroscopy).

ASTRONOMICAL SPECTROSCOPY : The use of spectrographs in conjunction with telescopes to obtain observational data on the velocities and physical conditions of astronomical objects.

ASTRONOMY : The science which treats of the celestial bodies, their nature, magnitudes, motions, distances, periods of revolution etc.

ASTRONUCLEAR AND ASTRO PARTICLE PHYSICS : Study of nuclear and other particles from space.

ASTROPHYSICS : The branch of astronomy concerned with the physical processes associated with the celestial bodies and the intervening regions of space. It deals principally with the energy of stellar systems and the relation between this energy and the evolution of the system.

ASYNCHRONOUS TRANSFER MODE (ATM) : It provides viable solutions to transfer voice data and relay sensitive information over the same computer network. Therefore ATM stands out as a solution that could reach every desk top, lap top, counter shop, set-top and pocket world-wide. As the key transport technology for the third generation mobile communications network ATM is playing a central role for multimedia handling and efficient network construction.

ATHLETICS : Exercises to enhance agility and strength.

ATMOLOGY : That branch of science which treats of the laws and phenomena of aqueous vapour.

ATMOSPHERIC CHEMISTRY : The study of the production, transport, modification and removal of atmospheric constituents in the troposphere and stratosphere.

ATMOSPHERIC DYNAMICS : The movement and other changes taking place in the atmosphere.

ATMOSPHERIC PHYSICS : The study of the physical phenomena of the atmosphere.

ATMOSPHERIC SCIENCES : Meteorology, climatology and allied sciences concerned with the study of the atmosphere.

ATOMIC MINERALS : Exploration of minerals useful for obtaining atomic energy like Uranium, Nobium, Tantalum, Beryllium etc.

ATOMIC PHYSICS : Branch of physics concerned with the structure of the atom, the characteristics of the electrons and other elementary particles of which the atom is composed, the arrangement of the atom's energy states and the processes involved in the radiation of light and X-rays.

ATOMIC SPECTROSCOPY : Branch of physics concerned with production, measurement and interpretation of spectra arising from electromagnetic radiation, by atoms,

AUDIO ENGINEERING : Engineering branch concerned with recording and transmitting audible sounds.

AUDIOLOGY : The science of hearing.

AUDIOMETRY : Measurement of hearing capacity by means of audiometers.

AUDIO-VISUAL EDUCATION : Teaching of which the use of audio and/or visual aids is an integral part or supplementary part.

AUDITING : To make an examination into accounts or dealings with money or property by proper officers or persons appointed for that purpose, hence a calling to account.

AUGURY : The art of proactive foretelling events by omens.

AUROLOGY : 1. The study of diseases of the ear 2. The science of auras, the ethereal radiations, emanating from living beings.

AUTECOLOGY : Study of the relations between a plant species and its environment.

AUTO BODY AND FRAME DESIGNING : Preparing designs for the manufacture of the body and frame of automobile vehicle.

AUTO BODY AND FRAME MANUFACTURING : Manufacturing technology of the body and frame of automobile vehicles.

AUTOELECTRICIAN COURSE : Study and training in arranging electrical fittings in automobile vehicles.

AUTOMATION TECHNOLOGY : Technology of devising and utilizing automation methods and techniques in industry.

AUTOMOBILE ENGINEERING : Branch of engineering concerned with the manufacture and maintenance of automobile vehicles.

AUTOMOTIVE ELECTRONICS : Electronics is now a virtually functional area of automobile vehicles including ignition systems, engine control modules, chasis and interior. There are embedded controllers for engine, transmission, braking, steering, suspension, climate, radio and instrumentation controls besides safety products like smart air bags and collision avoidance radar navigation and communication systems using voice recognition and hands free operations.

AUTOMOTIVE ENGINE TECHNOLOGY : Technology of design and manufacture of automotive engines and other equipments.

AUXONOGRPHY : The study of growth inhibiting or growth promoting agents by means of anxonograms which are plate cultures provided with variable growth conditions to determine the specific environmental factors.

AVIATION : The operation of planes and other aircrafts.

AVIATION ENGINEERING : Branch of engineering concerned with aerial navigation by machines heavier than air.

AVIATION MEDICINE : Branch of medicine concerned with the health and diseases of the crew and other passengers of aircraft and the study of effects of air travel on man.

AVIATION METEOROLOGY : Branch of meteorology concerned with supplying weather information and warnings to aviation vehicles and personnel.

AVIATION TECHNOLOGY : Study and development of technology used in aircraft.

AVICULTURE : The breeding and rearing of birds including poultry.

AVIONCS : 1. Electronic control of flight in air. 2. The invention and application of electronic and electrical devices in aeroplanes and missiles.

AYURVEDIC MEDICINE : A 5000 year old system of healing from India that balances the three doshas- vata, pitta and kapha.

B

BACK REFLECTION PHOTOGRAPHY : A method of a studying crystalline structure of X-ray diffraction in which the photographic film is placed between the source of X-rays and the crystal specimen.

BACTERIAL BIOTECHNOLOGY : The development of techniques for the application of bacterial processes to the production of materials of use in medicine and industry like, for example, antibiotics etc.

BACTERIAL GENETICS : Study of genetic principles and processes as exemplified by bacteria. Since it is possible to study several generations of bacteria in a short time scientists have found it convenient to study genetic phenomena employing bacteria as experimental organisms.

BACTERIAL PHYSIOLOGY : Study of the physiological processes in bacteria. It is of particular interest to biologists since bacteria occupy an important place in the economy of nature. Besides bacteria exhibit a wide range of autotrophic and heterotrophic modes of nutrition and are adapted to extreme living conditions.

BACTERIOLOGY : Branch of science concerned with the study of bacteria, their life history, physiology, genetics, ecology and economic importance. It plays an important role in medicine, ecology, biotechnology and industry.

BAKERY TECHNOLOGY : Technology involved in the manufacture of bakery products like bread, biscuits, cakes, pastry etc.

BALLISTICS : Branch of applied mechanics which deals with the motion and behaviour characteristics of missiles, that is, projectiles, bombs, rockets, guided missiles and so forth and of accompanying phenomena.

BANK BRANCH MANAGEMENT : A branch of banking concerned with the management of individual bank branches and a network of branches.

BANKING : The business or profession of conducting banking transactions like lending money (loans), accepting deposits, clearing cheques, maintaining the bank accounts of customers etc.

BANKING : CLIENT SERVER TECHNOLOGY : Designing banking software. Total bank automotion with various languages like Oracle, Visual basic etc.

BANKING LAW : Law pertaining to banking business.

BANKING TECHNOLOGY : Modern technological methods being adopted in the banking sector involving computers and their applications.

BANK MANAGEMENT : Management of banks is a highly specialized branch of management science involving the wide range of activities being undertaken by banks.

BARIATRICS : Branch of medicine concerned with obesity problems.

BARODYNAMICS : Mechanics of heavy structures which may collapse under their own weight.

BAROMETRY : The study of the measurement of atmospheric pressure with particular reference to ascertaining and correcting the errors of different types of barometers.

BASIC : Acronym for Beginner's All : Purpose Symbolic Instruction Code, which is a computer language. Because of its simplicity and comparative power the language is much used on personal computers.

BASIC EDUCATION : It is devised as a means of providing a general education through the life and work of village communities.

BASKETRY : It is the art of using two connected elements, the warp and the woof to make an object. There are many kinds of baskets.

BATHYMETRY : The science of measuring ocean depths in order to determine the sea floor topography.

BATTERIES AND FUEL CELLS : Design, assembly and testing of batteries, modern battery systems, new materials for batteries, applications of batteries and fuel cells.

BEAUTICIAN COURSE : A course of study in the methods of enhancing and maintaining beauty, particularly of skin and hair.

BEAUTY CULTURE : Scientific treatments, processes and methods to maintain and enhance beauty.

BEAUTY THERAPY : Skin and hair care, facials , different types of hair styles, bleaching, threading and waxing methods etc.

BEHAVIOURAL ECOLOGY : Study of the influence of environmental factors on behaviour.

BEHAVIOURAL EPIDEMIOLOGY : Study of the behavior, attitudes and opinions of people at the time of outbreak of epidemic and infectious diseases.

BEHAVIOURAL GENETICS : The branch of genetics concerned with determining the relative importance of the genetic constitution of animals as compared to environmental factors in influencing animal behaviour.

BEHAVIOURAL MEDICINE : Variously defined. Most simply as application of psychology to branches of medicine other than psychiatry.

BEHAVIOURAL NEUROSCIENCE : Study of neurosciences in relation to their role in controlling behaviour.

BEHAVIOURAL SCIENCE : Science concerned with the study of behaviour like, for example, psychology, psychiatry, sociology etc.

BEHAVIOUR THERAPY : Treatment of psychoneuroses by attempts to modify behaviour, for example, by gradual exposure to object of phobia.

BETA TAXONOMY : The level of taxonomic study dealing with the arrangement of species into lower and higher taxa.

BIBLE STUDIES : Studies pertaining to various aspects of the holy bible.

BIBLIOGRAPHY : A history or description of books or manuscripts, with notices of the different editions, the times when they were printed etc. Treated as a branch of library science.

BIBLIOLOGY : Variously defined : 1. Biblical literature, doctrine or theology 2. A treatise on books. 3. Bibliography.

BIBLIOMETRICS : Quantitative study of library science.

BIBLIOTHERAPY : Use of selected reading materials as a therapeutic method in medicine, psychiatry and education.

BIOACOUSTICS : 1. The study of the relation between living organisms and sound. 2. Study of the frequency or pitch, soundness, loudness, and duration of animal sounds to learn animal behaviour.

BIOARCHEOLOGY : Study of evolution through germline mutations in lineages.

BIOASTRONAUTICS : The study of biological, behavioural and medical problems pertaining to astronautics.

BIOBEHAVIOURAL HEALTH : Study of the behaviour of living beings as reflected in their health.

BIOCATALYSIS AND APPLIED MICROBIOLOGY : New drug development and screening, vaccines, extremophiles and their metabolites, enzymes in organic synthesis.

BIOCENOLOGY : The study of natural communities and of their interactions.

BIOCHEMICAL ENGINEERING : Application of engineering principles and methods in devising biochemical experiments and plants and machinery.

BIOCHEMICAL GENETICS : Study of the genetic processes through a study of the biochemical reactions taking place at the cellular level. Since genes express their effects through the biochemical reactions mediated by them, this study assumes importance.

BIOCHEMICAL TAXONOMY : Studies similarities in the structure of certain proteins and nucleic acids and determines the taxonomic positions and relationships of organisms on the basis of biochemical similarities.

BIOCHEMICAL TECHNOLOGY : Application of biochemistry in technology and industry.

BIOCHEMISTRY : Study of the structure of the chemical constituents of cells and their chemical reaction pathways.

BIOCHEMORPHOLOGY : The science dealing with the chemical structure of foods and drugs and their reactions on living organisms.

BIOCHRONOLOGY : The relative age dating of rock units based on their fossil content.

BIOCLIMATOLOGY : The study of the effects of natural environment on living organisms.

BIOCOMPUTING : Cross fertilization of biotechnology with information technology reveals the inherent connection between theories of natural life sciences and high-end computational technologies. Efforts have been made to compile full scale genetic information stored in the nucleus and the mitochondria as digital depositories of information. Genomics is the main constituent of bio-informatic research that aims to decide code of life in its fundamental unit, a cell.

BIODIVERSITY AND CONSERVATION BIOLOGY : Study of diversity of plant and animal species on the earth, particularly the centres of maximum diversity and methods of saving them and promoting their well being.

BIODYNAMICS : The doctrine of vital forces which no longer finds favour with scientists.

BIOELECTROCHEMISTRY : Study of the control of biological growth and repair processes by electrical stimulation.

BIOELECTROMAGNETICS : Study of the electromagnetic field generated by the body as an indication of disease imbalance and pathway to healing.

BIOELECTRONICS : Application of electronic theories and techniques to the problems of biology.

BIOENERGETICS : Study of the flow and transformations of energy that occur in living organisms.

BIOENERGY : Utilization of animal energy in agricultural operations and production of biogas from agricultural waste and cattle dung. A branch of agricultural engineering.

BIOENGINEERING : 1. The use of artificial tissues, organs and organ components to replace parts of body that are damaged, lost or malfunctioning, for example, artificial limbs, heart valves and heart pace maker. 2. The application of engineering knowledge to medicine and biology.

BIOETHICS : Ethical principles that should be followed while performing experiments and conducting research with living organisms. For example, study of the ethical implications involved in cloning human beings. Several recent experiments like fertilization involving humans have raised many important ethical questions and controversies.

BIOFEEDBACK : Relaying back to the person tangible evidence of various physiological systems such as brain waves, skin temperature or sweat pore response in an attempt to help manage stressful conditions.

BIOFERTILIZER TECHNOLOGY : The term biofertilizers denotes all nutrient inputs for plant growth which are of biological origin. In a narrower sense biofertilizer technology now is being defined as application of preparations containing live or latent cells of efficient strains of nitrogen fixing, phosphorus solubilizing or cellulolytic microorganisms used for application to seed, soil or composting areas with the objective of increasing the numbers of such organisms and accelerate certain microbial processes to augment the extent of availability of nutrients in a form which can be easily assimilated by plants.

BIOGAS TECHNOLOGY : The production of biogas from agricultural waste for the use of villagers as fuel and energy source.

BIOGEOCHEMICAL PROSPECTING : A prospecting technique for subsurface ore deposits based on interpretation of the growth of certain plants which reflect subsoil concentrations of some elements.

BIOGEOCHEMISTRY : A branch of geochemistry that is concerned with biological materials and their relation to earth chemicals in an area.

BIOGEOGRAPHY : Branch of geography concerned with the geographical distribution of animals and plants.

BIOGEOSCIENCE : Branch of science concerned with the study of biologic materials and their relation to earth characteristics.

BIOGRAPHY : The history of the life and character of a particular person, as a department of literature.

BIOHYDROLOGY : Study of the interactions between water, plants and animals including the effects of water on biota as well as the physical and chemical changes in water or its environment produced by biota.

BIOINFORMATICS : 1. Information science pertaining to living organisms and their characters, distribution, etc., and more particularly their genomes, 2. Application of information technology to biological science.

BIOINORGANIC CHEMISTRY : Role of metallic ions and their transport in biological systems particularly in photosynthesis, nitrogen fixation etc.

BIOLINGUISTICS : Scientific examination of language with special emphasis on the neurophysiological and genetic factors.

BIOLOGICAL ANTHROPOLOGY : Biological study of man and his origins.

BIOLOGICAL CHEMISTRY : Also known as biochemistry.

BIOLOGICAL CONTROL : 1. Introduction or encouragement of one species to eliminate or reduce another. 2. Natural or applied regulation of pest organisms especially through the role or use of natural enemies.

BIOLOGICAL OCEANOGRAPHY : The study of the flora and fauna of oceans in relation to the marine environment.

BIOLOGICAL SCIENCES : Sciences concerned with the study of living organisms like botany, zoology, microbiology, biochemistry, genetics, molecular biology, biotechnology, evolution etc. See Life sciences.

BIOLOGICAL WARFARE : Using pathogenic microorganisms such as those causing anthrax, smallpox, cholera etc., to kill enemy population on a large scale.

BIOLOGY : The science of life or which treats generally of the life of animals and plants including their morphology, physiology, origin, development and distribution.

BIOMATERIALS : Materials used in making parts for implantation in the human body.

BIOMATHEMATICS : Application of mathematics in biology, as for example in genetics.

BIOMECHANICS : 1. Study of the effects of exercise, on muscular movements and changes in muscles and other body parts and their structure. 2. Study of the mechanics of living things.

BIOMEDICAL ENGINEERING : 1. Application of engineering principles and methods in biology and medicine. 2. Utilization of engineering knowledge in the manufacture of artificial organs and parts of organs for transplantation in the human body.

BIOMEDICAL INSTRUMENTATION : Manufacture and maintenance of instruments and equipment used in biology and medicine, particularly in the diagnosis and treatment of diseases.

BIOMEDICAL MODELLING : Preparation of computer models for study of epidemiology of diseases.

BIOMEDICAL SCIENCES : The following subjects are classified as biomedical sciences: medical chemistry, biochemistry, bioinorganic chemistry, bioorganic chemistry, medical biotechnology, pharmaceutics, reproductive biology, developmental biology, chemistry and biology of heme, molecular genetics, microbiology, cell biology, immunology etc.

BIOMEDICAL WASTE MANAGEMENT : Disposal of hospital waste materials without causing environmental pollution.

BIOMEDICINE : Study of interaction between biology and medicine.

BIOMETEOROLOGY : The study of the relationship between living organisms and atmospheric phenomena.

BIOMETRICAL GENETICS : Application of mathematics and statistics in the study of genetics.

BIOMETRY : Application of statistical methods to biological data.

BIOMETRICS : The authentication of identities through unique physical or behavioral traits of individuals; common physical biometrics include finger prints, hand or palm geometry and retina, iris or facial characteristics. Behavioral characteristics include signature, voice, key stroke pattern and gait.

BIOMIMETIC CHEMISTRY : Study of the chemical processes resembling those taking place in living organisms.

BIOMOLECULAR ELECTRONICS : Study of electrical behaviour of DNA with respect to sequence, length, orientation etc., for designing and fabrication of DNA based electronic components, study of DNA based high density, memory devices, study of DNA electrical characteristics to understand DNA damage chemistry related diseases.

BIOMOLECULAR SCIENCES : All those sciences which study biomolecules like nucleic acids, hormones, proteins etc., Example: Molecular biology, Protein chemistry, nucleic acid chemistry etc.

BIOMOLECULAR SPECTROSCOPY: Spectroscopic study of biological molecules.

BIOMORPHIC ART : It is a type of designs on small stones by men of the Paleolithic age.

BIOMUSIC : Study of the evolutionary development of musical skills in the animal kingdom.

BIONAVIGATION : The ability of animals such as birds to find their way back to their roost even if the land marks on the outward bound trip were effectively concealed from them.

BIONICS : The science which deals with the transformation of the functions of living systems into electronic, mechanical and other analogues.

BIONOMICS : The branch of biology which studies the relations of organisms to their environment.

BIOORGANIC CHEMISTRY : Branch of chemistry concerned with the study of biologically active organic compounds like proteins.

BIOPESTICIDE TECHNOLOGY : Use of environmentally friendly pesticides of biological origin primarily in the form of extracts of plants such as neem, custard apple etc. Certain viruses like nuclear polyhedral virus (NPV) are also being employed to control crop pests.

BIOPHARMACEUTICALS : Study of drugs derived from plants, animals and other living beings.

BIOPHYSICS : Application of physical principles and methods to the study of biological phenomena and processes.

BIOPROCESSING : Use of organisms to bring about the breakdown of explosives such as TNT and dinitroglycerine. Clearing of waste materials by growing special plants in the polluted area.

BIOPROCESS TECHNOLOGY : Technologies based on biological processes. For example, utilization of Fermentation process for the production of vitamins, enzymes, etc., on a large scale.

BIOREMEDIATION : The use of organisms to clean up the pollution caused by man.

BIORHEOLOGY: The study of the reformation and flow of biological fluids such as blood, mucus and synovial fluid.

BIOSCIENCES : See Biological Sciences.

BIOSTATISTICS : Application of statistical methods for the analysis and interpretation of biological data.

BIOSTRATIGRAPHY : A part of paleontology concerned with the study of the conditions and deposition order of sedimentary rocks.

BIOSYSTEMATICS: Experimental study of diversity especially at the specific level.

BIOTECHNOLOGY : The development of techniques for the application of biological processes to the production of materials of use in medicines, industry and agriculture. For example: the production of antibiotics, cheese and wine relying on various fungi and bacteria.

BISCUIT TECHNOLOGY : The technology of large scale manufacture of biscuits from raw materials.

BLACK ART : It means sorcery in general or the imagined power of performing wonderful feats by means derived from the help of evil spirits or of the devil.

BLOOD BANKING TECHNOLOGY : Receiving blood from donors, testing it, determining the blood group, preserving it and giving to the needy persons.

BLOOD CHEMISTRY : Study of the chemical constituents of blood and their chemical reactions.

BLOOD DISEASES : Branch of medicine concerned with the study and treatment of diseases of blood like leukemia.

BOAT BUILDING : The art and technology of building boats of various sizes for navigation in canals, rivers, lakes and sea.

BOMB BALLISTICS : The special branch of ballistics concerned with bombs dropped from aircraft.

BONSAI : The japanese art of keeping trees reduced to a small size permanently in which state they flower and fruit.

BOOK BINDING : Design and production of covers for books. Book binding has now developed into an advanced technology employing sophisticated machinery for the processes involved at various stages.

BOOK-KEEPING : Book-Keeping is the science and art of identifying and recording accounting transactions systematically in the proper books.

BOOK PRODUCTION : Study of various processes involved in book production like editing, printing, proof correction, binding etc.

BOOK PUBLISHING : Study of various processes involved in book publication like selection of titles, authors, editors, scrutiny of manuscripts, getting art work prepared etc.

BOOK SELLING : Sales promotion and advertising, computer applications, keeping accounts etc.

BOOLEAN ALGEBRA : Named after the mathematician George Boole (1815-64), it uses algebraic notation to express logical relations in the same way that conventional algebra is used to express mathematical relationships. It is applied in computers.

BORDER MANAGEMENT : Management of land and maritime boundaries, island territories, territorial waters, preserving the sanctity of air space, dealing with entry of narcotics, illegal migrants, terrorists and arms.

BOSE-EINSTEIN STATISTICS : A theory of fundamental particles developed by the Indian Mathematician and Physicist. Satyendra Nath Bose in collaboration with Albert Einstein. It deals with the statistical mechanics of a system of indistinguishable particles for which there is no restriction on the number of particles that may exist in the same state simultaneously.

BOTANY : The Science which treats of the Vegetable Kingdom, dealing with the forms, structure and tissues of plants, the laws and conditions which regulate their growth and development, the functions of their various organs, the classification of plants, their distribution over the face of the globe and their condition at various ecological epochs.

BOUNDARY LAYER PHYSICS : A branch of space science dealing with physical characteristics and phenomena pertaining to the boundary layer.

BOXING : A game in which two persons fight with their fists.

BRACHYTHERAPHY : Short range radiotherapy as by radiation needles and surface applicators.

BRAIN MAPPING : Mapping of parts of the brain and their networking by means of various types of scanning.

BRAND MANAGEMENT : Promoting a product of a company by making its brand name popular with the help of advertising and other techniques.

BRAND VALUATION : The methodology adopted for brand valuation can be classified into 3 broad categories. 1. Cost based 2. Market-based 3. Economics based.

BREATHARANISM : The idea of living for thousands of years without food based on the premise that everybody who eats dies.

BREWING AND DISTILLING : The art and science of manufacturing alcoholic beverages.

BRIDGES ENGINEERING : Branch of civil engineering concerned with designing and building bridges.

BRITISH HISTORY : Study of the history of the British empire and its transformation into the British commonwealth.

BROADCAST ENGINEERING : Engineering concerned with the recording and transmission of radio programs.

BROADCAST JOURNALISM : A branch of journalism concerned with reporting and recording news stories and preparing commentaries and discussions for radio broadcasting.

BROADCAST TECHNOLOGY : Technology of manufacturing the equipment used in broadcasting radio programs.

BROMATOTHERAPY : The regulation or use of diet in treating diseases.

BRONCHOLOGY : Branch of medicine concerned with bronchial disease.

BRONCHOSCOPY : Branch of medical science concerned with the study and observation of bronchi which form part of the respiratory system, by means of an optical instrument called bronchoscope.

BRYOLOGY : The science of mosses, their structure, affinities, classification etc., See MUSCOLOGY a branch of botany.

BUDDISTIC STUDIES : Study of the philosophy founded by Gautam Buddha known otherwise as Sakyamuni, the sacred name of the founder of the system, who lived in the 6th century B.C. The religious system founded by Buddha, one of the most prominent doctrines of which is that *nirvana* or an absolute release from existence is the chief good. It prevails in China, Japan, Tibet, Myanmar, Srilanka, India etc., its adherents at one time comprising a third of the human race.

BUILDING AND REAL ESTATE MANAGEMENT : Branch of management science concerned with the management of buildings and real estate on a large scale, like leasing, accounting the income and investment and connected matters.

BUILDING CLIMATOLOGY : Study of the architectural and engineering aspects of building construction in order to make the building climatologically hospitable.

BUILDING MAINTENANCE MANAGEMENT: Maintenance, repairs, renovations, alterations, additions etc., on a large scale.

BUILDING SERVICES ENGINEERING : Branch of engineering concerned with providing amenities in buildings, like electricity, water, drainage, air-conditioning and other services.

BUILT ENVIRONMENT STUDIES : Study of environmental factors and causes and sources of pollution in built-up areas like buildings, factories, offices, hotels, hospitals theaters etc.,

BULK DRUGS : Branch of Pharmaceutical science concerned with the manufacture of medicines in large quantities for supply to other companies for their use in preparing their own formulations.

BURNS AND PLASTIC SURGERY : Plastics surgery performed on patients whose bodies have been damaged due to burns. Transplantation of skin is done to cover the burnt portions and disfigurement of the organs is rectified.

BUSINESS : Any enterprise which makes, distributes, or provides any article or service which the other members of the community need and are able and willing to pay for.

BUSINESS ADMINISTRATION : Concerned with the formulation of policies and programs involving business. In this process decision making is an attribute of administration.

BUSINESS ANALYSIS AND VALUATION : Analysis of assets and liabilities, income and expenditure, and suggesting measures for future improvements.

BUSINESS COMMUNICATIONS : Study of the different forms of communication used in commerce and industry, including correspondence report, writing etc.

BUSINESS ECONOMICS : Study of the economic problems that affect the organisation and operation of business firms, to forecast business trends and environments, interpret implication of economic and public policies on business.

BUSINESS ECOSYSTEM : Business networking to mutual advantage. A set of evolving trust relationships between its participants.

BUSINESS ENGLISH : Study of English used in business correspondence and transactions.

BUSINESS ENVIRONMENT : Study of internal and external factors and influences affecting business at any given time.

BUSINESS ETHICS : Ethical principles to be followed by business firms in order to earn the good will of customers and reputation.

BUSINESS FINANCE : Mobilising financial resources. Industry specific information for investment, interest and exchange rates, and stock exchange are the areas covered.

BUSINESS INFORMATION MANAGEMENT : Application of information technology to business.

BUSINESS INTELLIGENCE : It refers to the ability to leverage the data into meaningful information that will provide richer insights into business and allow one to sense its direction. BI solutions enable one to understand customer behavior, analyse the sales and identify opportunities for revenue generation, cutting costs and improve over all decision making. Additionally extensive analysis of historical data can be made to identify patterns of demand and understand the trends that may impact a business.

BUSINESS MANAGEMENT : Art and science of business management the important functions being providing inputs of financial, physical, human and technological resources, interactions with suppliers, customers, competitors, investors and political and social constraints including research and development.

BUSINESS MARKETING : Marketing of goods in business.

BUSINESS MATHEMATICS : Application of mathematical and statistical principles in business management.

BUSINESS ORGANIZATION : The primary aim of business organization is to organize the business into various departments and at various levels establishing beneficial relationships and specifying the grouping of work and jobs. The relationships between authority and responsibility and reporting levels are laid down in the process of organizing. This function streamlines the business into organized divisions or groups for attainment of the goals.

BUSINESS PROCESS REENGINEERING : The rethinking *ab initio* and radical redesign of business processes to achieve dramatic improvements and quantum jumps in critical contemporary measures of performance such as cost, quality, speed, service to the customers' satisfaction.

BUSINESS STUDIES : 1. Commercial and management studies. 2. A course of study concerned with various aspects of business.

C

CABINET MAKING : The art and craft of making high quality furniture.

CACOGENICS : Study of the effects of bad heredity.

CAD (COMPUTER AIDED DESIGN) : The process of applying computer technology so that a designer uses a computer terminal as window to bring necessary data to a draughting board.

CADASTRAL SURVEY TECHNOLOGY : A detailed survey of a country as the basis of an assessment for fiscal purposes etc.

CALCULUS : A method of computation in the higher branches of mathematics consisting of differentiation and integration.

CALLIGRAPHY : The art of beautiful writing; fair or elegant writing.

CALLISTHENICS : Systematic exercise for attaining strength and grace.

CAMPANOLOGY : The art or principles of bell ringing.

CANNING : The technique of preserving perishable vegetables and fruits in sealed air : tight cans.

CAPABALITY MATURITY MODEL : A computer model which provides a frame work that organisations can use to determine their ability to develop and maintain software.

CAPITAL MARKET AND INVESTMENT ANALYSIS : Analysis of investment choices on the basis of a study of capital market and make recommendations and suggestions for sound investment.

CAPTURE AND CULTURE FISHERIES : The study of methods of capturing and culturing food fishes.

CARBOHYDRATE CHEMISTRY : Study of the chemistry of a class of chemical substances known as carbohydrates which play an important role in nutrition and industry.

CARCINOLOGY : That department of zoology which interests itself with crustaceans or crabs, shrimps etc.

CARDIAC ARYTHMOLOGY : Study of irregularities of rhythms of the heart and their consequences and treatment.

CARDIAC ELECTROPHYSIOLOGY : Study of the electrical changes and behaviour of the heart.

CARDIAC LABORATORY TECHNOLOGY : Study of the techniques like electro cardiology, Echocardiography and other laboratory methods used in cardiology.

CARDIAC REHABILITATION : Rehabilitation of patients who suffered heart attacks and other heart diseases and complaints.

CARDIOANAESTHESIA : Branch of anaesthesiology specializing in heart surgery.

CARDIOELECTROPHYSIOLOGY : The science that is concerned with the mechanism, spread and interpretation of the electric currents which arise within the heart muscle tissue and initiate each heart muscle contraction.

CARDIOLOGY : Scientific study of the heart usually regarded as a branch of medical science.

CARDIO-RESPIRATORY PHYSIOLOGY : Study of the physiology of the connection between cardiac and respiratory activities.

CARDIOSURGERY : Department of surgery concerned with the surgical treatment of heart diseases.

CARDIOTHORACIC ANAESTHESIA : Branch of anaesthesiology concerned with cardiothoracic surgery.

CARDIOTHORACIC SURGERY : Branch of medical science concerned with the surgical treatment of heart and thoracic diseases.

CARDIOVASCULAR AND THORACIC NURSING : Branch of nursing concerned with patients undergoing treatment for cardiovascular and thoracic problems.

CARDIOVASCULAR SURGERY : Surgical treatment of disorders of the heart and associated blood vessels.

CAREER EDUCATION : Comprehensive educational programme that focusses on individual career development. See vocational education.

CAREER GUIDANCE : Guiding students and others about career opportunities and choices in keeping with their skills and aptitudes.

CARGO MANAGEMENT : A course of study pertaining to the management of lading or freight of a ship or airlines.

CARICATURE : An art form, either pictorial or descriptive in which beauties or defects are exaggerated so as to make the person or thing ridiculous while a general likeness is retained.

CARPENTARY : The art and craft of making useful objects with wood such as those used in construction and furniture.

CARPET TECHNOLOGY : The art, craft and technology of manufacturing carpets.

CARPOLOGY : Division of Botany concerned with the study of the structure of fruits and seeds.

CARTOGRAPHY : The science of the preparation of maps and charts.

CARTOMANCY : Reading of playing cards.

CARTOONING : An art form consisting of a pictorial sketch relating to any prevalent topic or events generally satirical in nature but always with a sense of humour.

CASE LAW : Branch of law built up on previous judicial decisions.

CASCADE ENGINEERING : Branch of engineering which involves carrying out reactions in a single pot reactor by choosing the appropriate reaction conditions with different modes of operation instead of conducting the several multistep reactions with intermittent separations and purifications.

CASH MANAGEMENT : Cash management is concerned with increasing the liquidity of firms by managing the cash inflows, outflows, debts and inventories to overcome the need to borrow from the market.

CASTING : The art of assigning the roles of a play or cinema to various actors. Forms part of a training course in stage and cinema direction.

CASTING TECHNOLOGY : 1. The technology of melting metals like iron and casting into pigs, ingots or moulds which renders the mental hard and non-malleable. 2. The technology of manufacturing articles with cast metals. Branch of engineering.

CATALOGUING : Branch of library science concerned with the preparation of catalogues of books classified according to their subjects.

CATARACT SURGERY : Branch of ophtholmology concerned with the removal of the lens affected by the disease known as cataract and fitting an artificial intraocular lens. Cataract may affect one or both eyes. If the affected eye is not operated upon the cataract will lead to blindness.

CATERING TECHNOLOGY : A branch of hotel management concerned with purveying food and beverages to customers.

CATHLAB TECHNOLOGY ; Branch of medical laboratory technology.

CATWALK CHOREOGRAPHY : Choreography concerned with the movements of models on the ramp.

CAVE ART : The art of upper palaeolithic Age. Also known as cro-magnon Art.

CELESTIAL GEODESY : The branch of geodesy which utilizes observations of near celestial bodies and earth satellites in order to determine the size and shape of the earth.

CELESTIAL MECHANICS : The study of he motions of forces between the celestial bodies.

CELL BIOLOGY : Branch of biology concerned with cell structure, growth, division, physiology, biochemistry etc.

CELL CULTURE : The technique of culturing cells taken from multicellular organisms in artificial nutrient medium containing growth substances intended to study fundamental problems of cell biology with potential applications in medicine.

CELL PHYSIOLOGY : Study of physiological processes at the cellular level.

CELLULOSE TECHNOLOGY : Extraction of cellulose from natural sources and its use in industry.

CEMENT TECHNOLOGY : Manufacture of cement and its use in construction and other industries.

CENTROGRAPHY : Statistical methods used to analyze geographical distributions.

CEPHALOMETRY : Branch of somatometry that involves measuring the face and head

CERAMIC DESIGN : The art of designing ceramic objects.

CERAMIC ENGINEERING : Application of engineering in ceramic industry.

CERAMICS : Art and science of making baked clay objects or the objects so made.

CERAMIC TECHNOLOGY : Use and application of ceramics in various fields.

CEREAL CROPS : Branch of agriculture concerned with the study of the morphology, cultivation, breeding and other aspects of cereal crops like rice, wheat, maize etc.

CEROGRAPHY : 1. The art of writing or engraving on wax. 2. The art of painting in wax colours.

CHARACTEROLOGY : Study of character and personality.

CHARTOGRAPHY : The art or practice of drawing maps or charts.

CHEMATOLOGY : See TRIBOCHEMISTRY :

CHEMICAL ANALYSIS AND QUALITY MANAGEMENT : Management of quality of products on the basis of their chemical analysis offered as a diploma course useful in industries, analytical sciences and electronics.

CHEMICAL BIOLOGY : Study of the chemical compounds present and chemical reactions taking place in living beings.

CHEMICAL CRYSTALLOGRAPHY : The geometric description and study of internal arrangement of atoms in crystals formed from chemical compounds.

CHEMICAL ECOLOGY : Study of the chemical changes taking place in the environment and their impact on the ecological conditions.

CHEMICAL ENGINEERING : The study of the design, manufacture and operation of plant and machinery for the industrial chemical processes.

CHEMICAL KINETICS : That branch of physical chemistry concerned with the mechanisms and rates of chemical reactions. Also known as reaction kinetics.

CHEMICAL MICROSCOPY : Application of the microscope to the solution of chemical problems.

CHEMICAL MINING : The extraction of valuable components of an ore body either within the mining area or elsewhere by chemical methods such as leaching.

CHEMICAL OCEANOGRAPHY : The study of the chemistry of ocean water, the dissolved and suspended substances in it, the level of acidity and the geographical and temporal variation of its chemical characteristics.

CHEMICAL PATHOLOGY : Study of chemical changes and processes involved in disease.

CHEMICAL PHYSICS : Study of the physical principles and laws involved in chemical processes.

CHEMICAL PLANT DESIGN : Branch of engineering concerned with designing plant and machinery used in chemical industries.

CHEMICAL PROCESS TECHNOLOGY : Study of industrial manufacturing chemical processes as, for example, in plastic, fibres, drugs, chemicals, oil refining etc.

CHEMICAL REACTION ENGINEERING : Modification of nature and rate of chemical reactions by engineering the physicochemical factors.

CHEMICAL SCIENCES : Sciences related to chemistry like, for example, chemical engineering, chemical technology, medicinal chemistry, industrial chemistry, applied chemistry etc.

CHEMICAL STRATIGRAPHY : Use of chemical characteristics in the study and classification of rock strata in the earth.

CHEMICAL TECHNOLOGY : Utilization of knowledge of chemistry in the manufacture of useful products.

CHEMICAL THERMODYNAMICS : Study of the thermodynamic principles and laws involved in chemical reactions and processes.

CHEMICAL ULTRASONICS : Use of ultrasound to induce chemical reactions. Also known as SONOCHEMISTRY.

CHEMICAL WARFARE : Using poisonous gases and other chemicals to kill enemy populations on a large scale. Terrorists are also using such methods.

CHEMISTRY : The science which seeks to discover the different kinds of matter of which the globe is composed and treats of the nature, laws of combination and mutual actions of the particles of matter and the properties of the compounds they form.

CHEMISTRY OF NATURAL PRODUCTS : Study of the chemistry of medicines, drugs, rubber, dyes, perfumes and several other plant and animal products obtained from nature and used by man.

CHEMOINFORMATICS : Molecular modelling structure based and *de novo* based drug design, toxicity, semiemperical and *ab initio* study of ligand docking, pharmacophore perception and computer software tools.

CHEMOMETRICS : Use of Computational and mathematical methods to extract information from analytical data in chemistry.

CHEMOTAXONOMY : Classification of organisms based on similarities and differences in their chemical products and biochemical pathways involved in their manufacture.

CHEMOTHERAPY : Branch of medicine concerned with the treatment of diseases by means of chemicals, particularly applicable to cancer treatment.

CHILD AND ADOLESCENT DEVELOPMENT : Study of the growth and development of child and adolescent stages with particular emphasis to their bearing on rearing children. Regarded as a branch of medicine, home science, psychology and allied subjects.

CHILD AND ADOLESCENT PSYCHIATRY : Branch of psychiatry concerned with the mental disorders of children and adolescents.

CHILD CARE : A course of study in which training is imparted in rearing children, including feeding, playing, putting them to sleep etc.

CHILD DEVELOPMENT : Branch of educational psychology which studies physical, intellectual, social and personality development of children.

CHILD HEALTH : Branch of medicine concerned with management of child health problems.

CHILD HEALTH NURSING : Branch of nursing science concerned with nursing services for sick children.

CHILD PSYCHIATRY : Medical study of abnormal behaviour in childhood and adolescence including Juvemile delinquents, drug addicts, etc.,

CHILD PSYCHOLOGY : Developmental study of human growth and behaviour from infancy to adolescence.

CHINESE MEDICINE : Includes herbalism and acupuncture in restoring balance to mind, body and spirit.

CHIRAL CHEMISTRY : Study of chemical compounds exhibiting stereoisomerism in their molecular structure, particularly those looking like mirror images having right and left-handed symmetry.

CHIROGRAPHY : 1. The art of writing; hand-writing. 2. The art of telling fortunes by examining the hand.

CHIROLOGY : The art or practice of communicating thoughts by signs made by the hands and fingers, much used by deaf-mutes.

CHIROMANCY : The art or practice of foretelling one's fortune by inspecting the lines and lineaments of his hand. Also known as palmistry. See CHIROGRAPHY.

CHIROPRACTIC : Healing that focusses on the adjustment of the spinal column as a treatment for many musculoskeletal pain problems.

CHIRUGERY : See SURGERY.

CHOCOLOGY : The science which studies the properties of various preparations made of cocoa like chocolates, beverages etc. and their effects on health and physiology.

CHONDRIOLOGY : The anatomical study of cartilage.

CHOREOGRAPHY : Conducting a band of dancers accompanied by their own singing or that of others.

CHOROGRAPHY : The art or practice of making maps of or describing particular regions, countries or districts.

CHOROLOGY : The study of how organisms are distributed geographically.

CHRISTIAN SCIENCE : A religious movement founded by Mrs. Eddy in 1866; the chief practical tenet of its creed is that pain and illness are illusions.

CHRISTIAN STUDIES : Study of christian scriptures and literature.

CHRISTOLOGY : See Christian Studies.

CHROMATOGRAPHY : Diverse groups of separation processes based on differences in rates at which individual components of a mixture migrate through a stationary phase.

CHROMATOLOGY : Science of colours.

CHROMODYNAMICS : A theory of interaction between quarks carrying colour in which the quarks exchange gluons in a manner analogous to the exchange of protons between charged particles in electrodynamics.

CHROMOLITHOGRAPHY : A method of producing coloured lithographic pictures by using stones having different portions of the picture drawn upon them with inks of different colours and so arranged as to blend into a complete picture.

CHRONOBIOLOGY : Effect of time on organisms and ecosystems especially of ciracadian and other rhythms.

CHRONOLOGY : The science of ascertaining the true periods or years when past events or transactions took place and arranging them in their proper order according to these dates.

CHRONOMETRY : The art and science of measuring time; the measuring of time by periods or divisions.

CHRONOTHERAPY : Treating sleep disorders by changing sleep timings.

CINEMATOGRAPHY : The art and science of producing motion pictures by means of movie photography. This has grown over the years into a highly advanced and specialized technology.

CIRCULAR PAPER CHROMATOGRAPHY : A paper chromatographic technique in which migration from a spot in the sheet takes place in 360° so that zones separate as a series of concentric rings.

CIVICS : Elementary form of political science.

CIVIL AVIATION : Air transportation planning and design based on publications of international civil aviation organization, federal aviation administration and other similar institutions.

CIVIL ENGINEERING : That branch of engineering which relates to the forming of roads, bridges, railroads, canals, aqueducts, harbours etc.

CIVIL ENGINEERING AND INFRASTRUCTURE TECHNOLOGY: Application of civil engineering in infrastructure development like laying roads, constructing bridges and buildings and arranging water supply, drainage etc., for starting any enterprises like industries, educational institutions, hospitals etc.

CIVILIAN BIODEFENCE STUDIES : Study of methods of protecting civilian population from dangers of biological warfare.

CLADISTICS : It is concerned with the study of the pattern produced by the evolutionary process, but is not concerned with the process that created it. It is a way of looking at the living world in terms of how they shared characteristics with one another without making unsustainable assumptions about ancestry and descent.

CLAIRYOYANCE : Visualizing objects hidden from the senses.

CLASSICAL ECONOMICS : The classical period in the study of economics ranged from 1776-1848. Classical economic theory was essentially about growth and development and set out to investigate the nature and causes of the wealth of nations and distribution of the national product among the factors of production within the framework of growing population and finite resources and of free competition in a private enterprise economy. Classical economics was also strongly oriented towards policy recommendations. Classical economics also examined micro-economic problems.

CLASSICAL FIELD THEORY : The study of the distribution of energy, matter and other physical quantities under circumstances where their discreet nature is unimportant and they may be regarded as (in general, complex) continuous functions of position. Also known as c-number theory, continuum mechanics, continuum physics.

CLASSICAL MECHANICS : Mechanics based on Newton's Laws of motion.

CLASSICAL PHYSICS : Theoretical physics upto approximately end of 19th Century.

CLASSICAL TAXONOMY : Taxonomic study based on morphology and anatomy.

CLASSICAL TECHNIQUES : A term used to describe standard statistical techniques in order to distinguish them particularly from Beyesian techniques. The feature of classical methods is that no information other than the sample data is used to make statistical inferences or with estimation of parameters of regression equations. It is generally used in economics.

CLASSICS : Study of Greek and Latin languages and classical civilization.

CLASSROOM ECOLOGY : Branch of educational research which studies problems in the real settings of the classroom environment.

CLIMATOCHRONOLOGY : The absolute age dating of recent geological events by using the oxygen isotope ratios in ice, shells and so on.

CLIMATOGRAPHY : A quantitative description of climate, particularly with reference to the tables and charts which show the climatic elements in an area.

CLIMATOLOGY : That branch of meteorology concerned with the mean physical state of the atmosphere in space and time as reflected in weather behaviour over a period of many years.

CLIMATOPHYSIOLOGY : The study of the interaction of the natural environment with physiologic factors.

CLINICAL BIOCHEMISTRY : Application of biochemistry in the diagnosis and treatment of diseases.

CLINICAL CHEMISTRY : Analysis and monitoring of changes in blood glucose and such other clinical chemical substances.

CLINICAL EPIDEMIOLOGY : Clinical investigation of epidemic diseases.

CLINICAL GENETICS : The study of biological inheritance by direct observation of living patients.

CLINICAL HAEMATOLOGY : Application of haematology in the diagnosis and treatment of diseases.

CLINICAL IMMUNOLOGY : Study of the immunological basis of diseases.

CLINICAL LINGUISTICS : Diagnosis of linguistic disorders such as inability to speak and to use language properly.

CLINICAL MEDICINE : Branch of medical science in which instruction is imparted to the student in a practical manner at the bed side of a patient.

CLINICAL MYCOLOGY : Branch of mycology concerned with the study of fungal diseases of man.

CLINICAL NEUROLOGY : Branch of medical science concerned with the study of the diseases of the nervous system.

CLINICAL NEUROPSYCHOLOGY : Diagnosis of brain impairement and how it affects thinking skills, emotions, behaviour and personality. Developing rehabilitation methods for brain impairement and interacting with other medical professionals.

CLINICAL NUTRITION : Diagnosis and treatment of nutritional disorders.

CLINICAL ONCOLOGY : Diagnosis and treatment of various types of cancer.

CLINICAL PATHOLOGY : Interpreting the results of various pathological tests for the diagnosis of diseases.

CLINICAL PHARMACOLOGY : Branch of pharmaceutical science concerned with the effects of drugs in treating diseases.

CLINICAL PSYCHOLOGY : Application of psychology in the diagnosis of mental illness.

CLINICAL RADIOTHERAPY : Use of radiations in the treatment of diseases like cancer.

CLINICAL SURGERY : Branch of medical science in which instruction is imparted to the student in a practical manner at the bedside of the patient.

CLINICAL VETERINARY MEDICINE : Branch of veterinary science concerned with the treatment of animal diseases.

CLINICAL VIROLOGY : Branch of virology concerned with the study of viral diseases of man.

CLONING TECHNOLOGY : A branch of reproductive technology in which the egg of a female animal is fertilised by a denucleated somatic cell of a male animal leading to the production of a progeny, in a series of further steps. The method was first successfully employed in a sheep and is now being, successfully replicated in several other animals. Attempts are being made to apply this technology to man.

CLOUD PHYSICS : The study of the physical and dynamical processes governing the structure and development of clouds and the release from them of snow, rain and hail.

C-NUMBER THEORY : See CLASSICAL FIELD THEORY.

COAL GEOLOGY : Branch of geology concerned with the structure, formation, mining and other aspects of fossil coal deposits.

COAL PALAEOBOTANY : A branch of palaeobotany concerned with the origin, composition, mode of occurrence and significance of fossil plant materials that occur in or are associated with coal deposits.

COAL PETROLOGY : The science that deals with the origin, history, occurrence, structure, chemical composition and classification of coal.

COASTAL HARBOUR HYDRAULICS AND ENGINEERING : Study of coastal harbors and their hydraulics and engineering problems.

COASTAL ZONE MANAGEMENT : Management of coastal zones from the point of view of natural resources.

COBOL : Short form of Common Business Oriented Language, an internationally accepted computer programming language for general commercial use.

COGNITIVE NEURO SCIENCE : Branch of neurology concerned with the role of the nervous system in conscious thought processes, mental structures and organizations.

COGNITIVE PSYCHOLOGY : Branch of psychology concerned with the study of conscious thought processes, mental structures and organizations, application of information processing models, intelligent human behaviour and adaptation to environment.

COGNITIVE PSYCHOPHARMACOLOGY : Study of the effects of drugs on conscious thought processes and psychological behaviour.

CONGNITIVE THERAPHY : It is a kind of therapy which is intermediate between behaviour therapy and dynamic psychotherapy with emphasis on conscious thought processes.

COLD CHAIN TECHNOLOGY : It is a technology for processing fruits and vegetables and to facilitate their transportation and establishing a chain of cold storage facilities at various points *en route*.

COLLOID CHEMISTRY : The scientific study of matter whose size is approximately 10-10,000 angstroms (1-1000 nanometers) and which exist as a suspension in a continuous medium especially a liquid, solid or gaseous substance.

COLO-PROCTOLOGY : Branch of medicine concerned with the diseases of the colon and rectum.

COLORIMETRY : The technique of measuring the depth of colour in a liquid by comparison with a standard liquid of the same tint. The method is applied for estimating the concentration of a substance in a solution. The technique may be photoelectric or indirect by means of spectrophotometry, used in physics and chemistry.

COMBAT VEHICLES : Study and manufacture of combat vehicles like tanks, bombing aircraft etc., used in warfare.

COMBINATORIAL CHEMISTRY : Use of automated equipment to systematically create and test thousands of chemical samples in about the same time it would have taken to test one sample with more conventional methods.

COMBINATORIAL MATHEMATICS : It is concerned with the number of ways in which one integer which means a whole number or a thing complete in itself can be expressed as the sum of smaller integers.

COMMERCE : A comprehensive term for all forms of trade wholesale, retail, import, export and all services which assist the carrying on of trade such as banking, insurance and transport.

COMMERCE NET : Computer applications in equity research and portfolio management, data extraction and analysis; intranet and extranet.

COMMERCIAL AND INDUSTRIAL LAW : Law applicable to commercial and industrial concerns and their activities.

COMMERCIAL GEOGRAPHY : Branch of geography concerned with the study of geographical distribution of commercial activities and the factors governing their distribution.

COMMON LAW : Law which is common to the whole country based on custom.

COMMONWEALTH LITERATURE : Literature of various countries of the British commonwealth

COMMUNICABLE DISEASES : Infectious diseases caused by pathogenic organisms and transmitted between individuals of same or different species.

COMMUNICATION ENGINEERING : Branch of engineering concerned with the design, manufacture, maintenance and operation of communication systems.

COMMUNICATION SYSTEMS : Study of means of transmission of information like telephone, radio, television, satellites etc.

COMMUNICATIVE DISORDERS : Speech and hearing disabilities and diseases.

COMMUNITY DENTISTRY : Study of dental problems of all members of a community with participation by and education of the community concerned.

COMMUNITY GASTROENTEROLOGY : Study of gastroenterological problems of a community with participation by and education of community concerned.

COMMUNITY HEALTH AND NUTRITION : Study of public health and nutrition with emphasis on participation by and education of the community concerned.

COMMUNITY HEALTH NURSING : Branch of nursing science which is concerned with community health : care.

COMMUNITY MEDICINE : Public health with emphasis on participation by and education of the community concerned.

COMPANY LAW : Law governing the establishment and conduct of companies.

COMPANY SECRETARYSHIP : A course of study for preparing persons to take up company secretaryship as a profession on passing the examination conducted by the institute of company secretaries.

COMPARATIVE CERAMICS : Technique of determining the chronology of ancient peoples by studying their ceramics.

COMPARATIVE CONSTITUTIONAL LAW : Comparative study of the constitutions of different countries.

COMPARATIVE DRAVIDIAN LITERATURE : Comparative study of the literature of dravidian languages.

COMPARATIVE EDUCATION : A study of educational problems and the solutions attempted in various countries. The outcomes and success or failure of educational reforms are studied. Special attention is paid to the problems of disadvantaged groups.

COMPARATIVE EMBRYOLOGY : A branch of embryology that deals with the similarities and differences in the development of embryo of animals or plants of different orders.

COMPARATIVE GENOMICS : Comparative study of the genomes of different organisms and groups of organisms in order to find kinships and evolutionary trends.

COMPARATIVE LINGUISTICS : Study of resemblances and differences between related languages.

COMPARATIVE LITERARY STUDIES : Study of poems, novels stories and plays written in 2 or more languages.

COMPARATIVE MEDICINE : Comparison of disease treatment between animals and humans.

COMPARATIVE PSYCHOLOGY : Applied usually to animal psychology as it uses comparative method.

COMPARATIVE RELIGION AND PHILOSOPHY : Comparative study of literatures of various countries of the world.

COMPETITION LAW : Law concerned with the regulation and promotion of competition among business institutions.

COMPLEX CLIMATOLOGY : Analysis of the climate of single space or comparison of the climates of 2 or more places.

COMPUTATIONAL BIOLOGY : Computer analysis of biological data espically for taxonomic and genetic studies.

COMPUTATIONAL CHEMISTRY : The use of calculations to predict molecular structure, properties and reactions.

COMPUTATIONAL FLUID DYNAMICS : Combination of fluid dynamics, mathematics and computation. It has a bearing on solid mechanics and nuclear physics. It plays a central role in trouble shooting in science.

COMPUTATIONAL GENOMICS : Computer analysis of genomes as an aid to determine the role of specific genes.

COMPUTATIONAL LIFE SCIENCES : Calculations involving growth, development and other life processes.

COMPUTATIONAL MATHEMATICS : Branch of mathematics concerned with computations.

COMPUTATIONAL SCIENCE : Study of science by means of computations of data pertaining to natural phenomena.

COMPUTER ACCOUNTANCY : The method of maintaining accounts with the help of a computer.

COMPUTER AIDED DESIGN : Short form CAD. Refers to the preparation of designs with the use of computer.

COMPUTER AIDED DRUG DESIGN : Drug designing aided by computers, specially suited to the disease causing protein molecule without side effects and drastically cutting down drug discovery research time and number of research personnel required, thus saving cost.

COMPUTER- AIDED LANGUAGE LEARNING : Use of computers in teaching and learning languages.

COMPUTER : AIDED MANAGEMENT : Use of computers in management.

COMPUTER-AIDED SURERY : Use of computer in formulating the procedure to be adopted in a surgical operation and predicting the outcome of the operation.

COMPUTER -AIDED TEXTILE AND GARMENT DESIGN : Use of computer in preparing designs for textile printing and designing garments.

COMPUTER APPLICATIONS : A general term for the uses to which a computer may be put.

COMPUTER APPLICATIONS IN COMMERCE : Computerised accounting, for example NGN WIN : 95, Office 97, and WIN NT, Computer applications inequity research and portfolio management, data extraction and analysis using Visual Basic, and RDBM's like SQL Server, e-Commerce, internet and extranet.

COMPUTER ARCHITECTURE : Design of the structure and construction of various types of computers like personal computers, desktop computers laptap computers, super computers etc.

COMPUTER COMMUNICATIONS : Use of computers in communications.

COMPUTER ELECTRONICS : Application of electronics in computers.

COMPUTER ENGINEERING : Study of the construction and mechanism of computers.

COMPUTER FORENSICS : Detection of computer crimes like hacking of websites, misuse of internet and intranet, causes of steganography, place of origin of e mails etc.

COMPUTER HARDWARE AND NET WORKING : Includes basic and electronics software institution and network installation.

COMPUTER INFORMATION SYSTEMS : Study of the information systems processed by a computer.

COMPUTER INTEGRATED MANUFACTURING : Use of computers for the integration of manufacturing techniques and processes.

COMPUTER LANGUAGES : Special languages used for computer programming examples : MS-Office, Unix, Visual Basic, Oracle etc.

COMPUTER LAW : Principles of law which govern dealings in and the use of computer technology including software.

COMPUTER MAINTENANCE : Maintenance of both hardware and software. The efficiency of any computer installation depends on effective maintenance.

COMPUTER NETWORK AND INTERNET APPLICATIONS : Computer networks LAN/WAN, creating web pages, internet protocol architecture networking applications for WWW.

COMPUTER PROGRAMMING : Programming is the process by which a set of instructions in the form of a computer language code for computer to make it perform a specified activity.

COMPUTER SCIENCE : Includes basic electronics, hardware, software and exposure to large computer systems.

COMPUTER SERVICING : The work of keeping the computer in an efficient working condition and undertaking repairs when necessary.

COMPUTERS IN MEDICINE : Use of computers in maintaining hospital records including diagnosis and treatment of patient's diseases as well as an aid in performing operations. Several instruments used in diagnosis and in surgery are computerised for increasing their efficiency and precision.

COMPUTER TECHNOLOGY : 1. Technological applications of computer. 2. Technology involved in the manufacture of computers.

COMPUTRONICS : Application of electronics in computers.

CONCHOLOGY : Study of the shells of mollusks.

CONCRETE TECHNOLOGY : Technology of manufacturing cement concrete and its use in construction work.

CONDENSED MATTER PHYSICS : Study of the physical properties of condensed matter like, for example under low temperatures and high magnetic fields.

CONFECTIONARY ARTS : Art of making sweetmeats, toffees etc.,

CONFLICT MANAGEMENT : Managing national and international conflict situations including insurgency, terrorism etc.

CONSERVATIVE DENTISTRY : Branch of dentistry concerned with the methods employed to save the dental structures from deterioration and eventual loss.

CONSTITUTIONAL LAW : Law pertaining to constitutional provisions and issues arising from them.

CONSTITUTIONAL JURISPRUDENCE : See constitutional law.

CONSTRUCTION CHEMICALS : Study of chemicals used in construction of buildings, bridges etc., like paints, varnishes, adhesives and other substances to prevent seepage of water etc.,

CONSTRUCTION CONTRACTING : Training course on contracting construction laws, bidding, tendering etc.

CONSTRUCTION ENGINEERING : Branch of civil engineering concerned with construction of buildings, bridges, dams, roads etc.

CONSTRUCTION EQUIPMENT MANAGEMENT : Management of equipment used in construction like concrete mixers etc.

CONSTRUCTION MANAGEMENT : Management of construction work involving employment and supervision of personnel and labour, payment of wages, procurement and supply of materials, maintaining accounts etc.

CONSTRUCTION PERSONNEL MANAGEMENT : Management of personnel employed in construction work like selection, supervision of their work, payment of wages, taking welfare measures etc.

CONSTRUCTION PROJECT MANAGEMENT : Management of all departments of construction projects.

CONSTRUCTION QUALITY MANAGEMENT : Management of quality control of construction projects involving quality of materials used in construction and quality of construction work in all its aspects.

CONSTRUCTION SAFETY MANAGEMENT : Management of safety of buildings, bridges, roads, dams etc., and of the safety of workers involved in construction work.

CONSTRUCTION TECHNOLOGY : Technological methods and innovations used in buildings and other constructions.

CONSUMER ECONOMICS : Branch of economics concerned with goods and services required for consumers, their availability, quality, prices etc.

CONSUMER ELECTRONICS : Branch of electronics concerned with electronic articles like radio, television, sound systems, VCR's, frigidaires, washing machines, microovens etc. commonly used by consumers.

CONSUMERISM : 1. A movement for the protection of consumers rights involving consumers associations, consumer forums, payment of compensation for deficiency in service by traders, service personnel and government departments etc. This is offered as a subject in some educational institutions. 2. Craze for consumer goods.

CONSUMER PROTECTION LAWS : Laws meant for protection of consumers interests.

CONTEMPORARY LITERATURE : Study of the literatures of contemporary times.

CONTEXT STUDIES : Liberal studies or minor subjects seen as helping to put students' major or main subjects in perspective.

CONTINUING EDUCATION : Extension of education part-time or full-time for young people and adults beyond the school leaving age.

CONTINUUM MECHANICS : See classical field theory.

CONTNUUM PHYSICS : See classical field theory.

CONTRACT LAW : Law pertaining to contracts.

CONTROL ENGINEERING : Study and development of automatic control in engineering based largely on mathematical laws.

CONTROL AND PROTECTION ENGINEERING : Branch of engineering concerned with controlling damage and protecting structures and machinery from depreciation and other destructive factors.

CONTROL SYSTEMS : A branch of electrical engineering.

CONVERGENCE LAW : Law covering the areas of telecommunication, broadcasting and net companies.

CONVERGENCE TECHNOLOGY : Convergence in multiservice technology where convergence of data, voice and video takes place. In other words computer, cable and content all merge into one common media and outlet.

COOKERY : The art of cooking.

COOPERATION : Study of co-operative institutions.

COOPERATIVE MANAGEMENT : Management of cooperative institutions.

COORDINATION CHEMISTRY : The chemistry of metal ions in their interactions with other molecules or ions.

COPERNICIAN ASTRONOMY : The system of astronamy proposed by the polish scientist Nicolas Copernicus (1473 : 1543) which rejected the notion that the earth was a stationery body at the centre of the universe but said that the sun was in the centre of the universe and earth was rotating around the sun.

COPROLOGY : Literary treatment of a base or dung- hill subject.

COPY EDITING : Editing manuscripts meant for publication.

CORONARY ANGIOPLASTY : Technique of removing blocks in the blood vessels of the heart.

CORONARY RADIOTHERAPY : Intracoronary radiotherapy to prevent restenosis after angioplasty by the use of radioactivity.

CORPORATE BANKING : Banking services dealing with large companies and government agencies.

CORPORATE COMMUNICATION : Maintaining good communication channels with shareholders is one of the important factors which determine good corporate governance.

CORPORATE ENVIRONMENTAL ECONOMICS : Study of the economic forces which continuously influence the organisation from the outside.

CORPORATE ENVIRONMENTAL MANAGEMENT : It is defined as a live function which deals with the management of external forces continuously influencing the operation of an organisation. The external forces are politics, administration, law and statute, society, religion, competition, business groups and media.

CORPORATE FINANCIAL MANAGEMENT : The application of financial principles within a corporation to create and maintain value through decision making and proper resource management.

CORPORATE GOVERNANCE : Corporate governance refers to management's recognition of its fiduciary responsibility to all shareholders. The framework for good corporate governance has a number of dimensions of which the most important are : 1. The regulatory concept; 2. Disclosure practices and communication. 3. Management objectives. 4. Structure of management's compensation.

CORPORATE LAW : Law applicable to business corporations.

CORPORATE SECRETARYSHIP : See company secretaryship.

CORPORATE STRATEGY : Study of the strategies to be adopted by corporations in making important decisions.

CORPORATION FINANCE : Study of the methods and ways to be adopted by corporations to secure financial resources for their business.

CORRESPONDENCE EDUCATION : See distance education.

CORROSION SCIENCE AND ENGINEERING : Study of the process of slow wearing away by the action of chemical and other factors primarily on metals and methods of preventing it from the standpoint of science and engineering.

COSMETIC CHEMISTRY : chemical study of cosmetics or beautifying substances.

COSMETIC DENTISTRY : Cosmetic or aesthetic dentistry is a multidisciplinary component of total facial harmony. Facial harmony applies to all the facial muscles around the mouth, the gums and the teeth. It involves the use of new techniques and innovative materials and includes bleaching, cosmetic cotouring, bonding inlays/outlays, aesthetic braces and implants.

COSMETIC SCIENCE : Study of the scientific aspects of preparations employed to render the skin soft, pure and white or to beautify and improve the complexion.

COSMETIC SURGERY : It is a kind of plastic surgery and includes all procedures adopted in plastic surgery to (beautify) improve the appearance of a person with normal function. Examples : breast augmentation in a woman with small breasts, rhinoplasty for improving the appearance of the nose.

COSMETOLOGY : Science concerned with beautifying and improving the complexion. See cosmetic science.

COSMOCHEMISTRY : Branch of cosmology concerned with the study of the chemical substances and reactions constituting the universe.

COSOMOLOGY : Study of origin, nature and evolution of the universe.

COST ACCOUNTANCY : To workout the unit cost of finished products taking into account not only variable costs but also a proportion of fixed costs.

COST ACCOUNTING : Detailed elements of cost for purposes of pricing, departmental budgeting and the control of manufacturing methods, material and labour.

COST ENGINEERING : Estimation of costs involved in engineering works and projects.

COSTING : See cost accounting.

COST MANAGEMENT : Analysis of costs in the manufacturing and other industries, business and government undertakings and taking measures to control the costs.

COSTUME DESIGNING : Designing costumes for actors in dramas, cinema, T.V. etc.

COST TECHNOLOGY : Short form for commercial off the shelf technology. It means purchasing equipment and materials from the private sector for defence and public sector needs.

COURSE DESIGNING : Branch of education concerned with designing courses of study for students.

CRAFT TRAINING : Training in a craft skill.

CRANIOLOGY : Study of crania and skulls including the measurement, photography or pictorial representation and description.

CREATIVE DESIGN : Academic discipline concerned with the development of craft.

CREATIVE WRITING : A course of study and training in the art of writing literary fiction like stories, novels, dramas etc.

CREDIT ANALYSIS : The process of analysing information on companies and bond issues in order to estimate the ability of the issues to live up to its future contractual obligations.

CRIME INVESTIGATION : Methods of investigation of various kinds of criminal acts like theft, forgery, financial frauds, murders etc. This study is useful to detectives and police personnel.

CIRMINAL JUSTICE : See criminal law.

CRIMINAL LAW : Law relating to criminal cases as opposed to civil cases. For example crimes like forgery, theft, murder, dacoity etc., are covered under this law.

CRIMINAL PSYCHOLOGY : Investigation of psychology of crimes and criminals and law pertaining to them.

CRIMINOLOGY : Study of crimes and criminals and law pertaining to them.

CRITICAL CARE MEDICINE : It is an important component of any hospital as it takes care of those patients whose life is threatened due to a variety of reasons like accidents, post-operative reasons, organ failures, infection etc. Seriously ill patients and their total needs such as nutrition, blood circulation, respiration etc, besides efforts to bring back the normal functioning of organs.

CRO-MAGNON ART : See cave art.

CROP BIOTECHNOLOGY : Molecular mapping, molecular marker-assisted plant breeding, transgenic plants etc., come under biotechnology.

CROP BOTANY : Study of the Botany of crop plants like rice, wheat maize, sugarcane etc.

CROP PHYSIOLOGY : Physiological study of crops pertaining to fertilizer, water requirements, soil factors, weather conditions, growth factors, productivity etc.

CROP PROTECTION : Control of crop pests and diseases.

CROP SCIENCES : Sciences concerned with cultivation and growth and yield of crops like plant breeding, crop protection, crop physiology, soil science, water relations etc.

CROP TECHNOLOGY : Use of modern machinery and methods for carrying out various agricultural operations like sowing seeds, weeding, watering, pesticides application, harvesting etc.

CROWD PSYCHOLOGY : Investigation of crowd statistics.

CRUSTACEOLOGY : Branch of zoology concerned with the study of custaceans comprising crabs, lobsters, shrimps etc. and characterised by having an external calcareous skeleton or shell in many pieces and capable of being moulted or cast, a number of jointed limbs, head and thorax united into a single mass, abdomen often forming a kind of tail.

CRUSTAL EVOLUTION : Study of the evolution of the structure of the crust of the earth.

CRYOBIOLOGY : 1. Study of organisms living at very low temperatures as in Antarctica. 2. The use of low temperature environments in the study of living plants and animals.

CRYOGENICS : Study of very low temperatures and the techniques for producing them.

CRYOGENIC ENGINEERING : Branch of engineering concerned with producing very low temperatures.

CRYOLITHOLOGY : Study of the development, physical characteristics and structure of underground ice especially in permafrost areas.

CRYOLOGY : Study of ice and snow.

CRYOPEDOLOGY : A branch of geology concerned with the study of intensive frost action and permanently frozen ground.

CRYOSCOPY : A phase equilibrium technique to determine molecular weight and other properties of a solute by dissolving it in liquid solvent and ascertaining the solvent's freezing point.

CRYOSURGERY : See cryotherapy.

CRYOTHERAPY : Treatment by local freezing chiefly for skin tumors and some otherwise inoperable cases.

CRYPTO CLIMATOLOGY : The science of climates of confined spaces; a form of microclimatology.

CRYPTOGAMIC BOTANY : Study of plants forming a large division of the plant kingdom, which do not bear true flowers consisting of true stamens and pistils and which are divided into cellular and vascular cryptogams, the former including algae, fungi, lichens, mosses etc., the latter, the ferns, the horsetails, lycopods etc.

CRYPTOLOGY : Secret or enigmatical language.

CRYSTAL CHEMISTRY : The study of the crystalline structure and properties of a mineral or other solid.

CRYSTAL DYNAMICS : See LATTICE DYNAMICS.

CRYSTAL ENGINEERING : Modification of crystal structure by various physical and chemical methods for intended purpose.

CRYSTAL GROWTH : Study of the growth of crystals.

CRYSTALLOGRAPHY : The science of crystallization, teaching the principles of the process and the forms and structure of crystals.

CRYSTAL OPTICS : Study of propagation of light in crystalline solids.

CULINARY ARTS : The art of cooking used in kitchens.

CULTURAL ANTHROPOLOGY : Study of the cultural evolution of man.

CULTURAL ECONOMICS : Analytical, theoretical and quantitative aspects of economics of art and culture covering areas such as demand and supply of a particular art form, price and income elasticity of performing arts, the market for art and culture, labour market in culture, need and rationale for public subvention in art and culture, resource mobilization and financing cultural organizations etc.

CULTURAL STUDIES : Study of the cultures of different societies or communities.

CULTUROLOGY : Science dealing with culture as a distinct class of phenomena.

CURRENCY : Strictly that component of a country's money stock that literally circulates from hand to hand, i.e., coins and bank notes. But the term is also used in the broader sense of a country's money, for example, sterling, franc, dollar, rupee etc, in which case it refers to the total money stock of that country.

CUSTOMER ASSET MANAGEMENT : A strategy aimed at retaining life long customer relationships through the use of computer technology. Also known as customer relationships management.

CUSTOMER RELATIONS MANAGEMENT : Short form CRM. It is a technology that makes customer interaction with a company quick and effortless. CRM technology helps businesses maintain an exhaustive information bank of customer preferences collected through previous contact with the customer, market survey, customer querries and direct sales thus making the whole process fast and friendly. CRM requires a customer centric business philosophy and culture to support effective marketing, sales and service processes.

The control of CRM through the internet is the main theme of eCRM. It is a web-driven technology.

CUSTOMS : Study of taxes on imports considered as a branch of economics and commerce.

CUSTOMS LAW : Law pertaining to customs..

CUTANEOUS BIOLOGY : Study of the skin or other covering of organisms.

CYANOMETRY : Study and measurement of the blueness of light.

CYBER LAWS : Law governing the use of internet.

CYBERNETICS : 1. Theory of communication systems and control mechanisms in living beings and machines. 2. One of the subjects of study in management sciences.

CYBERSPACE : A combination of the computer, communication, telecommunication and entertainment industries. The term cyberspace includes talk, computer, play, pay, shop and other activities (via) computers and work through computer networks.

CYCLADIC ART : The pre-Hellenic art of the Aegean islands.

CYCLEOLOGY : The determination and investigation of cycles in palaeontologic and geological phenomena.

CYCLOMETRY : The art of measuring circles.

CYNEGETICS : The art of hunting with dogs.

CYSTOSCOPY : The study of the interior of the urinary bladder and other parts of the urinogenital system with the help of an optical instrument known as cystoscope. Surgery is also performed with the use of the instrument.

CYTOCHEMISTRY : Study of the chemistry of the constituents of the living cell and primarily the location of chemical constituents and enzymes.

CYTOGENETICS : Comparative study of the mechanisms and behaviour of chromosomes in populations and taxa and the effect of chromosomes on inheritance and evolution.

CYTOLOGY : A branch of biological sciences which deals with the structure, behaviour and reproduction of cells and the growth, function, and chemistry of cell components.

CYTOPATHOLOGY : Study of diseases at the cellular level.

CYTOTAXONOMY : Science dealing with the study of classification and phylogenetic relationships of living beings on the basis of chromosome number, chromosome morphology and other cellular characteristics.

D

DACTYLIOGRAPHY : The art of gem engraving.

DACTYLIOLOGY : Knowledge of relating to the history and qualities of finger rings.

DACTYLOGRAPHY : Study of finger prints.

DACTYLOLOGY : Art of communication by means of signs with hands and fingers. The language of the deaf and the dump.

DAIMONLOGY : Deals with spirits, their involvement in the activities of human beings and methods for handling them.

DAIRY BUSINESS MANAGEMENT : Science of management pertaining to the business of milk, milk products and foods and beverages derived from milk.

DAIRY ENGINEERING : Engineering concerned with the preservation and transport of milk and production of various foods and beverages derived from milk, particularly the machinery employed in these various processes.

DAIRY MICROBIOLOGY : Study of microbiological principles and methods in the preservation of milk and the production of various derivatives of milk.

DAIRY SCIENCE : Study of rearing of milk producing cattle, physical, chemical and nutritional properties of milk and milk products and methods of production of milk derived foods and beverages etc.

DAIRY TECHNOLOGY : Technological aspects of production of milk products on a large scale.

DANCE DIRECTION : The art of directing dance sequences in plays and cinemas.

DARWINISM : The theories of origin of species and the descent of man proposed by Charles Darwin have come to be widely known as Darwinism.

DATA BASE ADMINISTRATION : Managing the database, querrying the huge bank of data, searching records that match specific criteria and creating reports accordingly.

DATABASE DESIGN AND ORACLE : Designing a database using the E.R. Model, Relational Model, Database decomposition, querry optimization, relational algebra, Relational calculus, File system recording from failures and cuncurrence control, Oracle memory architecture creating database.

DATABASE MANAGEMENT SYSTEMS : The software systems required to manage the data within the computer system.

DATA PROCESSING : 1. Condensation of scores or other data into tabular from by various methods by hand mechanically or by computer 2. The operations performed on data usually by automatic electric equipment in order to derive information or to achieve order among files.

DEBT MANAGEMENT : Term used generally in connection with Public debt to denote the action taken by the debt issuing authority or by the central bank acting for it to regulate the size and structure of the outstanding debt. Such management includes deciding the types of debt to be issued for example, short-term or long-term, marketable or non-marketable and the conditions of issue, for example, coupon, issue price, maturity data. An important objective is to control the term structure (relative amounts of different maturities). Because of large size, almost continuous growth of the management of the national debt is essential to control the country's money supply.

DECISION MAKING : The establishment of appropriate courses of action with the aim of achieving given objectives under specified circumstances which may be subject to uncertainity. Decision analyses lead to selection of appropriate criteria by which a course of action may be adjudged.

DECORATIVE ART : Refers to type of art which makes an artifact more attractive by adding embellishments that may not be functional.

DEEP CONTINENTAL STRUCTURE : Branch of geology concerned with the study of structure of continents at great depths.

DEFECT CHEMISTRY : Study of dynamic properties of crystal defects under particular conditions such as raising temperature or exposure to electro-magnetic particle radiation.

DEFENCE MACHINERY DESIGN : Design of machinery used in warfare like tanks, electronic and electric equipments etc.

DEFENCE MANAGEMENT : Management of strategies and their implementation for the defence of a country.

DEFENCE TECHNOLOGY : Deployment of sophisticated technological devices for surveillance and other purposes in the defence of a country.

DEFENSIVE MEDICINE : Clinical strategies to minimize risk of litigation. Chiefly U.S.A. usage.

DEMAND MANAGEMENT : The control of the aggregate level of demand in an economy through the use of monetary policy and/ or fiscal policy.

DEMOGRAPHY : 1. This is defined as the analysis of the size, structure and development of human population. 2. Study of birth and death rate trends and their effects on population trends. 3. The statistical study of populations with reference to nationality, mortality, migratory movements, age, and sex among other social, ethnic and economic factors.

DEMONOLOGY : Mythology and folklore dealing with demons and evil spirits.

DENDROCHRONOLOGY : The branch of Botany and Forestry dealing with the determination of age of trees in years on the basis of number of annual rings found in their stems.

DENDROLOGY : Branch of Botany and Forestry dealing with rearing of trees and allied subjects.

DENTAL ANATOMY : Study of the structure, arrangement and kinds of teeth in animals and man.

DENTAL MATERIALS : Materials used in dentistry for filling gaps, for making artificial teeth etc.,

DENTAL MEDICINE : Medicinal treatment of dental problems as different from dental surgery.

DENTAL PUBLIC HEALTH : Dental Check-up and treatment of members of a community.

DENTAL SCIENCES : Sciences dealing with different aspects of dentistry like orthodontics, dental surgery, periodontics, conservative dentistry, oral health etc.

DENTAL SURGERY : Refers mainly to the extraction of decayed and decaying teeth.

DENTISTRY : The profession of cleaning, extracting and repairing teeth when diseased and replace them when necessary by artificial ones.

DEONTOLOGY : The science of performance of duty.

DEPOSITARY OPERATIONS : Branch Banking and Finance concerned with deposits.

DERMATOGLYPHICS : 1. Diagnosis of chromosome abnormalities especially mongolism using finger prints, 2. The study of the integumentary patterns on the surface of finger tips, palms and sole.

DERMATOLOGY : The branch of science which deals with the skin and its diseases.

DERMOLIPECTOMY : The technique of surgical removal of excess fat from the body.

DESALINATION OF SEA WATER : The technology of reducing the salt level in sea water to make it potable to meet water shortage for drinking and agriculture.

DESCRIPTIVE ANATOMY : Study of the separate and individual portions of the body with regard to form, size, character and position.

DESCRIPTIVE BOTANY : The branch of botany that deals with diagnostic characters or systematic description of plants.

DESCRIPTIVE CLIMATOLOGY : Climatology as presented by graphic and verbal description without going into causes and theory.

DESCRIPTIVE ECONOMICS : An elementary study of economics devoted merely to a description of the working and functions of economic institutions such as the banking systems and IMF.

DESCRIPTIVE LINGUISTICS : Branch of linguistics concerned with the particular method of speech in a particular situation.

DESCRIPTIVE METEOROLOGY : Branch of meteorology dealing with atmosphere as a whole and its phenomena without going into theory. Also known as Aerography.

DESIGN OF CONCRETE STRUCTURES : Branch of civil engineering concerned with the preparation of designs for concrete structures.

DESIGN AND PRODUCTION OF THERMAL POWER EQUIPMENT : A field of engineering involving electrical and mechanical engineering and concerned with the design and manufacture of thermal power equipment for power generating plants.

DESK TOP PUBLISHING (DTP) : Printing with the help of computer.

DEVELOPMENT ADMINISTRATION : Science of administration concerned with the implementation of plans, schemes and projects intended to bring about economic development.

DEVELOPMENTAL BANKING : Branch of banking concerned with the promotion of economic development.

DEVELOPMENTAL BIOLOGY : Branch of biology concerned with the development and life history of living organisms.

DEVELOPMENTAL GENETICS : Genetic control of the process of differentiation of cells during development.

DEVELOPMENTAL PHARMACOLOGY : Study of the effects of drugs and their appropriate dosages in various stages of development of the organism.

DEVELOPMENTAL PSYCHOLOGY : Branch of psychology concerned with the study of mental and behavioural traits in various stages of development of man. It studies the psychological, cognitive and social development that takes place throughout one's life including behaviour during, child-hood and adolescence or changes that occur during maturity and old age. Also developmental disabilities, their effects and how one should cope with them. Developing ways to help elderly people stay as independent as possible.

DEVELOPMENTAL SEXOLOGY : Study of sexual characters during development.

DEVELOPMENT COMMUNICATION : Use of communication systems in the promotion of economic development and in disseminating information about development activities and achievements.

DEVELOPMENT ECONOMICS : Branch of economics concerned with the study of economic development.

DEVELOPMENT PLANNING : A plan is built up on the basis of a broad set of development aims, either referring to an economy as a whole, specific areas or sections. Plans can have various objectives, for example, target growth rates, solving unemployment problems, building up heavy industry, developing the rural sector or the implementation of particular techniques or strategies. Generally development is a long process.

DEVELOPMENT STATISTICS : Statistical analysis and study of data of economic development.

DEVELOPMENT STRATEGY : The approach taken to the problem of under development which will depend on which particular growth model is being used. There are many different strategies such as industrial development, import substitution, balanced growth of urban and rural areas, expanding and supporting agriculture in order to support the surplus population or developing the export sector in order to earn foreign exchange.

DEVELOPMENT STUDIES : Studies of the problems of social economic and technological development in developing countries.

DEVELOPMENT TRAINING : It is a branch of human resources development specializing in learner centered interactive and experiential approaches. The methodology is humanistic rather than behavioural working with people's attitudes and thus reorienting them with the appropriate knowledge and skills.

DEVOTIONAL STUDIES : Study of major religions, problems of ethics and values, in society, yoga and meditation practices.

DIABETOLOGY : Branch of medicine concerned with the diagnosis and treatment of diabetes and its various complications.

DIAGNOSTIC MEDICINE : Science and art of identifying cause of patient's trouble usually but not mentioning name of disease.

DIAGNOSTIC RADIOLOGY : Branch of medicine concerned with diagnosis of diseases with the use of X-rays and other radiations.

DIAGNOSTIC RADIOTECHNOLOGY : Refers to the machinery like X-ray machine employed in the radiological diagnosis of diseases.

DIAGNOSTICS : Branch of medicine concerned with the discrimination of diseases by their distinctive marks or symptoms. In modern times various biochemical tests and sophisticated instruments and machinery like X-rays, CAT-Scan, MRI (Magnetic Resonance Imaging) are being employed as an aid in diagnosis.

DIAGNOSTICS TECHNOLOGY : The various technological innovations employed in diagnostics. See Diagnostics.

DIALECTICS : 1. That branch of logic which teaches the rules and modes of reasoning or of distinguishing truth from error; 2. The art of using forms of reasoning so as to make fallacies pass for truth.

DIALECT STUDIES : Study of the form or idiom of a language peculiar to a province or to a region or people as distinguished from the literary language of the whole people.

DIALYSIS TECHNOLOGY : 1. Separation of materials of different molecular sizes by diffusing through membranes and application of this technique to therapeutic modification of body fluids. 2. Used also of separation of tissues (1944), for example, iris detachment.

DIAMAGNETISM : Study of materials which are repulsed by magnets.

DIAMOND GRADING : The technique and science of grading diamonds on the basis of their quality and other characteristics.

DIAMOND TECHNOLOGY : Cutting and polishing raw diamonds, industrial uses of diamonds, and use of diamonds in ornaments etc.

DIATHERMY : Generating heat in tissues by means of high frequency electric current for physiotherapy or surgery.

DIDACTICS : The art or science of teaching.

DIE MAKING : Branch of engineering concerned with making dies used in foundries for casting metals.

DIESEL MECHANISM : Study and training relating to the maintenance and repair of diesel engines.

DIETECTICS : That department of medicine which relates to the regulation of diet to the patients.

DIFFERENTIAL CALCULUS : 1. An important branch of higher mathematics which deals largely with the infinitely small differences of variable and mutually dependent quantities. 2. Study of slopes of curves, non-uniform velocities, acceleration, forces, maximum and minimum values of quantities.

DIFFERENTIAL EQUATIONS : A branch of mathematics concerning the study of equations having not more than two variables.

DIFFERENTIAL GEOMETRY : Study of the properties of curves and surfaces with the use of differential calculus. For example, study of slopes of curves, non-uniform velocities, acceleration, forces, maximum and minimum values of quantities.

DIFFERENTIAL PSYCHOLOGY : The branch of psychology which studies the differences between individuals, groups or races in fundamental psychological characteristics.

DIGITAL AUDIO TECHNOLOGY : Computer aided recording of sound as in audio cassettes etc., in the form of digits.

DIGITAL COMMUNICATION : Communication in the form of digits instead of words.

DIGITAL ELECTRONICS : Concerned with electronic machines employing digits like computers.

DIGITAL FILM MAKING : Using computer technology in the process of film making.

DIGITAL FORENSICS : Use of computers and internet in Crime detection and trying to decipher hidden or explicit information or messages pertaining to criminals or by criminals.

DIGITAL GEOGRAPHY : Analysing data from satellite imagery of the earth with the help of computers. Satellite imagery provides a whole gamut of information from the nature of forest cover, water bodies, soils and agricultural data and helps to pointing changes in the physical landscape.

DIGITAL IMAGERY ANALYSIS : Computer analysis of images obtained from satellites for remote sensing. The computer system takes inputs from any type of imagery including synthetic aperture and radar, satellite data, actual photo and infrared image data and amalgamates them with digitised maps and even non-graphic texts.

DIGITAL INDUSTRIAL TECHNOLOGY : It is the latest advance in non-destructive testing of industrial materials and products. Real time radioscopy and digital image processing techniques for on line inspection of welds in boiler tubes.

DIGITAL INSTRUMENTATION : Instrumentation involving use of computer technology.

DIGITAL LIBRARY SCIENCE : Includes information systems of all levels of digital content, and techniques of selection, connection and organisation of digital content, all kinds of digital genre and electronic publishing, searching and finding information, development and implementation, interface, designation.

DIGITAL PHOTOGRAPHY : Photography using digital cameras, digital photolab, computerised colour lab and other computer-aided devices.

DIGITAL SIGNAL PROCESSING : Short form DSP. The subject includes DSP architecture, embedded DSP systems, signal processing algorithms and associated practical work.

DIGITAL TRANSMISSION TECHNOLOGY : The digital or terrestrial technology enables, transmission of 4-6 programmes through the same aerial on T.V. It enables data broadcasting and only a set or box is required to receive the digital channel.

DIGITAL VASCULAR IMAGING : Computer analysis of images of blood vessels.

DILATOMETRY : The measurement of changes in the volume of a liquid or dimensions of a solid which occur in phenomena such as allotropic transformations, thermal expansion or compression creep or magnetostriction. It is a branch of physics.

DIMENSIONAL ANALYSIS : A technique that involves the study of dimensions, primarily as a tool for obtaining information about physical systems too complicated for full mathematical solutions to be feasible.

DIOPTRICS : The branch of physics that treats of the refraction of light especially by the transparent medium of the eye and by lenses.

DIPLOMATIC STUDIES : Practices and procedures of modern diplomacy management and information technology, diplomatic law and practice, perspectives on world politics and the changing global agenda.

DIRECT MARKETING : Marketing of goods and services by the producer or manufacturer are provided directly to the consumers without the intervention of middle men like agents, distributors, retailers etc.

DIRT ARCHAEOLOGY : Archaeology actually conducted by excavation.

DISARMAMENT STUDIES : Study of possibilities, prospects and consequences of reducing the race of nations to arm themselves, as a way to establish world peace.

DISASTER MANAGEMENT : Management of rescue and relief operations at the occurrence of disasters like cyclones, floods, fire accidents, earthquakes and other similar natural calamities.

DISEASE PROCESSES : Biological and physicochemical processes involved in the development and progress of disease.

DISTANCE EDUCATION : Education imparted from a distance without the need for students to attend classes by means of postal correspondence and through radio, T.V., internet and other modern audio-visual technologies like cassettes etc., previously known as correspondence education.

DIVING : The art or practice of descending into water; especially the art of descending below the surface of water and remaining at varying depths in order to remove or recover objects from the bottom.

DIVINING : The art of discovering hidden objects with the aid of certain experiments and observations. Usually practised by some persons to locate underground water, minerals etc.

DNA FINGER PRINTING : A method of confirming the identity of a person by a study of a sample of the 'DNA'. It is usually employed as a forenisc method to identify persons, especially to confirm the identity of criminals and to confirm the identity of a father in cases of doubtful parentage.

DOCUMENTATION : The term is used in computer programming and systems analysis. It means a record of input, output and types of processing and the way the Computer is to be operated. Similarly the various stages in systems analysis also are documented.

DOMESTIC ECONOMICS : See Home Economics.

DOMESTIC SCIENCE : Study concerned with house-hold skills such as catering, cookery and the use of cleaning materials. See Home Science.

DOUBLE ENTRY BOOK-KEEPING : The accounting systems in which every business transaction whether a receipt or payment of money, sale or purchase of goods and services gives rise to 2 entries; a debit and a corresponding credit on opposite pages of a ledger.

DOUBLE EXPOSURE HOLOGRAPHIC INTERFEROMETRY : The study of interference fringes generated by the superposition of two holograms of the same object-one with the object in on underformed state and the second after a small deformation.

DRAINAGE ENGINEERING : Branch of civil engineering concerned with the laying of drainage pipes for underground drainage and construction of other types of drainage in towns and cities and factories etc.

DRAMA : One of the fine arts.

DRAMATURGY : The science which treats of the rules of composing dramas and representing them on the stage.

DRAUGHTSMANSHIP : The work of drawing plans or designs. Primarily pertaining to engineering works and projects.

DREDGING : To remove sand, silt, mud, gravel etc., from the bottom of rivers, docks etc., by the use of a dredge or dredging vessel.

DRESS DESIGN : The art of designing dresses; now offered as a course of study.

DRILLING TECHNOLOGY : 1. Drilling holes in metal or wood as a part of handicraft or as an industrial process. 2. The method of drilling deep holes or pits or wells in the earth or sea bed for the exploration and exploitation of oil and natural gas resources.

DRUG DELIVERY TECHNOLOGY : Techniques employed for introducing drugs into the body for the treatment of diseases such as, for example, in the form of tablets, powders, syrups, injections, inhalers, patches on the skin etc.

DRY FARMING : The practice of producing crops under those conditions wherein the crop yield is limited by scanty rainfall and irrigation.

DRY LAND AGRICULTURE : See dry farming.

DUBBING : The technique of superimposing the sound track on an audio or video tape.

DVD AUTHORING : Short form for digital versatile Disk authoring. Authoring is generally defined as the process of preparing content, encoding video and creating the final DVD image. In the case of DVD authoring it is a complex process since it involves the laying out of multiple audio tracks and a video tract, generation of sub-titles, main pages, parental lock-out features, interactive functions such as programme search, time search, seamless play and pause and finally editing of video and audio.

DYEING : To give a new and permanent colour particularly to cloth or the materials of cloth as wool, cotton, silk and linen; also to hair, skins etc.

DYE TECHNOLOGY : Manufacture of materials used in dyeing.

DYNAMIC CLIMATOLOGY : The climatology of atmospheric dynamics and thermodynamics.

DYNAMIC ECONOMICS : The intertemporal analysis of the economic system. The economy may be passing from one equilibrium point to the other (i.e. two comparative static equilibria) or it may be continuing through time without reaching a state of static equilibrium. Effectively any economic model which simultaeously contains variables in more than one time period may be considered dynamic.

DYNAMIC GEOMORPHOLOGY : The quantitative analysis of steady state, self-regulatory geomorphic processes. Also known as analytical geomorphology.

DYNAMIC LINGUISTICS : Study of languages in the light of their development and history.

DYNAMIC PSYCHOLOGY : A psychology emphasizing motives and drives.

DYNAMICS (KINETICS) : Branch of mechanics concerned with the motion of a systems of material particles under the action of forces, especially those which originate outside the system under consideration.

DYSTELEOLOGY : Study of organs which do not seen to have any function and have become vestigial.

E

EARLY CHILDHOOD CARE : Course of study and training in the care of children below one year of age. A branch of home science, psychology and medicine.

EARLY CHILDHOOD EDUCATION : Education of children at the pre-school, nursery and kindergarten stages. Branch of education.

EAR, NOSE, THROAT (E.N.T) : Branch of medicine concerned with ear, nose and throat diseases. See otorhinolaryngology.

EARTH QUAKE ENGINEERING : Branch of engineering concerned with the restoration of buildings and other structures damaged by earthquake and constructing earthquake resistant buildings and other structures.

EARTH SCIENCES : A group of sciences concerned with the study of earth like Geology, Geography, Oceanography, Meteorology, Geophysics, Geochemistry, Geodesy etc.

EASEMENT LAW : A privilege without profit which one proprietor has in the estate of another proprietor, distinct from the ownership of the soil, as a way, water course. etc.

ECCLESIOLOGY : 1. The science of antiquities as applied to chruches and other ecclesiatical foundations. 2. The science and theory of church building and decoration.

ECHOCARDIOGRAPHIC TECHNOLOGY : Technology pertaining to the special equipment used to record the functioning of the heart and any abnormalities in the same.

ECOGENETICS : Deals with the adjustment and adaptations of populations to the environment, particularly in the field of nutritional ecology and infectious diseases. It is a study of genetically determined differences in susceptibility to the action of physical, chemical and infectious agents in the environment.

ECOLOGICAL ANATOMY : Anatomical adaptations of plants and animals in response to environmental conditions.

ECOLOGICAL CLIMATOLOGY : A branch of bioclimatology including the physiological adaptation of plants and animals in relation to climate.

ECOLOGICAL ECONOMICS : See environmental economics.

ECOLOGICAL PHYSIOLOGY : Study of the physiological changes taking place in animals and plants in response to changes in the environment.

ECOLOGICAL SCIENCES : The following branches of science may be grouped together as ecological sciences : Plant Ecology, Animal ecology, Ecological climatology, Ecological physiology, Ecological genetics, Human ecology etc.

ECOLOGY : Study of the relations of plants and animals to their surroundings.

E-COMMERCE : Electronic Commerce which employs various electronic devices and means in carrying out commercial transactions. It is considered as a potential gold mine for commercial organisations. Different E-commerce technologies are available.

ECONOMETRICS : A branch of statistics concerned with the testing of economic hypotheses mainly through the use of multiple regression techniques and sometimes through the use of more sophisticated methodology.

ECONOMIC BOTANY : Branch of Botany dealing with the study of economically useful plants and plant products.

ECONOMIC DEVELOPMENT : The process of improving the standard of living and well being of the population by raising per capita income. This is usually achieved by an increase in industialization relative to reliance on the agricultural sector.

ECONOMIC DYNAMICS : That part of economics which analyses the movement of economic systems through time.

ECONOMIC ENTOMOLOGY : Branch of entomology concerned with the study of losses of economically important animals and plants due to insect predation.

ECONOMIC GEOGRAPHY : Relations of physical environment and economic conditions to the manufacture and distribution of commodities.

ECONOMIC GEOLOGY : Application of geology to mineral usage and principles of engineering.

ECONOMIC HISTORY : Study of history from the point of view of economic development of societies.

ECONOMIC LEGISLATION : Legislation concerned with economic and financial matters.

ECONOMIC PLANNING : This may be classified as imperative or indicative. Imperative planning applies to a centralised macro economic plan in an economy dominated by the Public sector. In a fully planned economy the government takes control of output, price and waste control. Indicative planning refers to the indication of a series of goals by the government.

ECONOMICS : Science concerned with those aspects of social behaviour and those institutions which are involved in the use of scarce resources to produce and distribute goods and services in the satisfaction of human wants.

ECONOMIC SOCIOLOGY : The study of the relations between economic and non-economic aspects of social life.

ECONOMICS OF EDUCATION : Study of education from the economist's point of view. Here usually the criteria are 1) Economy in resources and time 2) Efficiency of the education system 3) Its effectiveness in achieving national objectives and social and economic development.

ECONOMIC THEORY : A body of economic principles built up as a result of logical reasoning ; it provides the tools of economic analysis.

ECONOMIC THEORY OF POLITICS : A model of political behaviour which assumes that votes are utility maximizers and that political parties are vote maximizers.

ECONOMIC THOUGHT : The branch of economics which is concerned with the development of economic ideas through the writings of the great economists of each period.

ECOPEDOLOGY : Study of soils and soil erosion from ecological point of view.

ECOTOXICOLOGY : Study of the effects of poisonous substances in the environment on people and other living organisms.

EDUCATION : 1. Teacher training. 2. Total process of developing human ability and behaviour 3. Education as a discipline.

EDUCATIONAL ADMINISTRATION : Refers to the entire process through which appropriate human and material resources are procured, made available and applied for the realization of certain predetermined educational goals.

EDUCATIONAL FINANCE : Provision of economic resources required to run educational Institutions.

EDUCATIONAL MANAGEMENT : Study of the running, handling, conducting or controlling the educational organization both structurally and functionally.

EDUCATIONAL ORGANIZATION : Refers to the systematic arrangement or available human and material resources for a definite purpose; a structural framework for education.

EDUCATIONAL PLANNING : Refers to selection of content and materials for imparting education at various levels.

EDUCATIONAL PSYCHOLOGY : That branch of applied psychology which is concerned with the application to education of psychological principles and findings together with the Psychological study of problems of education.

EDUCATIONAL SOCIOLOGY : Contribution of education to social mobility and social class differences in educational attainments.

EDUCATIONAL STATISTICS : 1) To interpret data on student characteristics 2) Certain statistics are used to describe test characteristics 3) Knowledge of statistical concepts assists in research.

EDUCATIONAL TECHNOLOGY : 1. Use of films, film strips and similar audio-visual aids in education 2. Design of implementation of system of teaching. 3. Educational technology utilizes scientific and technological methods and concepts that are developed in psychology and other related fields to enrich the teaching-learning process.

EDUCOLOGY : Theoretical study of teaching skills or the theory of teaching practice.

EFFLUENT TREATMENT : Methods of treating effluents from factories and other industrial establishments to make them free from poisonous and harmful substances.

EGYPTIAN ART : Refers to the architecture, sculpture and painting of ancient Egypt which were among the most important in the entire history of art.

EGYPTOLOGY : 1. The science of Egyptian antiquities 2. That branch of knowledge which treats of the ancient language, history etc., of Egypt.

ELASTODYNAMICS : Study of the mechanical properties of elastic waves.

ELASTOMER TECHNOLOGY : Technology of manufacture of natural and synthetic rubber. See Rubber technology.

ELECTRICAL ASSEMBLY : A course of study and training in assembling electric machines.

ELECTRICAL ENGINEERING : Branch of engineering concerned with the generation, transmission and distribution of electricity.

ELECTRICAL ENGINEERING TECHNOLOGY : Technological applications of electrical engineering.

ELECTRICAL INSTALLATION : Study of the methods of installation of electric machinery.

ELECTRICAL MEASUREMENT : Branch of electrical engineering concerned with the measurement of electricity generated and consumed.

ELECTRICAL MACHINES : 1. Branch of electrical engineering concerned with the study of machines used for generating electricity by friction or by induction. 2. Study of electric generators.

ELECTRICAL POWER SYSTEMS : Branch of electrical engineering concerned with the study of power systems.

ELECTRICAL SCIENCES : The following are included under electrical sciences- electrical and electronic Engineering, electronics and communication engineering, computer science and engineering.

ELECTRICIAN COURSE : A course of study and training in house wiring, repairing electrical appliances, motor winding and repairing etc.,

ELECTRICITY : The science of physical phenomena involving electrical charges and their effects when at rest and when in motion.

ELECTROBIOLOGY : That branch of biology concerned with electric currents developed in living organisms.

ELECTROCHEMICAL ENGINEERING : Branch of engineering concerned with electrochemical reactions and generation of electrochemical energy.

ELECTROCHEMICAL MATERIAL SCIENCE : Study of materials used in electrochemical systems.

ELECTROCHEMICALS : Electrochemical synthesis of organic and inorganic chemicals.

ELECTROCHEMICAL THERMODYNAMICS : The application of the laws of thermodynamics to electrochemical systems.

ELECTROCHEMISTRY : Study of chemical properties and reactions involving ions in solution including electrolysis and electric cells.

ELECTROCONVULSIVE THERAPY : Treatment of mental illness especially depression by passing electric current through brain to produce convulsions.

ELECTRODICS AND ELECTRO CATALYSIS : Pollution control in electrochemical processes; pollution control by electrochemical methods.

ELECTRODYNAMICS : Study of electric charges in motion, the forces created by electric and magnetic fields and the relationship between them.

ELECTRO GAS DYNAMICS : Conversion of the kinetic energy of a moving gas to electricity, for such applications as high voltage electric power generation, air-pollution control and paint spraying.

ELECTRO HYDROMETALLUGRY : Secondary recovery of non-ferrous metals, electromelting and electrowinnowing of metals.

ELECTROKINETICS : The study of the motion of electric charges especially of steady currents in electric circuits and of the motion of electrified particles in electric or magnetic fields.

ELECTROMAGENETISM : 1.That branch of electrical science which deals with the relations between electricity and magnetism as shown, for example, in the action of dynamos and electric motors, 2. Magnetism produced by an electric current rather than by a permanent magnet.

ELECTROMAGNETIC THEORY : The theory which explains the relations between electricity and magnetism plays an important role in electrical science. The theory attributes the phenomena of light to periodic changes in the electric and magnetic condition of the ether propagated with finite velocity as electromagnetic waves.

ELECTROMETALLURGY : Use of electrical processes in the separation of metals from their ores, the refining of metals or the forming and plating of metals.

ELECTROMYOGRAPHY : Study of muscular movements by electrical means.

ELECTRON ACOUSTIC MICROSCOPY : A technique for producing images that show variation in an object's thermal and elastic properties. An electron beam generates ultrasonic waves in the specimen, which are detected by a piezoelectric transducer whose output controls the brightness of a spot sweeping a Cathode ray tube in synchronization with the electron beam.

ELECTRON BEAM WELDING : Method of welding with the help of electron beams.

ELECTRONIC DESIGN : Designing electronic circuits on silicon chips. The most promising technique in electronics today is Very Large Scale Integration (VLSI) with the power of integrating millions of transistors on a single silicon chip as also advanced digital design.

ELECTRONIC LEARNING : Method of learning with electronic devices including internet.

ELECTRONIC PAYMENT SYSTEM : Payment of money by crediting to bank account through a computer network.

ELECTRONICS : Science pertaining to the study and design of control, communication and computing devices which depend on movements of electrons in circuits consisting of semiconductors, thermionic valves, resistors, capacitors and inductors.

ELECTRONICS ENGINEERING : Engineering aspects of making and maintenance of electronic devices and instruments.

ELECTRONICS SERVICE ENGINEERING : Includes basic and digital electronics, colour TV, VCD, telephone servicing and computer hardware servicing etc.

ELECTRONICS TECHNOLOGY : Application of electronics in the manufacture of electronic appliances and instruments.

ELECTRON MICROSCOPY : Study of ultra structure as revealed by the electron microscope at magnifications of several thousand times.

ELECTRON OPTICS : The study of the use of electron lenses in the electron microscope, cathode ray tubes and other similar devices.

ELECTRON SPECTROSCOPY : 1. Techniques that measure the energies of electrons ejected from solids or gases after excitation by protons. 2. The study of the energy spectra of photelectrons or Auger electrons emitted from a substance upon bombardment by electromagnetic radiation, electrons or ions used to investigate atomic, molecular or solid state structures and in chemical analysis.

ELECTRO-OPTICS : Study of the influence of an electric field on optical phenomena as in electro-optical Kerr effect and the Stark effect. Also known as Optoelectronics.

ELECTROPHYSIOLOGY : That branch of science which treats of electrical phenomena produced through physiological agencies.

ELECTROPLATING TECHNOLOGY : A method of plating one metal with another by electrodeposition.

ELECTROPYROMETALLURGY : Electrolytic production of metals from molten salt electrolysis.

ELECTROSTATICS : Study of electric charges at rest, their electric fields and potentials.

ELECTROTHERAPEUTICS : The treatment of diseases by means of electricity. Also known as electrotherapy.

ELECTROTYPING : The act of producing copies of types, wood cuts, medals etc., by means of the electric deposition of copper upon a mould taken from the original.

ELEMENTOLOGY : The study of the effect of elements like Zn, Al, Cd, Cu, etc., on health.

EMBEDDED SYSTEMS : Embedded computer software for telecommunications, control, medical applications, consumer products etc.

EMBOLIZATION THERAPY : Use of emboli introduced by selective arteriography to treat vascular tumors etc.

EMBROIDERY : Work in gold, silver, silk or other thread, formed by the needle on cloth, stuff and muslin into various figures.

EMBRYOLOGY : The study of the development of embryo in plants and animals.

EMERGENCY MEDICINE : That branch of medicine which is concerned with the treatment of emergency cases.

EMPLOYER : EMPLOYEE RELATIONS : Branch of the science of personnel management which treats of the relations between the employer and employees both in public and Private sectors.

ENCRYPTION : Encrypting a message by means of manipulaing the original text so that it can be read only by providing a key that unlocks the encryption and makes the text readable. The encryption system in which there are two keys-public and private. The user of the system distributes the public key to his clients/friends so that they can encrypt the messages intended to the user who is the owner of the public key. The message encrypted this way can only be decrypted by the corresponding private key. No other person can read the encrypted message.

ENDOCRINOLOGY : Study of the physiology and biochemistry of endocrine or ductless glands, the material secreted by which is not conveyed by a duct but through the veins. The chief examples are : the adrenal, thyroid, parathyroid and pituitary gland.

ENDODONTICS : Branch of dentistry concerned with root canal therapy.

ENDOSCOPY : Study of the internal structure of the internal organs and their surgery without cutting the body open, with the help of the optical instrument known as the endoscope. It has vast applications in cardiology, gastroenterology, neurology, orthopaedics, urology, paediatrics etc. An endoscopic sewing machine is also available.

ENDOUROLOGY : Branch of medical science concerned with the study of the internal structure and diseases of the urinary system. See UROLOGY, NEPHROLOGY.

ENERGY AUDITING : To examine the energy needs and utilization in relation to one another in order to determine shortages and wastages and means of enhancing generation in a given organization.

ENERGY CONVERSION : Study of the methods of converting energy from one form to another in order to augment energy sources.

ENERGY ENGINEERING : Branch of engineering concerned with the utilization and generation of various forms of energy like mechanical, electrical, thermal, chemical, solar, wind, tidal etc., from renewable and non-renewable sources.

ENERGY MANAGEMENT : Economic project managing, formulation of energy policy, impact of energy audit and energy conservation. See Energy Engineering.

ENERGY METABOLISM : Study of the conversion and utilization of energy in living organisms, through various physiological and biochemical processes.

ENERGY STUDIES : Courses and investigations on the sources available, transport, storage and efficient use of energy.

ENERGY TECHNOLOGY : Study of the methods of energy distribution, storage and uses of energy for diverse purposes.

ENGINEERING : 1. The art of constructing and using engines or machines 2. The art of executing such works as are the objects of civil and military architecture in which machinery is in general extensively employed.

ENGINEERING AND MANUFACTURING MANAGEMENT : Application of engineering techniques in the management of manufacturing industry.

ENGINEERING CHEMISTRY : Knowledge of chemistry employed in various branches of engineering study and practice.

ENGINEERING DRAWING : Drawings used in engineering works and studies.

ENGINEERING GEOLOGY : Branch of geology which is utilized for the study of soil conditions at the time of construction of dams, buildings, roads, bridges, tunnels etc.

ENGINEERING INFORMATICS : Branch of information technology concerned with information pertaining to various branches of engineering and their computerization and networking.

ENGINEERING MANAGEMENT : Study of management science meant for engineers to improve their management skills.

ENGINEERING MATHEMATICS : Application of mathematics in various branches of engineering.

ENGINEERING MECHANICS : It covers a wide range of engineering problems such as analysis of structures, vibration of bridges, turbulence, hydrodynamics, lubrication and boundary value problems.

ENGINEERING MEDICINE : Branches of medicine dependent on complex devices such as those used in artificial respiration, heart fabrillation etc.,

ENGINEERING METHOD : A method used in statistical cost analysis where engineer's estimates of the input-output relationships form the basis upon which to calculate minimum production cost at different levels of output. The advantages of this method are that input prices and technology can be held constant.

ENGINEERING STATISTICS : Branch of statistics concerned with the application of statistical methods in preparing engineering estimates and analysis.

ENGINEERING STUDIES : Such studies as architecture, landscape design, town planning, atmospheric pollution, noise pollution, traffic management etc.

ENGYSEISMOLOGY : Seismology dealing with earthquake records made close to the disturbance. See Seismology.

ENTEROLOGY : Study of the internal parts or viscera of the body.

ENTERPRENEURAL STUDIES : Study and investigations concerning problems and performance of enterpreneurs. See ENTERPRENEUR EDUCATION

ENTERPRENEUR EDUCATION : Imparting knowledge concerning setting up of new industries to enterprising individuals wishing to do so.

ENTERPRENEURSHIP : Study of the role of enterpreneurs in business and industry offered as a course at university level.

ENTERTAINMENT ELECTRONICS : Application of electronics in the field of entertainment as, for example, radio, TV, cinema, sound systems etc.

ENTOMOLOGY : That branch of Zoology which treats of the structure, habits and classification of insects.

ENTOZOOLOGY : That branch of Zoology which treats of animals living in some part of another animals.

ENVIRONMENTAL AUDIT : Auditing environmental management systems in institutions.

ENVIRONMENTAL BIOLOGY : Branch of biology concerned with the study of the mutual effects and inter-relationships between environment and living organisms.

ENVIRONMENTAL BIOTECHNOLOGY : The mutual interactions, effects and influences of organisms modified or created by biotechnological methods and the environment.

ENVIRONMENTAL CHEMISTRY : Study of the chemical substances present naturally in the environment and those chemicals which are added by man to the environment in the soil, water and atmosphere which cause pollution and harm the environment.

ENVIRONMENTAL CRIME : Causing environmental pollution by releasing harmful substances into the soil, water and atmosphere such as industrial emission and effluents, radioactive materials, hospital wastes etc.

ENVIRONMENTAL ECONOMICS : Assessment of the value forgone by the society due to environmental destruction and other economic aspects of environmental pollution and protection.

ENVIRONMENTAL EDUCATION : Imparting knowledge of the environment and the need to conserve and protect the environment to all sections of the population including children.

ENVIRONMENTAL ENGINEERING : That branch of engineering which is concerned with the measures to be taken for preventing and protecting against environmental pollution of water, air and soil caused by chemicals, radiation, sound etc.

ENVIRONMENTAL EPIDEMIOLOGY : Branch of medical science concerned with the methods of investigating epidemic diseases caused by environmental factors.

ENVIRONMENTAL GEOMECHANICS : Study of effects of environmental factors on the durability of geomaterials like natural stone, concrete and bricks as also seismic behaviour of dams and slopes.

ENVIRONMENTAL GEOPHYSICS : Assessing the impact of human activity on the earth, finding ways of putting it right and monitoring public and industrial use of the earth's resources.

ENVIRONMENTAL HEALTH SCIENCE : Science concerned with the study of health problems caused by environmental factors. Various medical and public health sciences are involved in this area.

ENVIRONMENTAL IMPACT ANALYSIS : An analysis which seeks to identify the effects on the whole environment of any investment project or public works project. This would include the forecasting of potential pollution emission, loss of visual acuity etc.

ENVIRONMENTAL LAW : Law concerned with the regulations to be followed by institutions to prevent environmental pollution likely to be caused by their actions and activities and penalties for their violation.

ENVIRONMENTAL MANAGEMENT : Study of the management of the environment in order to prevent pollution and degradation and promote healthy environmental conditions.

ENVIRONMENTAL MEDICINE : Treatment of diseases caused by environmental factors.

ENVIRONMENTAL MICROBIOLOGY : Study of the microbes present in the environment including soil, water, air etc., and their role in health, disease, medicine and industry.

ENVIRONMENTAL MYCOLOGY : Study of the fungi and their role in environmental protection and degradation.

ENVIRONMENTAL PLANNING : Planning cities, towns, villages, houses, factories, offices and all other structures and constructions taking into consideration the sustainability of the environment.

ENVIRONMENTAL QUALITY MAPPING : Determining the environmental quality of a given area and more especially the different parts of an area.

ENVIRONMENTAL REMOTE SENSING : Study of the environment by means of remote sensing technologies.

ENVIRONMENTAL SCIENCE : Study of environmental degradation and its effects on man and other living and non-living objects and methods of preventing and controlling them.

ENVIRONMENTAL SOCIOLOGY : Study of the environmental factors on human societies and influence of society on environmental degradation.

ENVIRONMENTAL TECHNOLOGY : Use of technological methods, particularly civil engineering methods in environmental conservation and protection.

ENVIRONMENTAL TOXICOLOGY : Study of poisonous substances present in the environment and their effects on man and other living beings.

ENVIRONMENTOLOGY : Branch of science concerned with the study of environment and its effect on man and other living and non-living objects. See Environmental Science.

ENZYME ENGINEERING : Modification of the actions of enzymes by changing the physical and chemical factors.

ENZYME KINETICS : Study of the rate of enzyme reactions which show biphasic kinetics.

ENZYME TECHNOLOGY : Use of industrial enzymes in the pharmaceutical, chemical and other manufacturing processes.

ENZYMOLOGY : Branch of science concerned with the study of enzyme structure, properties and reactions mediated by them in living systems.

EPIDEMIOLOGY : 1. Branch of medical science concerned with the methods of investigating epidemics. 2. Study of the behaviour of large groups of people affected with a particular disease.

EPIGENETICS : The study of those processes by which genetic information ultimately results in distinctive physical and behavioural characteristics.

EPIGRAPHY : That branch of knowledge which deals with the deciphering and explaining of inscriptions.

EPILEPTOLOGY -Branch of medicine concerned with the disease known as epilepsy.

EPISTEMOLOGY : The methods of scientific procedures which lead to the acquisition of knowledge.

ERGOLOGY : Study of the effects of work on the human organism from a physiological and psychological point of view.

ERGOMETRICS : Science of measurement of work output.

ERGONOMICS : Study of working environment especially in relation to efficiency.

E.R.P. : Short form for ENTERPRISE RESOURCE PLANNING which is a set of application software that brings manufacturing, finance, sales, distribution, human resources and other business functions into balance.

ESCHATOLOLOGY : The study of last or final things as death, judgement etc.,

ESTHETICS : The science or that branch of philosophy which deals with the beautiful.

ESTUARINE OCEANOGRAPHY : The study of the chemical, physical, biological and geological properties of estuaries.

ETHICS : The science which treats of the nature and grounds of moral obligation.

ETHNICITY AND RACISM STUDIES : Study of the sociological, biological, anthropological and legal aspects of ethnicity and racism throughout the world.

ETHNOBIOLOGY : Study of ethnology in its relation to physical anthropology.

ETHNOBOTANY : Branch of botany concerned with the study of plants used by tribals and villagers, primarily the medicinal uses of such plants.

ETHNOGRAPHY : The direct observation of the activity of members of a particular social group and the description and evaluation of such activity.

ETHNOHISTORY : Use of the records of literate groups to help write their history.

ETHNOLINGUISTICS : Systematic investigation of the relationship between languages and ethnology.

ETHNOLOGY : That branch of science which investigates the mental and physical differences of mankind and the organic laws on which they depend.

ETHNOMEDICINE : Medicine used and practiced by tribals and villagers.
ETHNOMETHODOLOGY : Branch of sociology which investigates how people construct their society.
ETHNOMUSICOLOGY : Comparative study of musicology
ETHNOPHARMACOLOGY : Branch of pharmacology concerned with the study of the properties, effects and uses of drugs used by tribals and villagers.
ETHNOPSYCHOLOGY : Primarily the psychology of races and particularly primitive races.
ETHNOSOCIOLOGY : Sociology applied to primitive man.
ETHOLOGY : 1. Branch of science which extends the study of animal behaviour to objective investigations of human behaviour. 2. The study of animal behaviour in a natural context.
ETIOLOGY : 1. Investigation of the causes of a given phenomenon. 2. Medically the investigation of the causes of a disease.
ETYMOLOGY : 1. That branch of linguistics which explains the origin and derivation of words. 2. That branch of grammar which comprehends the various inflections and modifications of words.
EUCLIDIAN GEOMETRY : Study of geometry based on the assumptions of the celebrated mathematician Euclid.
EUGENICS : Study of improving the quality of human populations by the application of genetic principles.
EUPHENICS : The production of a satisfactory phenotype by means other than eugenics.
EUROPEAN STUDIES : Study of the civilization, culture, literature, history etc., of european countries.
EUTHENICS : Same as Eugenics.
EVOLUTION : The process of biological and organic change in organisms by which descendants come to differ from their ancestors and a history of the sequence of such change.
EVOLUTIONARY ANTHROPOLOGY : Study of the biological evolution of man.
EVOLUTIONARY BIOLOGY : That branch of biology concerned with the study of evolutionary trends among living beings.
EXCAVATION ARCHAEOLOGY : Study of ancient monuments, buildings and other structures discovered by digging the earth.
EXCHANGE : Traditionally one of the main divisions of economics; the basis of the greater part of economic study being exchange of goods and currencies.

EXCISE : Study of taxes on all goods produced or manufactured in a country including relevant rules and procedures.

EXCISE LAW : Law pertaining to and applicable to excise duties.

EXECUTIVE MANAGEMENT : Comprises international marketing, international finance, E-commerce, internet technology, derivative trading etc.

EXERCISE PHYSIOLOGY : Study of physiological changes taking place in the body while exercising and as a result of exercising.

EXERCISE PSYCHOLOGY : Study of the effects of physical exercise on mental state and disposition.

EXERCISE SCIENCE : The study of the effects of systematic exertion of the body as conducive to health.

EXFOLIATIVE CYTOLOGY : Study of cells shed or scrapped from epitheilial surfaces for detection of diseases especially precancer.

EXHIBIION DESIGN : A course of study and training in designing exhibitions.

EXOBIOLOGY : Study and investigation of the possibility of the existence of extra – terrestrial life in the universe.

EXOLINGUISTICS : Study of the relation between a language and the rest of the culture of which it forms a part.

EXPENDITURE CONTROL AND MANAGEMENT : Control and management of expenditure in a given institution or government to see that unnecessary and wasteful expenditure is not incurred leading to losses

EXPERIMENTAL ASTRONOMY : Study of Astronomy with the help of X-rays, gamma rays, 1R and optical instruments.

EXPERIMENTAL EMBRYOLOGY : Experimental study of the effects of various physico-chemical and biological and physiological factors on the development of the embryo and the culturing of the embryo under artificial conditions in the laboratory.

EXPERIMENTAL MEDICINE : Experimental study of diseases and their treatment in the laboratory.

EXPERIMENTAL MORPHOLOGY : Experimental study of various physical and chemical and biological factors on morphologocal characters of organisms.

EXPERIMENTAL PETROLOGY : A branch of petrology in which phenomena that occur during petrological processes are reproduced and studied in the laboratory.

EXPERIMENTAL PSYCHOLOGY : Employment of experimental methods to obtain psychological data or to solve psychological problems. Studies behaviour differences between human beings and animals like rats, monkeys and pigeons. Prominent areas of study include motivation, learning and memory, sensory and perceptual processes, effects of substance abuse and genetic and neurological factors affecting behaviour.

EXPLORATION GEOPHYSICS : Applications of geophysical principles and methods to the exploration of minerals, oil and natural gas.

EXPLOSIVES : Branch of military and armament science concerned with the study of explosives used in warfare.

EXPORT MANAGEMENT : Course of study dealing with export promotion and management of various operations concerned with exports like shipping, and marine insurance, finance for exports, government policies on exports and documentation.

EXPORT PROMOTION : The main alternative strategy to the import substitution strategy. The idea is to develop industries where main markets are overseas. The provision of an efficient infrastructure such as transport and communication network is necessary.

EXTENSION EDUCATION : Educating the people about developments in various fields through the media, street plays, practical demonstrations, pamphlets etc., for example, educating the farmers about agricultural research results and their application in the field.

EXTERIOR BALLISTICS : Science concerned with behaviour of a projectile after leaving the muzzle of the firing weapon.

F

FABRICATION : A branch of engineering concerned with connecting various parts to make a whole, mainly in civil and mechanical engineering.

FABRIC PAINTING : The art of painting on cloth.

FABRIC STUDIES : Study of quality of cloth and the factors which govern quality.

FACILITIES MANAGEMENT : Management of facilities in a community such as water supply, sanitation, roads etc.

FACTOR ANALYSIS : A branch of multivariate analysis in statistics.

FACTORY LAW : Study of the acts concerning safety precautions to be taken in factories and the rights and responsibilities of factory workers.

FAMILY AND MARRIAGE COUNSELLING : Counseling by sociology and psychology experts about problems of discord and adjustment to married and about to be married couples.

FAMILY DISPUTE RESOLUTION : It covers family and its institutions, matrimonial remedies, law and unfair practices in family relations, family and property relations, family disputes and adjudicatory mechanisms and family counseling, resolutions of all family related disputes such as partition, settlements, maintenance and adoption.

FAMILY MEDICINE : Branch of general medicine concerned with health and diseases of members of a family taken as a unit.

FAMILY RELATIONS : Branch of sociology dealing with the mutual relations of the members of a family taken as a sociological unit.

FAMILY RESOURCE MANAGEMENT : Branch of home science concerned with management of both financial and human resources of a family.

FAMILY STUDIES : Branch of sociology concerned with the study of family organization in various races and cultures.

FARM MANAGEMENT : Branch of agriculture concerned with the management of farm involving materials procurement, engaging agricultural labour, payment of wages for carrying out agricultural operations and maintaining the accounts of income from sale of produce and expenditure incurred.

FASHION ARTS : Arts like sketching designs for printing of fabrics, embroidery, preparing designs for jewellery etc., to cater to the needs of the fashion world.

FASHION DESIGN : Designing fashionable dresses and ornaments presently being offered as a course of study.

FASHION JOURNALISM : Writing features about fashions and reporting about fashion events for newspapers and magazines.

FASHION PHOTOGRAPHY : Taking photographs of models displaying fashions in textiles and jewellery, hair styles etc.

FASHION TECHNOLOGY : Manufacturing technology of fashionable dresses, ornaments etc.

FEED AND FODDER TECHNOLOGY : Branch of animal husbandry concerned with the preparation of feed and fodder for cattle.

FEMINISM : STUDIES : Study of the feminist movement and literature pertaining thereto.

FEMTOCHEMISTRY : Branch of physical chemistry concerned with the study of changes taking place at the molecular and atomic level during the course of a chemical reaction at the time scale on which the reactions actually happen, namely femtoseconds. One femtosecond is 10^{-15} seconds. Femtochemistry enables us to know why certain reactions take place but not others.

FERMENTATION SCIENCE : Science concerned with carrying out fermentation with the help of microorganisms for the manufacture of vitamins, antibiotics, organic acids and other useful products.

FERMENTATION TECHNOLOGY : Technology aspects of conducting fermentations for the purpose of manufacturing various useful chemical substances as by products on an industrial scale.

FERTILITY STUDIES : Study of the causes of infertility in men and women and methods of restoring fertility.

FERTILIZER TECHNOLOGY : Study of the technology of manufacture of chemical fertilizers for use in agriculture.

FIBRE CROPS : Branch of agriculture concerned with the cultivation and use of fiber yielding crops like cotton, jute, agave, hibiscus etc.

FIBRE OPTICS : 1. Use of fibres to transmit information in the form of coded pulses. 2. The technique of transmitting light through long, thin, flexible, fibre of glass, plastic or other transparent materials; bundles of parallel fibres can be used to transmit complete images.

FIBRE SCIENCE AND TECHNOLOGY : Concerned with the characters and utilization of natural and synthetic fibres like cotton, silk wool, terrylene, nylon, polyester etc. Study of fibre forming processes, processing and extraction of fibres and filament yarns, processing of textile fibres etc.

FIELD ARCHAEOLOGY : Study of the remains of the past that are visible on the surface or through examining soil discoloration and crop growth. It does not include excavations.

FILE TRANSFER PROTOCOL (FTP) : This programme helps file operations and transfer between computers in a network. FTP also helps in transferring files between machines with different operating systems. An operating system software drives the computer to do operations.

FILM DIRECTION : The art and technique of directing the production of movie films offered as a course of study.

FILM EDITING : The art and technique of editing movie films, offered as a course of study.

FILM JOURNALISM : Reporting about film production activities from studios, interviewing film personalities, reporting news about films and reviewing films for journals.

FILM PROCESSING TECHNOLOGY : Technique of processing motion picture films after they are shot; offered as a course of study.

FILM STUDIES : Study of motion pictures to critically evaluate their technical quality, story, direction, acting and other aspects from a comparative and historical perspective.

FILTRATION TECHNOLOGY : Methods of application of filtration of substances in industry and other purification processes.

FINANCE : A branch of economics. Narrowly interpreted it signifies capital in monetary form, that is in the form of funds lent or borrowed normally for capital purposes through financial markets or institutions. But in common parlance the term is applied to funds from almost any source used to undertake any kind of expenditure.

FINANCE AND CONTROL : Comprises corporate finance, investment analysis, portfolio management, financial services, international finance, equity research, treasury management, insurance, mutual funds and related areas.

FINANCIAL ANALYSIS : Also called securities analysis and investment analysis, it is concerned with the analysis of financial statements, interviewing corporate executives and attending trade shows, writing reports, recommending either purchasing, selling or holding various stocks.

FINANCIAL ENGINEERING : Combining or dividing existing instruments to create new financial products.

FINANCIAL MANAGEMENT : Management of financial resources and their utilization in corporate institutions.

FIANANCIAL MARKETS AND SERVICES : Study of stock markets mutual funds and investment brokering and allied financial services.

FINANCIAL PLANNING : The process of evaluating the investing and financing options available to a firm. It includes attempting to make optimal decisions, projecting the consequences of these decisions for the firm in the form of a financial plan and then comparing future performance against that plan.

FINE ARTS : Those that appeal to the taste or sense of beauty as painting, sculpturing, music etc.

FINGERPRINT SCIENCE : The science of deciphering finger prints and identifying the persons on the basis of their finger prints. It is extensively used in criminology to identify criminals.

FIRE ENGINEERING : Preventive strategies to keep organistions fire proof, miniminizing damages and loss including study of fire fighting equipment.

FIRE FIGHTING : The profession of putting out fires in towns, cities, industrial establishments etc., using various methods for the purpose.

FISCAL POLICY : Use of taxation and government expenditure to regulate the aggregate level of economic activity. Income and expenditure taxes may be levied for the purpose. The overall effect on economic activity will depend on the size of tax cut and the multiplier.

FISCAL STUDY : Study of income and expenditure of a government and methods of regulating economic activity.

FISH CAPTURE TECHNOLOGY : Technological methods employed in capturing fish, for the purpose of utilizing the fishery resources to the maximum extent.

FISHERIES ENGINEERING : Branch of engineering concerned with the design and manufacture of equipment used in catching fish.

FISHERIES NAUTICAL SCIENCE : Branch of science concerned with fishing boats and vessels and navigation for catching fish.

FISHERIES TECHNOLOGY : Technology concerned with the utilization and preservation of fish and manufacture of fish products.

FISHERY BIOLOGY : Branch of biology concerned with the study of fish used as food and for other purposes.

FISHERY ECONOMICS : Study of the economics of fisheries like production, marketing, distribution, export, import etc.

FISHERY OCEANORAPHY : Study of oceanography from the standpoint of fishery output, factors influencing fisheries etc.

FISH PROCESSING TECHNOLOGY : Methods of producing various products from fish used in food and industry.

FLAME PHOTOMETRY : A branch of spectrochemical analysis in which samples in solution are excited by introducing into a flame to induce line emission spectra.

FLASH SPECTROSCOPY : The study of electronic states of molecules after they absorb energy from an intense, brief light flash.

FLEET MANAGEMENT : Management of a fleet of vehicles and vessels in an organisation.

FLORAL ANATOMY : Study of the internal structure of flowers particularly with reference to their vascular supply.

FLORAL MORPHOLOGY : Study of the structure of flowers with a view to interpret their evolutionary significance.

FLORICULTURE : Branch of horticulture concerned with the cultivation of flower producing plants primarily for their aesthetic and ornamental value.

FLORISTICS : Study and cataloguing of plant species occurring in a given area.

FLORISTRY : Flower arrangement, decoration and other artistic uses of flowers.

FLOWER ARRANGEMENT : Art of arranging flowers in an aesthetic manner for ornamental purposes.

FLOUR MILLING TECHNOLOGY : Preparing flours of various grains by milling.

FLUID DYNAMICS : The science of fluids in motion.

FLUID ENGINEERING : Branch of engineering involving fluids, their flow rates and other characteristics.

FLUID GEOMETRY : Fluid distribution in reservoir strata.

FLUID MECHANICS : The science concerned with fluids either at rest or in motion and dealing with pressures, velocities and accelerations or expansion in the fluid including fluid deformation and compression.

FLUID STATICS : Determination of pressure intensities and forces exerted by fluids at rest.

FLUOROSCOPY : It is a kind of imaging in which a phosphorescent screen sensitive to X-rays is used instead of photographic film. A visible image is formed on the screen as X-rays passing through the subject cause the screen to glow. Flouroscopy allows a doctor to view the internal structure of the subject's body as it moves.

FLUVIOLOGY : The science of rivers.

FODDER CROPS : Branch of agriculture concerned with the cultivation of crops used as fodder.

FOETAL MEDICINE : Study of the diseases of the foetus and their treatment

FETOSCOPY : Examination of the foetus with the help of an optical instrument in the amniotic cavity allowing biopsy and blood sampling.

FOLKLORE : Common orally transmitted traditions, myths festivals, songs, superstitions and stories of all peoples.

FOLK LITERATURE : Orally transmitted literature of rural folk in the form of songs, poetry, stories etc.

FOLK MEDICINE : Common orally transmitted remedies used by tribals and villagers.

FOLK MUSIC : Common orally transmitted songs of all peoples.

FOLK PSYCHOLOGY : Psychology of peoples, psychological study of the beliefs, customs, conventions, etc., of peoples.

FOOD ADMINISTRATION : Distribution, quality control and nutritional evaluation of food.

FOOD ENGINEERING : Techniques of producing various kinds of food substances.

FOOD POLICY ECONOMICS : Economics concerned with sustainable food production and distribution to eliminate food scarcity, malnutrition, hunger and starvation deaths throughout the world.

FOOD PROCESSING TECHNOLOGY : Techniques of converting raw food materials into value added, easily consumable, tasty products with long shelf life.

FOOD QUALITY MANAGEMENT : Monitoring food quality at every stage of preparation, processing and packaging.

FOOD SCIENCE : Concerned with the study of nature of food stuffs, kinds of foods, nutritive values of foods, food processing etc.

FOOD TECHNOLOGY : Study of the properties and preparation of foods particularly in industrial processes. See Food Science.

FOOTWEAR DESIGNING : Designing footwear of various kinds to suit specific needs of people of all ages, for all seasons, climates, fashions, purposes etc.

FOOTWEAR MAKING : Vocational training course in footwear making.

FOOTWEAR SCIENCE AND ENGINEERING : Study of scientific and engineering principles and methods involved in designing and manufacturing footwear.

FOOTWEAR TECHNOLOGY : Technology of footwear manufacture.

FOREIGN EXHANGE MANAGEMENT : Study of currencies of various countries and their exchange rates, their fluctuations and factors influencing exchange rates and concerned banking regulations etc.

FOREIGN RELATIONS : See international relations.

FOREIGN TRADE : Study of trade between nations.

FORENSIC ACCOUNTING AND AUDITING : To study the monetary transactions of suspected criminals and economic offenders for the purpose of submitting in a court of law.

FORENSIC ANTHROPOLOGY : Study of the body features and measurements of suspected criminals and dead bodies as evidences in cases of murders and other crimes to be submitted in a court of law. Identification of the dead, whether the remains are human or not, determining sex, age, state of health, ancestral background etc; and recreating the face and history behind the unidentifiable remains.

FORENSIC DENTISTRY : Identification of deceased persons through dental remains, bite mark analysis and examination of oral, facial structures for determination of injury, possible malpractices or insurance fraud.

FORENSIC DNA TECHNOLOGY : Identification of suspected criminals on the basis of their DNA analysis to be submitted in a court of law. This technology is also used in the case of doubtful parentage.

FORENSIC ENGINEERING : Application of engineering evidence in disputed cases including murder, suicide or natural death, before a court of law.

FORENSIC MEDICINE : Application of medical science in law and police investigations. An important example is the post-mortem examination of dead bodies in doubtful or disputed cases of death.

FORENSIC PATHOLOY : Use of pathological evidence in legal cases, primarily for determining cause of death, time of death etc., in disputed cases.

FORENSIC PHYSICS : Application of knowledge of physics for legal purposes.

FORENSIC PSYCHOLOGY : Study of the psychological features of criminals and their victims as an aid in investigation and legal proceedings.

FORENSIC PSYCHIATRY AND BEHAVIOURAL SCIENCE : A broad range of legal issues is addressed by forensic psychiatry and behavioural science for example, the patient's competence to stand trial, determining the mental condition of the accused juvenile delinquency, child custody parental fitness, spouse abuse etc.

FORENSIC SCIENCE : Applications of science in the investigation of crime and in legal cases.

FORENSIC TOXICOLOGY : Application of knowledge of poisons and poisoning in criminal investigation and in legal cases. Study of the harmful effects of chemical drugs on living systems with emphasis on the conditions under which they occur. It involves the interpretation of analytical, clinical and environmental data and the medical history of the victim, identification of the toxin, blood, urine or gastric contents.

FOREST CONSERVATION : Those measures concerned with the protection and preservation of forest lands and resources.

FOREST ECOLOGY : The science that deals with the study of forests and their relationships to the environment. Takes a look at related topics like bio-climatic variability and forest vegetation, rainfall, environment and forests; air and soil temperatures, winds, solar radiation, snow, dew and frost, soil moisture regime etc.

FOREST MANAGEMENT : Prevention of deforestation, promotion of afforestation and proper utilization of forest produce and preservation of wild life are included in forest management.

FOREST NUTRITION : Study of nutritional requirements, deficiency diseases and remedial measures of forest trees and other species.

FORESTRY : The management of forest lands for wood, forages, water, wild life and recreation.

FOREST SCIENCE : Includes study of Botany, genetics, physiology, pathology, entomology of forest trees, wood technology, forest soils etc.,

FOREX MANAGEMENT : Management of foreign exchange transactions in banks and export and import businesses.

FORGING BUSINESSES : Branch of mechanical engineering concerned with shaping metals in the desired manner by the application of heat and other means.

FORMAL SOCIOLOGY : Study of social relationships as the object of analysis.

FORMULATION TECHNOLOGY : Developing new dosage forms of drugs, advanced drug delivery systems, especially injectables, coating technologies, aerosols, transdermal patches etc.

FORTRAN : Short form for Formula Translation. It is a problem oriented high level computer programming for scientific and mathematical use.

FOUNDATION ENGINEERING : Branch of civil engineering concerned with the foundation of buildings, bridges, and other constructions.

FOUNDRY ENGINEERING : Branch of engineering concerned with the machinery and works used in casting of metals.

FOUNDRY TECHNOLOGY : Methods of casting metals.

FOURIER SERIES : The mathematical hypothesis proposed by the french mathematical physicist Fourier. It has extensive applications.

FRACTURE MECHANICS : Branch of engineering concerned with the cracking and breaking of metals and metallic structures.

FRAGMENTOGRAPHY : Identification of complex substances by disintegration and making the fragments volatile.

FRAGRANCE AND FLAVOUR DEVELOPMENT : Development of fragrance and flavours in various preparations by the addition of appropriate chemicals in suitable proportions.

FREE ELECTRON LASER : It is a type of laser which works by passing a stream of electrons travelling at nearly the speed of light though a wiggler, a device that produces alternating magnetic fields. These fields cause the electrons to vibrate at a specific frequency which stimulates them to emit a beam of laser light. This has been used in surgery.

FRONT OFFICE MANAGEMENT : Management of reservations of rooms, allotment of rooms, registering customers, keeping a register of arrivals and departures, collecting the room charges etc from customers and other related functions in large hotels and lodging houses, guest houses etc.

FRUIT AND VEGETABLE PROCESSING : Application of various treatments and processes to prepare diverse value added products with greater shelf life.

FUNCTIONAL MANAGEMENT : Application of management principles to other areas like personnel management, financial management, marketing management, advertising etc.

FUNCTIONAL MATHEMATICS : Use of mathematics for various purposes.

FUNCTIONAL PSYCHOLOGY : A type of psychology which emphasizes the functions rather than the mere facts of mental phenomena.

FUNDAMENTAL ANALYSIS : Security analysis that seeks to detect misvalued securities by an analysis of the firm's business prospects. Research analysis often focusses on earnings, dividend prospects, expenditure for future interest rates and risk evaluation of the firm.

FUNGAL BIOTECHNOLOGY : Utilization of fungi for the production of antibiotics and other chemicals, for industrial purpose and for food production.

FUNGAL GENETICS : Study of the genetics of fungi made considerable contribution to our understanding of genetic principles, since results can be obtained in a short time span and culturing fungi is relatively easy.

FUNGAL PHYSIOLOGY : Fungi, a group of organisms which are devoid of chlorophyll exhibit saprophytic, parasitic and symbiotic mode of life and are a source of antibiotics and other useful substances. Hence the study of physiology of fungi is of interest not only from the biological point of view but also for industrial purposes.

FUNGICIDE TECHNOLOGY : Manufacture of chemical fungicides for eradicating fungi which cause diseases of crop plants, animals and man and those which spoil foodstuffs, buildings and monuments, and cause harm to several articles and equipments used by man.

FURNACE TECHNOLOGY : The technology of using the furnace which is an inclosed structure in which is kept a strong fire for melting ores or metals, heating the boiler of a steam engine and other such purposes.

FURNITURE DESIGN : The art of designing furniture to suit diverse tastes and functions.

FUTURE STUDIES : Visualising and forecasting probable future developments and events in science, technology, economics, politics, sociology and other fields on the basis of the existing knowledge and historical evidence. Also known as futurology.

FUTUROLOGY : See future studies.

FUZZY LOGIC TECHNOLOGY : Fuzzy logic deals with problems which are uncertain and vague. It basically translates and implements human thinking and uses sound mathematical theory to solve problems. It has wide applications in industries, factories the military operations as well as in the medical field to diagnose diseases.

G

GAME THEORY : The science of strategic decision making offers powerful insights on how to anticipate and counter the moves of rivals. Its frameworks are apt for a variety of business situations such as pricing, negotiating and cooperating. This is considered a must for today's focussed manager, irrespective of the industry or business.

GAMMA TAXONOMY : The level of taxonomic study concerned with biological aspects of taxa including intra specific populations, speciation and evolutionary rates and trends.

GANDHIAN THOUGHT AND PEACE STUDIES : Study of Mahatma Gandhi's ideas and thinking and their bearing on world peace.

GARDENING : The art and practice of cultivating gardens and growing flowers, vegetables and fruits; a branch of horticulture.

GARMENT EXPORT MANAGEMENT : Exporting ready made garments to other countries forms part of export management business and requires knowledge of market conditions and requirements of various countries and government regulations governing export of garments in the country of origin and the importing countries.

GARMENT MAKING TECHNOLOGY : Fundamentals of apparel production, garment construction, pattern making and grading, textile science, equipment technology, cutting room procedure, product development and quality assurance, fabric dyeing and printing, garment production control and computer aided design.

GAS ANALYSIS : Analysis of the constituents or properties of a gas (either pure or mixed) by various methods to find out heating value, molecular weight, density and viscosity.

GAS ENGINEERING : Branch of engineering concerned with the supply, storage and use of gas (normally hydrocarbons used for heating)

GAS DYNAMICS : The study of the motion of gases and of its causes, which takes into account thermal effects generated by the motion.

GAS MECHANICS : The study of the action of forces on gases.

GASTROENTEROLOGY : Branch of medicine concerned with the diseases of the stomach and intestines.

GASTROLOGY : The art of cooking

GAS TURBINE PROPULSION ENGINEERING : Branch of aeronautical engineering concerned with propulsion by means of a gas turbine used in aircraft.

GEM CRAFT : The art of polishing precious stones like ruby, topaz, emerald, diamond etc and fixing them in ornaments.

GEM IDENTIFACTION : Identification of precious stones on the basis of their characteristics.

GEMMOLOGY : Science of studying the properties of precious stones like diamond, ruby, topaz etc and determining their value.

GEM STONES CARVING : The techniques of carving gem stones in order to fix them in ornaments.

GENDER AND SOCIETY : Theory and politics of gender issues in different societies, cross cultural study of gender, feminism and social theory, gender and development and issues and controversies in social and political theory.

GENEALOGY : The study of pedigrees or family history.

GENECOLOGY : The study of species and their genetic subdivisions, their place in nature and the genetic and ecological factors controlling speciation.

GENESIOLOGY : The science of the origin of the world and of man.

GENERAL EDUCATION : 1. A non-examinable syllabus. 2. Area of knowledge which should be common to all pupils.

GENERAL GEOLOGY : Study of the geological features and phenomena of the earth, origin of the earth etc.

GENERAL PSYCHOLOGY : A systematic discussion of general principles and laws governing mental life in general as distinct from peculiarities characteristic of the individual.

GENERAL SCIENCE : Combination of aspects of physics, chemistry and biology taught as a single subject

GENERAL STUDIES : Programme of studies designed to broaden the education of students beyond the main or major subjects.

GENE THERAPY : Application of genetic engineering techniques to alter or replace defective genes.

GENETIC COUNSELLING : Counselling of patients about genetic diseases, counselling of parents about the probability of their offspring inheriting genetic diseases and defects, counselling of brides and grooms about their genetic compatibility etc. With the recent unveiling of the human genome the possibilities and potentialities of genetic counselling have increased enormously.

GENETIC ENGINEERING : 1. Modification of bacterial cells to synthesize completely new substances, for example, insulin. 2. The intentional production of new genes and alteration of genomes by the substitution or addition of new genetic material.

GENETIC FINGERPRINTING : Identification of chemical entities in animal tissues as indicative of the presence of specific genes.

GENETIC MEDICINE : Medical treatment based on genome studies.

GENETICS : The branch of biology dealing with heredity.

GENETICS AND PLANT BREEDING : The application of genetic principles and methods to the improvement of crop varieties, a branch of botany and agriculture.

GENETIC TOXICOLOGY : Study of the effect of toxic substances on the genetic material. Some toxic substances may induce genetic mutations.

GENITOGRAPHY : Investigation of doubtful sex.

GENITOURINARY SURGERY : Surgical treatment of disorders of the reproductive and urinary systems which are closely related.

GENOMICS : Study of the genome or the complete genetic composition of an organism. The complete genome of man and of a few other animals and plants has been analysed and the sequence of the genes in the chromosomes revealed till now.

GEO-ACOUSTICS : The study of the acoustic properties of rocks mainly to explore the possible use of the rock system as a carrier of seismic signals in a communication system.

GEOBOTANICAL PROSPECTING : The use of the distribution, appearance and growth anomalies of plants in locating ore deposits.

GEOBOTANY : The study of plants as related to their geological environment.

GEOCHEMICAL PROSPECTING : Use of geochemical and biogeochemical principles and data in the search for economic deposits of minerals, petroleum and natural gas.

GEOCHEMISTRY : Study of the chemical composition of various phases of the earth and the physical and chemical processes which have produced the observed distribution of elements.

GEOCHRONOLOGY : The dating of events in earth's history.

GEOCHRONOMETRY : Study of the absolute age or the actual age of rocks.

GEOCOSMOGENY : Study of the origin of the earth.

GEODESY : 1. The science concerned with surveying and mapping the earth's surface to determine, for example, its exact size, shape and gravitational field. 2. That branch of applied mathematics which determines the figures and areas of large portions of the earth's surface, the general figure of the earth and the variations of the intensity of gravity in different regions.

GEODETIC ASTRONOMY : The branch of geodesy which utilizes astronomic observations to extract geodetic information.

GEODYNAMICS : The science of the forces and processes of the earth's interior.

GEOECONOMY : The study of economic conditions that are influenced by geographic factors.

GEOELECTRICAL ENGINEERING : Branch of electrical engineering concerned with the production of electricity from geothermal energy.

GEOENVIRONMENTAL ENGINEERING : Branch of environmental engineering concerned with environmental effects on the earth.

GEOEXPLORATION : Exploration of the interior of the earth for minerals, petroleum and other hydrocarbons.

GEOGNOSY : The science dealing with the solid body of the earth as a whole, occurrence of minerals and rocks and their origin.

GEOGRAPHIC INFORMATION SYSTEMS : Short form GIS. It is an earth information technology to help boost agricultural production, predict climate changes, preserve biodiversity and help disaster relief management and even traffic management.

GEOGRAPHY : Study of the features of the earth's surface, their distributions and interactions and the interaction of man with them.

GEOGRAPHICAL BOTANY : See plant geography.

GEOHYDROLOGY : Science dealing with underground water, often referred to as hydrogeology.

GEOINFORMATICS : Science concerned with the collection, storage and utilization of information pertaining to the earth. It encompasses survey and mapping geographical information system, global positioning system, high resolution imagery and digital cartography. It has wide applications from planning for road widening in urban areas to identifying land suitable for cultivation in rural areas.

GEOLOGICAL OCEANOGRAPHY : The study of the floors and margins of the oceans.

GEOLOGY : 1. The science which deals with the structure especially the internal structure of the crust of the globe and of the substances which compose it. 2. The science which treats of the minerals, rocks, earths or other substances composing the globe, the relations which the several constituent masses bear to each other, their formation, structure, position and history together with the successive changes that have taken place in organic and inorganic kingdoms of nature as illustrated by fossils or otherwise.

GEOMAGNETISM : Science concerned with the earth's magnetic field.

GEOMATICS : Branch of science concerned with making available cartographic data in digital form.

GEOMETRICAL OPTICS : Study of the geometry of the path of light rays and their imagery through optical systems.

GEOMETRY : 1. The science of magnitude. 2. That science which treats of the properties of lines, angles and surfaces. 3. That branch of mathematics which treats of the properties and relations of magnitudes.

GEOMORPHOLOGY : 1. Study of origin and development of land forms excluding the major forms of the earth's surface (for example, mountain chains and ocean chains. 2. The study of the origin of secondary topographic features which are caused by erosion in the primary elements and built up of the erosional debris.

GEONOMY : The science of the physical laws relating to the earth, including geology and physical geography.

GEOPHYSICAL ENGINEERING : A branch of engineering that applies scientific methods for locating mineral deposits.

GEOPHYSICAL INSTRUMENTATION : Design, development and manufacture of modern instruments for use in the study of earthquakes and prospecting for minerals, oil, and natural gas.

GEOPHYSICAL OCEANOGRAPHY : Branch of oceanography which describes the shape and material of the sea floor. It seeks to understand the origin of sea floor sediments and rocks and their patterns. It involves the study of the geological and geophysical characteristics of coastal margins for the exploitation of deep sea mineral resources as well as the selection of suitable locations of marine structures. See geological oceanography.

GEOPHYSICAL PROSPECTING : Application of quantitative concepts and principles of physics and mathematics in geological explorations to discover mineral resources.

GEOPHYSICS : Principles of mathematics and physics applied to the study of earth's crust and interior.

GEOPONICS : The art or science of cultivation of crops on land.

GEOSCIENTIFIC INSTRUMENTATION : Seismological studies, snow sensors, artificial recharging of ground water, snow/glacier parameters, measurements for assessment and forecasting of snow bound run off water.

GEOSTATISTICS : Study of facts pertaining to the earth like dimensions of the earth, gravity, mass etc.

GEOTECHNICAL ENGINEERING : Application of engineering methods in the study of the earth.

GEOTECHNOLOGY : Includes soil mechanics and foundation engineering.

GEOTHERMAL PROSPECTING : Exploration for sources of geothermal energy.

GERIATRIC HOME CARE : A course of study and training in home care for the aged who are suffering from chromic diseases like Alzheimer's disease, Parkinson's disease etc.

GERIATRICS : Branch of medicine concerned with the health and treatment of diseases of old people.

GERIOPSYCHIATRY : Branch of psychiatry concerned with mental diseases of old people.

GERONTOLOGY : Branch of science concerned with the study of ageing and problems of old age.

GLACIAL GEOLOGY : Study of land features resulting from glaciation.

GIACIOLOGY : Study of existing or modern glaciers in their entirety.

GLASS BLOWING : The art of blowing and fashioning glass vessels. It is used in fashioning glass apparatus for scientific experiments.

GLASS CUTTING : The art of cutting glass or grinding it into ornamental or useful forms.

GLASS DESIGNING : Making glass objects in various designs and decorations.

GLASS PAINTING : The art of producing designs in colour on or in glass.

GLASS TECHNOLOGY : The technology of manufacturing glass from raw materials and of making glass objects.

GLOBAL MANAGEMENT : Primarily applied to management of business activities at the international level. Globalization gaining increasing importance in every field, scope of global management is becoming widened and extended.

GLOBAL NAVIGATION SATELLITE SYSTEM : Conceived by the international civil aviation organization of the UNO it is a conceptual body of future air navigation systems also known as communication, navigation and surveillance of air traffic management system. It means taking navigation from ground base to satellite base.

GLOBAL POSITIONING SYSTEM : It is a modern technology in which receivers are used to study the strain in the earth with the help of satellite information to pinpoint location of strains with an accuracy of 3 mm or less. This technology can be helpful in predicting earthquakes.

GLOBAL STRATEGIC MANAGEMENT : Management of strategies in the political, economic and defence fields on a global scale.

GLOSSOLOGY : The definition and explanation of terms as of a science. See terminology.

GLOTTOCHRONOLOGY : Chronological comparison of languages by comparing their basic vocabulary sampled at different times.

GLOTTOLOGY : The science of language; comparative philology. See linguistics.

GLYPHOGRAPHY : An electrotype process by which a design in relief is obtained from an etched plate.

GLYPTOGRAPHY : The art or process of engraving on precious stones.

GNATHOLOGY : Branch of dentistry concerned with the study of the jaw and its diseases.

GNOMONICS : The art or science of dialing in order to find the altitudes, declinations etc. of the sun and stars.

GNOTOBIOLOGY : 1. The branch of biology dealing with known living forms. 2. The study of higher organisms in the absence of all demonstrable, viable micro-organisms except those known to be present.

GONIOMETRY : The art of measuring solid angles, particularly the angles formed by the faces of mineral crystals.

GOVERNMENT : Branch of politics and public administration concerned with the study of structure and functioning of government.

GRAMMAR : Branch of linguistics that deals with the meaningful arrangement of a language form and with word classes and their relations with each other and their relation in large units.

GRAPHEMICS : Systematic investigation of methods of writing and the relationship of writing systems to systems of language; also known as graphonomy.

GRAPHIC ARTS MANAGEMENT: Management of various forms of graphic art like drawing pictures, painting, computer graphics etc.

GRAPHIC ARTS TECHNOLOGY: Study of technological methods and practices and processes used in graphic arts.

GRAPHIC DESIGNING: Preparing designs in the form of pictures.

GRAPHICS: The art of expressing ideas in the form of pictures. See computer graphics.

GRAPHOLOGY: Study of hand writing in relation to specific qualities and attitudes of a person

GRAPHONOMY: See Graphemics.

GRAPHOTHERAPY: A method of treatment to help better one's attitude through hand writing.

GRAPHOTHOLOGY: The Scientific investigation of changes in handwriting indicative of physical or mental abnormality or disorder.

GREASING AND LUBRICATION: Application of grease and lubricants to machinery.

GRINDING TECHNOLOGY: Manufacture and use of grinding machines and grinding wheels as a part of machine tools manufacturing industry.

GROSS ANATOMY: Anatomy that deals with the naked eye appearance of tissues.

GROUND WATER MICROBIOLOGY: Study of the microorganisms present in ground water. Treated as a branch of Microbiology and geology.

GROUND WATER TECHNOLOGY : Technology involving the exploration, utilization, recharging and quality monitoring and control of ground water.

GROUP DYNAMICS: Study of behavior of groups of people and of the interaction of behavior of individuals with the development of common perceptions.

GROUP THEORY: Theory of the collections of mathematical elements. Branch of mathematics.

GROUP THERAPY: Psychotherapy with 5-10 Patients and 1-2 therapists.

GROWTH ECONOMICS: Branch of economics concerned with theories of economic growth.

GROWTH THEORY: Branch of economics concerned with the analysis of the determinants of the rate at which an economy will grow over time like changes in capital stock, population size, age profile of the labour force and technical progress.

GUIDANCE AND COUNSELLING: Branch of education concerned with providing guidance to students regarding choice of courses in relation to their aptitudes and potentialities.

GUIDANCE SERVICES: Concerned with the Provision of information and guidance to students about employment opportunities available in their respective fields of specialization.

GYMNASTICS : The art of performing athletic exercises. See athletics.

GYMNOSPERMS: Branch of botany concerned with the study of plants in which seds are not enclosed in fruits but are exposed. Examples : Cycas, Pinus etc.

GYNAECOLOGICAL ONCOLOGY: Branch of medicine concerned with the study of cancer of the female reproductive system.

GYNAECOLOGY: Branch of medicine concerned with the study of female ailments and bodily peculiarities.

GYROSCOPICS: The branch of mechanics concerned with gyroscopes and their use in the control of ships, aircraft etc.

H

HAEMATICS : The branch of Physiology that treats of blood. Also known as haematology.

HAEMATOLOGY : Branch of Physiology and medicine concerned with the study of physicochemical properties of blood, blood groups, blood transfusion and diseases of blood.

HEAMATO-ONCOLOGY: Branch of medicine concerned with cancers of the blood.

HAEMODIALYSIS ENGINEERING: Branch of biomedical engineering concerned with equipment used for the dialysis of blood.

HAEMODYNAMICS : A branch of physiology concerned with circulatory movements of the blood and the forces involved in circulation.

HAEMORHEOLOGY : Study of the flow of blood and of effects of changes in blood constituents on blood flow.

HAGIOLOGY : That branch of literature which has to do with the lives and legends of the saints.

HAIR-STYLING : The art and profession of cutting and arranging hair in a stylish and fashionable manner.

HARDWARE ENGINEERING : Engineering concerned with the construction and maintenance of the electronic and mechanical gadgets of a computer.

HARDWARE MAINTENANCE : Study and practical training in the maintenance of computer hardware.

HARDWARE TECHNOLOGY : Technology concerned with all the electronic and mechanical gadgets which together form a computer system as distinct from the set of instructions which are used to operate them.

HAZARDOUS WASTE MANAGEMENT : Disposal of dangerous waste generated in industries and hospitals in a safe manner.

HEALTH AND FERTILITY : Branch of population studies concerned with the health and fertility status of a population.

These parameters constitute important factors in population growth.

HEALTH AND MORTALITY : Branch of population studies concerned with the relation between health and mortality rates which constitute important factors in population growth.

HEALTH ANTHROPOLOGY : Study of the health characteristics and status of different races.

HEALTH CARE ADMINISTRATION : Administration of health care services to the community.

HEALTH COUNSELLING : Professional course of study and training in providing advice and guidance regarding health problems.

HEALTH ECONOMICS : Branch of medicine concerned with the cost of medical treatment and prevention of disease.

HELATH EDUCATION : Education about health at various levels like children, adults, women and the elderly.

HEALTH INFORMATICS : Health internet system administration.

HEALTH MANAGEMENT : Management of health service.

HEALTH PHYSICS : Branch of medical physics concerned with the protection of medical, scientific, and industrial workers from the hazards of ionizing radiation and other dangers associated with atomic physics.

HEALTH PSYCHOLOGY : Study of attitudes of people towards health and disease, psychology of patients etc.

HEALTH SCIENCES : Sciences connected with health like, for example public health, sanitary science, social and preventive medicine etc.

HEALTH STATISTICS : Statistics about the state of health, incidence of disease, mortality, longevity etc, in a community, state or country.

HEARING SCIENCE : Branch of science concerned with physiology of hearing, hearing defects, loss of hearing, hearing aids and treatment of hearing disorders.

HEAT TRANSFER : Branch of physics and thermal engineering concerned with transfer of heat from one body to another.

HEAVY ENGINEERING : Branch of engineering concerned with heavy machinery, heavy electric generators, heavy vehicles, heavy earth moving equipment etc.

HEAVY EQUIPMENT OPERATION : Driving and maintaining heavy vehicles, tractors, cranes, drills etc.

HEAVY WATER TECHNOLOGY : Process development, design, engineering construction and operation of plants for production of heavy water to support nuclear power programme.

HEDONICS : Psychology of pain and pleasure.

HELICOPTER SYSTEM : Branch of aeronautical engineering concerned with the manufacture and maintenance of helicopters.

HELIOTHERAPY : Treatment of diseases by exposure to sunlight.

HELLINISTIC ART : Greek art during the period of geographical expansion.

HELIMINTHOLOGY : Branch of zoology concerned with the study of disease causing parasitic worms known as helminths. Also of importance in medicine, microbiology and parasitology.

HEPATICOLOGY : Branch of Botany concerned with liverworts or Hepaticae, a sub-division of Bryoplyta. These plants got the name liverworts due to their supposed resemblance in shape to the liver.

HEPATO BILIARY IMAGING : Imaging of liver, bile ducts, gall bladder and pancreas.

HEPATOLOGY : Branch of medicine concerned with the diseases of the liver.

HERBAL FOLKLORE : Study of herbs used in folklore.

HERBOLOGY : Study of herbs and their healing effects. Native American systems classify plants as food, medicine or poison.

HEREDITY : The study of hereditary transmission of qualities like those of the parent. The doctrine that the offspring inherits the characteristics of the parent or parents. See genetics.

HERMENEUTICS : Theory and method of interpreting human action in sociology.

HERPETOLOGY : Branch of zoology concerned with the study of reptiles comprising lizards, snakes, crocodiles and dinasaurs.

HIEROGLYPHICS : The art of conveying meaning by means of a figure of an animal, plant or other objects which may be used to stand for an alphabetical character.

HIEROLOGY : Knowledge of sacred writings.

HIGH ENERGY PHYSICS : See particles physics.

HIGH PRESSURE CHEMISTRY : The study of chemical reactions that occur at pressures exceeding 10000 bars.

HIGH PRESSURE PHYSICS : The study of effects of high pressure on matter.

HIGH TEMPERATURE CHEMISTRY : The study of chemical phenomena occurring above 500°K.

HIGH VOLTAGE ENGINEERING : Branch of electrical engineering concerned with high voltage machines.

HIGHWAY ENGINEERING : Branch of civil engineering concerned with the design, construction and co-ordination of highway projects.

HINDUISM : The doctrine and rites of Hindus, Brahminism. Hindu from sanskrit Sindhu river or Indus.

HINDU LAW : Law applicable to Hindus in the spheres of marriages, divorce, property rights, adoption etc.

HISTOCHEMISTRY : Study of the distribution of chemical compounds of tissues by means of their chemical reactions of importance in pathology.

HISTOLOGY : Branch of biology concerned with the study of tissues of animals and plants. Also of importance in medicine. See Histopathology.

HISTOPATHOLOGY : Branch of pathology concerned with the study of diseases at the tissue level. Study of changes in tissue structure and chemistry helps in diagnosis and treatment of diseases.

HISTOPHYSIOLOGY : The science of tissue functions.

HISTORADIOGRAPHY : A technique for taking X-ray pictures of cells, tissues or sometimes of whole small organisms.

HISTORICAL ARCHAEOLOGY : Study of history based on archaeological findings.

HISTORICAL GEOGRAPHY : Branch of geography concerned with the changes taking place in geographical boundaries capital cities, utilization of natural resources and other geographical features over time.

HISTORICAL GEOLOGY : A branch of geology concerned with the systematic study of fossils and their locations in a sequence of bedded rocks.

HISTORICAL LINGUISTICS : Refers to the study of history of a language.

HISTORICAL SCIENCES : History, ancient history and archaeology.

HISTORICAL SOCIOLOGY : Study of sociology from the historical perspective.

HISTORIOGRAPHY : The art of writing history.

HISTORY : Systematic study of the origin and progress of peoples, nations, institutions, disciplines etc.

HISTORY OF BOTANY : Study of the development of knowledge of plants and their uses from the time of the earliest man to the present day through various stages.

HISTORY OF EDUCATION : Study of the past development of educational systems, educational theory and educational institutions.

HISTORY OF MEDICINE : Collection and study of historical evidences for the growth and development of medical systems and institution from ancient times.

HISTORY OF SCIENCE : Study of the development of science and its various branches in various countries through history.

HISTRIONICS : The art of theatrical representation. See theater arts, dramaturgy.

HOLOGRAPHY : Production of 2-dimensional films from which 3-dimensioned images can be derived using interference between laser beams.

HOME ART : Art such as sculptures and engravings; counting of objects that actually come from the homes of man.

HOME DESIGNING : It covers designing colours, lighting, Fengshui, glass painting, flower arrangements, draperies etc., knowledge of computer aided design and auto CAD are useful tools in home designing.

HOME ECONOMICS : Study of domestic science with additional attention to budgeting and planning.

HOME GARDENING : Growing ornamental vegetable and fruit plants in the back yards of homes as a bobby.

HOME MANAGEMENT : Branch of home science concerned with the management of household affairs like home decoration, provision of facilities for the members of the family and the upkeep of the home etc.

HOME NURSING : Branch of nursing science concerned with nursing sick and elderly people at their homes, staying in the house of the patient as a member of the family.

HOME SCIENCE : Branch of science concerned with management of home and its upkeep and includes food and nutrition, child development, human physiology, bio-chemistry, psychology and other allied subjects.

HOMEOPATHY : A system of medicine developed in the early 1800 and based on the notion that similar substances in infinitesimal doses could prompt a natural response in a person with diseases. Homeopathic medicines are given in accordance with the patient personality characters.

HOROLOGY : The art of constructing machines for measuring time such as watches, clocks, dials etc.

HOROSCOPY : The predicting of future events by the disposition of the stars and planets.

HORTICULTURAL ENGINEERING : Creation of new varieties of horticultural plants by various methods like cutting, grafting crossing etc.

HORTICULTURAL NURSERY MANAGEMENT : Management of nurseries for raising seedlings, cuttings, grafts, etc. used in horticultural gardens.

HORTICULTURAL SCIENCE : Science of growing vegetables fruits and ornamental flowers.

HORTICULTURAL THERAPY : Branch of occupational therapy dealing with the therapeutic properties of horticultural plants.

HORTICULTURE : See horticultural science.

HOSPITAL AUTOMATION : Use of computer software in hospital management.

HOSPITAL ADMINISTRATION : Course of study and training in administration of a hospital.

HOSPITAL AND HEALTH SYSTEMS MANAGEMENT : Management of hospitals and health systems in a given area or jurisdiction.

HOSPITAL MANAGEMENT : Course of study and training in the management of the various departments and activities of a hospital.

HOSPITALITY AND CATERING SERVICES : Food and beverage production and service, front office, house keeping, hotel economics and hygiene and nutrition, principles of management, hospitality, accounting and finance, computers and business law, accommodation management, human resource management, hospitality marketing and sales, travel and tourism managements.

HOSPITALITY MANAGEMENT : Management of hospitality services as in hotels, guest houses, air lines etc. See hospitality and catering services.

HOSPITAL PHARMACY : Dispensing medicines to patients in a hospital.

HOTEL CATERING AND HOSPITALITY : Course of study and special training in catering and attending to the needs and comforts of the guests in hotels.

HOTEL MANAGEMENT : Course of study and training in managing various departments of a hotel.

HOUSE KEEPING : Branch of hotel management dealing with the up keep and maintenance of rooms, dining hall interiors and the premises of a hotel.

HOUSING : Study of the various aspects of planning, construction and financing of provision of living accommodation to people in a given area or jurisdiction.

HOUSING LAW : Law governing flats, apartments, promoters, builders, developers, cooperative housing societies, environment, slums and consumer forums.

HRD AUDIT : Evaluating the human resources function for business improvement.

HUMAN BEHAVIOUR : Branch of Psychology concerned with human behaviour including abnormal behaviour and mental illness.

HUMAN BIOLOGY : Branch of biology concerned particularly with the human body.

HUMAN DEVELOPMENT : 1. Developmental stages of man from the embryonal stage onwards. 2. Development of man from primitive condition through civilization.

HUMAN DEVELOPMENT AND FAMILY STUDIES : Branch of sociology concerned with the social development of man and family systems.

HUMAN ECOLOGY : The branch of ecology that considers the relations of individual persons and of human communities with their particular environment.

HUMAN GENETICS : Study of inheritance of human characters including hereditary defects and diseases.

HUMAN GENOMICS : Branch of science concerned with the analysis of the human genome and the genes constituting it.

HUMAN GEOGRAPHY : Branch of geography concerned with the study of geographical distribution of man and factors governing the distribution.

HUMAN NUTRITION : Study of the nutritional requirements, deficiency diseases and their prevention and cure in man.

HUMAN PALAEONTOLOGY : Study of the evolution and development of man on the basis of fossil history.

HUMANITIES : Studies dealing with man as the central concern, for example, literature, history, philosophy, languages etc.

HUMAN PHYSIOLOGY : Study of the various functional systems of man like digestive, excretory, respiratory, circulatory, sensory, nervous, reproductive etc., forms part of biology, medicine and allied sciences.

HUMAN RELATIONS AND ADMINISTRATION : Maintaining proper relations between the employees and administrators in government and private institutions

HUMAN REPRODUCTION : Study of the reproductive processes in humans including experiments involving the production of test tube babies.

HUMAN RESOURCES DEVELOPMENT : Developing the productivity and capability of people by imparting education and training in various skills.

HUMAN RESOURCES MANAGEMENT : Management of the human resources of an institution with the aim of obtaining their maximum co-operation in fulfilling the objectives of the institution.

HUMAN RIGHTS AND SOCIAL ACTION : A course of study dealing with social action in protection of human rights.

HUMAN RIGHTS STUDIES : Study of human rights as enshrined in the United nations charter and their violation, organisations and institutions engaged in securing human rights.

HUMAN SERVICES : Studies of services aimed at the provision of minimum human needs like food, health, education, housing, employment etc.

HYDRAULICS : Branch of science and technology concerned with the mechanics of fluids, especially liquids.

HYDRAULICS AND WATER RESOURCE ENGINEERING : Application of hydraulics in the management of water resources by constructing dams, canals etc, using engineering methods.

HYDROACOUSTICS : See underwater acoustics.

HYDRO BIOLOGY : Biology of aquatic organisms.

HYDRODYNAMICS : Study of motion of a fluid and of the interaction of fluid with its boundaries.

HYDROGEOCHEMISTRTY : Study of the chemical characteristics of ground and surface waters as related to areal and regional geology.

HYDROGEOLOGY : Science dealing with the occurrence of ground and surface water, its utilization and its functions in modifying the earth.

HYDROGRAPHY : Study of the waters of the earth's surface including oceans, seas, lakes and rivers.

HYDROKINETICS : Study of the forces produced by a liquid as a consequence of its motion.

HYDROLOGY : Study of terrestrial water, in particular inland water before its discharge into the ocean or evaporation into the atmosphere.

HYDROMAGNETICS : See magnetohydrodynamics.

HYDROMECHANICS : Study of liquids traditionally water as a medium for the transmission of forces.

HYDROMETALLURGY : The process of assaying or reducing ores by liquid reagents.

HYDROMETEOROLOGY : That part of meteorology concerned with hydrologic problems particularly flood control, hydroelectric power, irrigation and similar fields of engineering and water resources.

HYDROMETRY : The science and technology of measuring specific gravities, particularly of liquids.

HYDROPATHY : The treatment of disease by the use of cold water externally or internally also know as Hydrotherapy.

HYDROPHYSICS : Study of physical properties of water.

HYDROPHYTOLOGY : Botany of water plants.

HYDROPONICS : Science concerned with growing plants in nutrient solutions in contrast to geoponics or growing plants in soil.

HYDROSTATICS : 1. The science which treats of the weight and equilibrium of fluids, particularly of water 2. That branch of science which treats of the properties of fluids at rest.

HYDROTHERAPY : See Hydropathy.

HYETOGRAPHY : The study of the annual variation and geographical distribution of precipitation.

HYGIENE : A system of principles or rules designed for thee promotion of health, especially the health of households or communities.

HYGIENICS : Sanitary science. See Hygiene.
HYGROLOGY : Study concerned with water vapor content of the atmosphere.
HYGROMETRY : Study concerned with measurements of the humidity of atmosphere and other gases.
HYMENOLOGY : Study of the membranes of the animal systems.
HYPERSONICS : Production and utilization of sound waves of frequencies above 500 megahertz.
HYPNOLOGY : Scientific study of sleep.
HYPNOTHERAPY : Use of hypnosis in treatment of disease.
HYPNOTISM : The art of inducing artificially a sleep like condition often by the person fixing his attention upon some bright object being accompanied by more or less unconsciousness.
HYPSOMETRY : The art of measuring the heights of places upon the surfaces of the earth.

I

ICHNOLOGY : Study of foot marks of animals.

ICHTHYOLOGY : Branch of Zoology concerned with the study of fishes.

ICONOGRAPHY : That branch of knowledge which treats of ancient statues, busts, paintings in fresco mosaic works, engraving on gems or metals and the like.

IDEAL AERODYNAMICS : A branch of aerodynamics that deals with simplifying assumptions that help explain some air flow problems and provide approximate answers.

IDEALOGY : See Ideology.

IDENTIFICATION AND VALUATION OF GEMS : A branch of the science of gemmology that is concerned with the identifying features of gems and their evaluation.

IDEOGRAPHY : System of writing, using pictures or symbols for ideas instead of letters or syllable sounds.

IDEOLOGY : The science of ideas also written as IDEALOGY .

IKEBANA : Japanese art of flower arrangement.

IMAGE AUDIT : Assessing the internal and external images of business /organizations (commercial and non-commercial), including political parties.

IMAGEOLOGY : The technique of observing and studying the internal parts of the body by obtaining their images by various mechanical and optical devices. The images are also projected on a screen. By this method it is possible to observe the internal details merely by making an incision on the body.

IMAGE PROCESSING : Physico chemical processing of images obtained on a film in order to make prints.

IMMUNOBIOLOGY : That branch of biology and medicine which is concerned with the study of the immune systems.

IMMUNOCHEMISTRY : Branch of Immunology and medicine concerned with blood groups etc.

IMMUNO DIAGNOSTICS : Branch of medicine concerned with the diagnosis of diseases on the basis of antigenic differences as well as diagnosis of diseases of immune system.

IMMUNOGENETICS : Genetics of antigenic differences and blood groups.

IMMUNOHAEMATOLOGY : That branch of immunology which is concerned with the study of the relation between the immune system and blood including blood transfusion.

IMMUNOLOGY : 1. Branch of medicine concerned with the study of the mechanism of conferring immunity to diseases by the use of vaccines. 2. A branch of biological science concerned with the native or acquired resistance of higher animal forms and humans to infection with micro organisms.

IMMUNOPATHOLOGY : Branch of pathology concerned with the study of immunity to diseases and also diseases of the immune system.

IMMUNOTHERAPY : Therapy to modify the immune system.

IMMUNO TOXICOLOGY : Study of the effect of toxins and poisons on the immune system.

IMPLANT DENTISTRY : Branch of dentistry concerned with implanting artificial teeth in the place of diseased or lost teeth.

IMPLANT SURGERY : See implantology.

IMPLANTOLOGY : Branch of medicine concerned with inserting parts or organs of the body in the place of those which have become dysfunctional or lost.

INCOME TAX : A branch of economics and commerce. Income is regarded as suitable for taxation although definition of taxable income is problematic.

INCOME TAX LAW : Law pertaining to the levy and collection of income tax.

INDEXING : Branch of library science concerned with the preparation of lists of books arranged in alphabetical order like subject index, author index, title index etc.

INDIRECT TAXES : These are defined as taxes levied on goods and services and their payment is only indirect. Excise and customs duties, value-added taxes are examples of indirect taxes.

INDIAN HERITAGE AND CULTURE : Study of the ancient Indian arts and culture.

INDIAN HISTORY : Study of the history of the country and people of India

INDIAN OCEAN STUDIES : Study of the nations bordering Indian ocean like India, Bangladesh, Myanmar etc.

INDIVIDUAL PSYCHOLOGY : The psychology of individual differences.

INDOLOGY : Study of the civilization, culture, languages etc, of India.

INDOOR GARDENING- Growing potted plants inside homes, offices, business establishments and other buildings for ornamental purpose and also for providing fresh air and removing pollution.

INDUSTRIAL ARCHITECTURE : Branch of architecture concerned with designing factories, offices and other buildings of industrial concerns.

INDUSTRIAL AND OPERATIONS MANAGEMENT : Study of management of industries and operations concerned with industries.

INDUSTRIAL AND WASTE WATER TREATMENT : Treatment of industrial effluents and waste water to make them less hazardous.

INDUSTRIAL AUTOMATION : Industrial automation systems like advance programmable logic : controllers, digital DC and AC drives and windows-based colour graphic systems.

INDUSTRIAL BIOTECHNOLOGY : Application of biotechnological techniques for industrial uses like production of medicines etc.

INDUSTRIAL CATALYSTS : Use of catalysts for industrial purposes.

INDUSTRIAL CHEMISTRY : Application of chemistry in industry.

INDUSTRIAL CLIMATOLOGY : A type of applied climatology which studies the effect of climate and weather on industrial operations; The goal is to provide industry with a sound basis for administrative and operational decisions which involve a weather factor.

INDUSTRIAL COUNSELLING : Providing guidance to enterpreneurs about starting and running an industry.

INDUSTRIAL ECOLOGY : It involves engineering and management as it tracks the flow of materials and energy consumed in production process for producing a balance sheet. It turns engineers into resource accountants in manufacturing industry.

INDUSTRIAL ECONOMICS : Branch of applied economics dealing with factors affecting the structure of industry and the way it is owned and managed.

INSUSTRIAL ELELCTORNICS : Application of electronics in industries.

INDUSTRIAL ENGINEERING : Application of engineering techniques for improving productivity.

INDUSTRIAL ENVIRONMENTAL ECONOMICS : Study of the economics of controlling the environmental factors involved in industries including treatment of harmful effluents and other hazardous environmental pollutants.

INDUSTRIAL FAN ENGINEERING : Manufacture of industrial fans including centrifugal, axial, mixed flow and other types of fans.

INDUSTRIAL FINANCE : Mobilizing financial resources for industries.

INDUSTRIAL FISHERIES : Development of value added products and by products from low cost fish and processing wastes from fish and shell fish.

INDSUTRIAL GEOGRAPHY : Branch of geography that deals with location, raw materials, products and distribution as influenced by geography.

INDUSTRIAL HYGIENE : Maintenance of cleanliness, sanitation and other conditions for protecting the health of industrial workers.

INDUSTRIAL LAW : Study of legal enactments applicable to industries and industrial workers.

INDUSTRIAL MANAGEMENT : Includes systems, marketing, operations, logistics, finance and human resources management.

INDUSTRIAL MARKETING : Marketing of industrial products, machinery and inputs used in industries. Marketing of technical and specialty engineering goods, pharmaceuticals etc.

INDUSTRIAL MATHEMATICS : Application of mathematics for improving quality and productivity in industry.

INDUSTRIAL MEDICINE : Branch of medicine concerned with the treatment of industrial diseases of workers.

INDUSTRIAL METAL FINISHING : The technique of finishing metals and metal products in industries.

INDSUTRIAL METALLURGY : Extraction and purification of metals used in industries.

INDUSTRIAL METEOROLOGY : Application of meteorological information and techniques to industrial problems.

INDUSTRIAL MICROBIOLOGY : The study, utilization and manipulation of those microorganisms capable of economically producing desirable substances or changes in substances and the control of undesirable microorganisms.

INDUSTRIAL PLASMA TECHNOLOGY : Industrial material processing technologies assisted by plasma.

INDUSTRIAL POLLUTION CONTROL EINGINEERING : Engineering methods for the prevention, control and removal of pollution in industries.

INDUSTRIAL PROCESS INSTRUMENTATION : Design and manufacture of instruments used in carrying out industrial processes.

INDUSTRIAL PSYCHOLOGY : 1. The study of man in relation to his work covering such matters as suitability for different types of employment, the effect on efficiency of his working environment and human relationships in industry. 2. Application of psychological methods to problems arising in the industrial field. 3. Applies principles of psychology and research methods in the work place with the aim of improving productivity and the quality of the work place, screening applicants, getting involved in in-house training and development, counselling, organizational behaviour analysis and development.

INDUSTRIAL RADIOGRAPHY : Use of x-rays for nondestructive testing of industrial products including computed tomography (CT), phase contrast radiography and tomography.

INDUSTRIAL RELATIONS : Relations between workers, work groups, worker organizations and managers, companies and employer organizations regarding pay, employment and disciplinary rules.

INDUSTRIAL SAFETY : Study of safety measures and precautions to prevent accidents in industries which may cause injuries to workers and loss of life and property.

INDUSTRIAL SECURITY : Safeguarding the property and personnel from thieves, dacoits, terrorists and other antisocial elements. For this purpose many industries employ special security forces in addition to those provided by the government.

INDUSTRIAL SOCIOLOGY : Study of social relations involved in industry.

INDUSTRIAL STATISTICS : 1. Application of statistics in industry 2. Statistical data pertaining to the industries in a country, or a state or on a global scale.

INDUSTRIAL TOXICOLOGY : Study of poisonous substances produced in industries and their antidotes.

INDUSTRIAL TRIBOLOGY : Study of friction between rubbing surfaces in industries and the use of lubricants.

INFANT PSYCHOLOGY : Psychology of the period of infancy.

INFECTIOLOGY : Branch of medicine concerned with infections caused by pathogenic organisms.

INFORMAL EDUCATION : Education in which two distinct parties (for example, teacher and learner) cannot be distinguished with formal school attendance.

INFORMATICS : Information science and technology developed with the use of computers.

INFORMATION ARCHTECTURE : It is an emerging field that explores ways that content can be grouped (organization), how to refer to the content groups (labelling) and how to move between the groups (navigation). As we move from storing information in books to creating electronic libraries, which are multidirectional and use multimedia, information architects have an important responsibility to organise the data in ways that users can access quickly and easily. A branch of library science.

INFORMATION ECONOMICS : Study of the role of exchange of information in markets. Lack of proper information is a disadvantage in marketing. This discipline has countless applications extending from traditional agricultural markets in developing countries to modern financial markets in developed countries.

INFORMATION SCIENCE : Equated with library science but a wider view regards it as the study of information and communication systems of all types including mechanised data, computerised information and documentation of all types.

INFORMATION SYSTEMS : Study of information systems of all types including mechanised data and computerised information.

INFORMATION SYSTEMS CONSULTANCY : Giving suggestions and guidance to the needy institutions about organizing their information systems in accordance with their requirements.

INFORMATION TECHNOLOGY : Computerising information and networking to facilitate maximum and efficient utilization of information in all spheres of activity.

INFORMATION TECHNOLOGY LAW : Law pertaining to the use and abuse of information technology involving infringement of the rights of various parties.

INFORMATION WARE HOUSING : Storing information in an organised manner to facilitate retrieval with the use of computers.

INFORMATION WARFARE : It aims at attacking the enemy computer systems while protecting one's own networks

INFORMETRICS : Quantitative study of information science.

INFRARED ASTRONOMY : Study of radiation from space in the infrared region.

INFRARED SPECTROSCOPY : The study of properties of material systems by means of their interaction with infrared radiation; ordinarily the radiation is dispersed into a spectrum after passing through the material.

INFRASTRUCTURE DEVELOPMENT : Building facilities like highways, ports, Aviation, power plants etc., which are prerequisites for economic development. Concerned with engineering and economics.

INFRASTRUCTURE : Operation and maintenance of infrastructure facilities like highways, power, Aviation, power plants, communication systems etc.

INFRASTRUCTURE SYSTEMS : Study of infrastructure systems like highways, railways, aviation, power plants, ports, communication and transport systems.

INNOVATION TECHNOLOGY : Design and development of novel technological methods and materials in response to newer needs.

INORGANIC CHEMISTRY : The chemistry of elements and of compounds other than those of carbon.

INPUT-OUTPUT ANALYSIS : A branch of economics concerned with the structure of production relationships in an economy.

INSECT PATHOLOGY : A biological discipline embracing the general principles of pathology as applied to the diseases of insects.

INSECT PHYSIOLOGY : Study of the physiology of insects which constitute a diverse and economically important group in animal kingdom; development of insecticides to kill harmful insects is related to the physiology of insects.

INSECT TOXICOLOGY : Study of the toxins produced by insects and the effects of poisons on insects.

INSECTICIDE TECHNOLOGY : Design, development, manufacture and application, of insecticides to destroy harmful insects.

INSECTICIDE TOXICOLOGY : Study of the effects of insecticides on insects and humans.

INSOLVENCY LAW : Law pertaining to winding of companies, liquidation, management of companies after winding up, adjudication of insolvency; and sale of assets of liquidated companies.

INSTITUTIONAL ECONOMICS : A school of economic thought which flourished in the 1920's in U.S.A. which believed that there is a need for economists to recognise the relevance of other disciplines like sociology, politics, law etc.

INSTRUCTIONAL DESIGN : It is a branch of education concerned with the systematic process of translating general principles of learning and instruction into plans for instructional materials and learning. It combines theory and practice from the fields of psychology, management, educational technology and communication.

INSTRUCTIONAL MANAGEMENT : It is a computer software system that facilitates online distributed learning activities such as locating and using educational content, tracking learner progress, reporting learner performance and exchanging student records between administrative systems.

INSTRUMENTAL METHODS OF ANALYSIS : Chemical analysis with the help of analytical instruments like flame photometer, spectrophotometer, spectroscopy etc.

INSTRUMENTAL MUSIC : Music produced by playing certain instruments like violin, flute, saxaphone, clarinet, various kinds of drums etc.

INSTRUMENTATION TECHNOLOGY : Design, development and manufacture of modern instruments for use in scientific research and medicine.

INSTRUMENT RATING : A term primarily used in the evaluation of performance of instruments used in aircraft.

INSURANCE MANAGEMENT : Management of various departments of insurance business.

INSURANCE : It is a type of business which permits individuals and institutions to exchange the risk of a large loss for the certainty of a small loss. The losses most commonly insured against are loss of property, life and income which may occur due to various unpredictable factors.

INTEGRAL CALCULUS : Branch of mathematics concerned with the application of calculus to finding areas, volumes, equations of curves, solutions of differential equations etc.

INTEGRATED PEST MANAGEMENT : Pest control involving use of various methods aimed at minimising excessive use of insecticides.

INTEGRATIVE MEDICINE : Medical treatment involving more than one system of medicine like, Allopathy, homeopathy, Ayurveda etc.

INTELLECTUAL PROPERTY LAW : Study of law concerned with intellectual property rights and patent rights including copy right.

INTELLIGENCE STUDIES : Study of subversive activities, enemy propaganda, military or political conditions in foreign countries and recording, analysing factual, strategic or technical intelligence information.

INTENSIVE CARE MEDICINE : Branch of medicine concerned with special care of patients under certain conditions as, for example, after undergoing major surgery.

INTENSIVE CORONARY CARE : Branch of cardiology concerned with special care of patients suffering from coronary diseases as, for example, immediately after suffering a heart attack or after undergoing a heart surgery.

INTERFACE SCIENCE AND ENGINEERING : Study of interface phenomena as for example, those occurring at the interface between immiscible liquids or between liquid surface and the outside atmosphere and their applications.

INTERIOR BALLISTICS : Science concerned with the combustion of power, development of pressure and movement of projectile in the bore of a gun.

INTERION DECORATION : The art of decorating inside homes, offices, hotels, theaters and other buildings.

INTERIOR DESIGN : Designing the interiors of homes, offices, hostels, theaters and other buildings not only to provide facilities and enhance the utility but also to make them more attractive and convenient. If necessary it entails the demolition of some structures and erecting new structures. It is closely linked with architecture and civil engineering.

INTERMEDIATES AND DYE STUFFS : Materials used to give a new and permanent colour to cloth or the materials of cloth as wool, cotton, silk and linen and also to hair, skin etc. Intermediates are substances obtained in the course of chemical reactions which can be used for various purposes.

INTERMEDIATE TECHNOLOGY : A set of techniques and technological processes which is half way between the highly capital intensive techniques of the western world and the indigenous techniques of developing countries.

INTERNAL COMBUSTION ENGINEERING : Branch of engineering concerned with the manufacture of combustion engines used in aircraft, motorcars etc. in which a mixture of petrol gas and air is exploded in the cylinder so that the explosive force acts directly on the piston.

INTERNAL MEDICINE : Medicine as practiced by specialist physicians (U.S.A.).

INTERNAL SECURITY MANAGEMENT : Management of insurgencies, terrorism, drug trafficking, cyber crime, cyber warfare etc.

INTERNATIONAL AFFAIRS : Study of political, economic, social and defence events taking place at the international level.

INTERNATIONAL AIR AND SPACE LAW : Law pertaining to aircraft movement across nations and to utilization of space for launching satellites and space craft.

INTERNATIONAL AIRLINES MANAGEMENT : A course of study and training in the principles and practical aspects of managing the activities of international airlines.

INTERNATIONAL BUSINESS : Study of business transactions carried on between nations.

INTERNATIONAL BUSINESS ADMINISTRATION : Branch of business administration concerned with business between nations.

INTERNATIONAL CONTRACTING AND PROJECT EXPORTS : Study of contracting of projects by one country or a company based in one country in another country involving differences in laws, procedures and infrastructure and raw-materials etc.

INTERNATIONAL COMMUNICATIONS : Methods of transmitting information between nations through various means like telex, E-mail, wireless, telephone, internet.

INTERNATIONAL ECONOMICS : That part of economics which deals with transactions between countries in the field of goods and services, financial flows etc. It is divided into two subject areas: pure theory and monetary theory. In the former attention is focussed on real magnitudes such as gains from trade, terms of trade, patterns of trade etc. While the latter is preoccupied with the determination of the exchange rate between currencies and with adjustment mechanisms for attaining equilibrium in the balance of payments.

INTERNATIONAL FINANCE : Study of financial transactions between nations and supply of finance for development through international financial institutions like world bank, international monetary fund etc.

INTERNATIONAL FISCAL STUDIES : Studies concerned with problems like transfer, pricing of cross border transactions, taxation of expatriate income, interpretation of double taxation avoidance agreements, taxation of e-commerce, use of low- tax regimes (tax havens) by multinationals etc.

INTERNATIONAL HUMAN RIGHTS : Study of violations of human rights of persons of one country occurring in other countries.

INTERNATIONAL HUMANITARIAN LAW : Law pertaining to the humanitarian treatment of persons of one nation in another nation when they are in distress, as for example, when they seek political asylum.

INTERNATIONAL INVESTMENT ANALYSIS : Analysis of investment prospects, problems and profitability in various countries particularly for multinational companies and those who want to invest in one or more foreign countries.

INTERNATIONAL LAW : Law applicable to relations and disputes between nations which are referred to the international court of justice.

INTERNATIONAL MARKETING : Marketing of goods across nations.

INTERNATIONAL RELATIONS : Study of political, economic, commercial, scientific and cultural relations between nations. Also known as foreign relations.

INTERNATIONAL TRADE : Trade between nations in goods and services. The essential difference between internal trade and international or foreign trade is that the latter involves the use of different currency and is subject to additional regulations such as tariffs, quotas and exchange control.

INTERNATIONAL TOURISM : Study of international tourism involves knowledge of the history, culture and interesting tourist spots of different countries.

INTERNET AND WEB DESIGN : Designing internet and web pages.

INTERNET SCIENCE AND ENGINEERING : Branch of computer science and engineering concerned with scientific and engineering aspects of internet working.

INTERNET TECHNOLOGY : Technology of building up and utilization of internet facility world wide.

INTERNIST : I : Computer diagnostic system for general medicine.

INTERPRETATION : The job of an interpreter is to relay the meaning of a speech often on complicated subjects almost simultaneously. There are various kinds of interpreters- Conference interpreters, business and specialist interpreters, general interpreters (guides) etc.

INTERVENTIONAL CARDIOLOGY : Branch of cardiology concerned with the treatment of heart disease with a view to stop it from taking a serious turn quickly.

INTERVENTIONAL RADIOLOGY : Addition of therapeutic measures to diagnostic techniques of radiology.

INTERVENTIONAL THERAPY : Treatment of serious medical conditions in order to intervene and prevent a quick turn for the worse.

INTRANET TECHNOLOGY : An intranet is a network of computers within an organization and uses internet technologies such as file transfer protocol and world wide web to share information. It may provide a path onto the internet.

INVENTORY ANALYSIS : A body of techniques which attempt to determine the optimum level of inventories, i.e. Stocks or stores of raw materials, components work in progress or finished goods.

INVENTORY MANAGEMENT : Stores purchase procedures, cutting costs in stores, purchases, documenting inventory flow, items available for sale or in the process of being made available for sale.

INVERTEBRATE PATHOLOGY : All studies having to do with the principles of pathology as applied to invertebrates.

INVERTEBRATE ZOOLOGY : Branch of zoology dealing with the study of animals lacking a vertebral column like protozoas, worms, insects etc.

INVESTMENT BANKING : Lending by banks to corporations and other business for purposes of investing for starting new ventures and for expanding existing business.

INVESTMENT FINANCIAL MARKET AND INFRASTRUCTURE LAW : Law pertaining to the financial market for investment in infrastructure projects.

INVESTMENT MANAGEMENT : Management of investment portfolios in order to get sound returns. Also called portfolio management and money management.

INVESTMENTS : As a discipline, it is the study of financial securities such, as stocks and bonds from the investor's point of view. This area deals with the firm's financing decision, but from the other side of transaction.

IRRIGATION ENGINEERING : Branch of civil engineering concerned with the construction of dams and canals and channels to supply water to the crops.

IRRIGATION WATER MANAGEMENT : Branch of civil engineering concerned with the regulation of water supply to the crops by opening and closing of sluice gates, utilization of ground water sources by constructing borewells, rain water conservation and water shed programmes.

ISLAMIC MEDICINE : A system of treatment of diseases within the framework of Quaran.

ISLAMIC STUDIES : Study of islamic religious precepts preached by prophet Mohammed.

ISOTOPIC CHEMISTRY : Branch of chemistry concerned with the study of isotopes which are defined as elements which have the same atomic number and the same chemical properties but different atomic weights. Some of the isotopes of some elements are radio active.

ISOTOPE HYDROLOGY AND GLACIOLOGY : Study of terrestrial water, in particular inland water resources and glaciers with the use of isotopes.

ISOTOPE MEDICINE : Use of isotopes including radioactive isotopes in the diagnosis and treatment of diseases.

ISOTOPE TECHNOLOGY : Manufacture of isotopes including radio-isotopes and their utilization in medicine, industry and scientific research.

IT MANAGEMENT : Managing information technology infrastructure and its applications.

J

JAINOLOGY : Study of the teachings of Mahaveer Jain.

JAPANESE MANAGEMENT : Japanese science of management consisting of ZD (zero defects), shifting of the use of statistics from SQC (Statistical quality control) to SPC (statistical process control), SMED (single minute exchange of dies), pokayoke (defining processes and operations in 2 dimensions, namely value added (VA) and non value added (non VA)

JAVA : Widely used as a web and e-business tool in computers.

JIGS AND FIXTURES DESIGN : Design of contrivances used in engineering shops for holding the work and guiding the cutting tools. Branch of mechanical engineering.

JOINT FOREST MANAGEMENT : Management of conservation of forests and utilization of forest resources jointly by the inhabitanis of forests and the government with an advisory role for non government organisations, if any.

JOURNALISM : The profession of publishing, writing in or conducting a journal or newspaper or magazines. Offered as a course of study in educational institutions including universities.

JURIDICAL SCIENCES : Pertaining to law and legal studies.

JURISPRUDENCE : Principles and knowledge of law.

JUTE TECHNOLOGY : Extracting the fibre from the stem of the jute plant (Corchorus species) and processing of the fibre. Also includes manufacture of cloth, bags, carpets etc with jute thread.

JEWELLERY DESIGN : The art of designing jewellery offered as a course of study.

K

KARYOLOGY : Branch of biology concerned with the study of the nucleolus, nucleus, chromosomes etc.

KERATOPLASTY : Corneal transplant surgery for curing corneal blindness.

KEYHOLE SURGERY : It is one of the latest developments in medicine, which allows surgeons to operate from outside the body and avoid extensive cuts on the surface. Patients need less anaesthesia, experience less post-operative pain and can go home soon.

KEYNESIAN ECONOMICS : Branch of economics concerned with the concepts and theories proposed by J.M. Keynes. The methodology of keynesian economics may be distinguished from neo-classical economics by its concern with aggregate behaviour especially the income generating effect of total expenditure and the emphasis placed on the investment component in determining the level of activity.

KHADI AND HANDLOOM TECHNOLOGY : Technology of manufacturing khadi cloth by spinning and weaving by hand with the help of hand operated looms.

KINANTHROPOMETRY : Anthropometry of sports. It evaluates physical structure of individuals by gross motor functions.

KINEMATICS : The branch of mechanics concerned with the motions of objects without being concerned with the forces that cause the motion.

KINESICS : Study of body language.

KINESIOLOGY : 1. Study of movement sensations in living beings. 2. The study of human motion through anatomical and mechanical principles.

KINETICS : The dynamics of material bodies.

KITCHEN MANAGEMENT : Art of preparing cuisine and culinary management.

KNITTING : The technique of preparing dress, bags and other articles by looping or knitting a continuous thread of cotton, wool, silk or plastic by means of wires or needles.

KNITTING TECHNOLOGY : The technique of knitting by means of machines. See knitting.

KNOWLEDGE ENVIRONMENT ENGINEERING : It focuses on designing successful knowledge processing environments. The primary focus of the subject is on how to model, design, measure and transform an environment to help an organization meet its goal fast and more effectively from a knowledge management perspective.

KNOWLEDGE MANAGEMENT : Knowledge management system is a value added internet with facilities to search and identify captured knowledge or identify experts who have the knowledge.

L

LABORATORY GENOMIC TECHNOLOGIES : Modern technologies for rapid determination of genome sequences.

LABORATORY MEDICINE : Branch of medicine concerned with laboratory experiments on medical problems.

LABOUR DEVELOPMENT : Enhancing the skills and productivity of labour by imparting training.

LABOUR ECONOMICS : The branch of economics that deals with the nature and determinants of pay and employment with emphasis on the role of institutions in determining the pattern and speed of adjustment in the labour market especially efficiency, redundancy, wages etc.

LABOUR EDUCATION : Imparting education to labour in their spare time. See worker education.

LABOUR LAW : Law relating to the duties and rights, wages, leave and other facilities of labour.

LABOUR MANAGEMENT : Management of labour dealing with their problems, demands, strikes etc.

LABOUR RELATIONS : See Industrial relations.

LABOUR WELFARE : Study of measures for the welfare of labour like providing drinking water, sanitary facilities, rest rooms, health facilities, housing etc.

LAKE BIOLOGY : Study of the life and ecology of organisms living in lakes.

LAMARCKISM : Theory of organic evolution involving inheritance of acquired characters proposed by Jean Baptiste Lamarck.

LAMINATION : Branch of mechanical engineering dealing with splitting into thin plates or layers.

LANDSCAPE ARCHITECTURE : The designing of beautiful buildings and cities or towns or groups of buildings resembling a natural scene.

LANDSCAPE GARDENING : The art of laying out, arranging trees, shrubbery etc, so as to produce the effect of natural landscape.

LAND SURVEYING : The determination of the area, shape etc. of a tract of a land, usually not of a very great extent.

LAND USE PLANNING : Determination and demarcation of various parts of a large area of land for various purposes like agriculture, housing, industries, recreation etc.

LANGUAGE TECHNOLOGY : Use of technology in the areas of understanding language and communication including translation from one language to another and training and research in the relevant areas.

LAPAROSCOPY : A technique of observing and treating, especially gynaecological disorders without cutting open the body by simply inserting an optical device known as laparoscope.

LASER : Acronym for light amplification by stimulated emission of radiation. Laser beams do not spread like ordinary light, i.e., they are highly directional. They are largely monochromatic, coherent and have high intensity.

LASER AND ELECTROOPTICAL ENGINEERING : Branch of engineering concerned with the design and manufacture of lasers and other electro optical equipment.

LASER APPLICATIONS IN INDUSTRY : Use of laser in welding, engraving, metal cutting etc.

LASER CHEMISTRY : Use of laser in chemistry to unravel the molecular structure and to bring about certain chemical reactions.

LASER PHYSICS : Branch of physics concerned with the production and properties of lasers.

LASER PRINTING : Printing carried out with the use of a laser.

LASER SPECTROSCOPY : A branch of spectroscopy in which a laser is used as an intense monochromatic light source; in particular it includes saturation spectroscopy as well as the application of laser sources to Raman spectroscopy and other techniques.

LASER SURGERY : Surgical operations performed by the use of laser without having to use a knife. With this kind of surgery bleeding and hospital stay can be avoided. It is being employed for eye surgery and certain other kinds of surgical treatments.

LASER SYSTEMS : Different kinds of lasers like carbon dioxide laser etc. used for different purposes.

LASER TECHNOLOGY : Use of the electrooptical equipment known as laser in medicine and other sciences and industries.

LASER WELDING : Industrial welding carried out with the use of laser beams.

LATTICE DYNAMICS : Study of thermal vibrations of a crystal lattice. Also known as Crystal dynamics.

LAUNCH VEHICLE TECHNOLOGY : Branch of space technology concerned with the study of Vehicles used for launching spacecraft into orbit.

LAUNDERING TECHNOLOGY : The technique of washing clothes, drying, ironing, removing stains, dry cleaning etc. Of late, washing and drying machines, various kinds of detergents, starches, stiffening agents, whitening agents, stain removers etc, have come into use.

LAW : Science dealing with legal enactments and procedures. See Jurisprudence.

LAW OF PATENTS : Law pertaining to the patent rights of inventions. It forms part of intellectual property rights.

LAW OF THE SEA : Law pertaining to the territorial rights of nations with regard to navigation and exploitation of marine resources.

LEAD ACID BATTERY TECHNOLOGY : Branch of electric engineering concerned with the storage of electric power in lead acid batteries and their applications.

LEADERSHIP : Branch of management science concerned with leadership qualities and their development and application in management.

LEATHER GARMENT TECHNOLOGY : A course of study and training in making garments of various types with leather.

LEATHER GOODS MAKING : A course of training in making various goods from leather like footwear, bags, valets, vests, belts etc.

LEATHER TECHNOLOGY : Study of the scientific methods of manufacturing leather from animal skins for specific purposes. It involves tanning of leather and application of various physical and chemical processes.

LEGAL MEDICINE : Application of medical science in solving criminal cases involving poisoning and similar offenses. See forensic medicine.

LEGAL METROLOGY : Checking the weights and measures used by traders to detect malpractices and enforce government regulations.

LEGAL STUDIES : Studies pertaining to law and jurisprudence.

LEGISLATIVE DRAFTING : Drafting bills to be placed before the legislature for approval as well as amendments, modifications etc.

LEISURE STUDIES : Study of ways of utilizing leisure in a productive and profitable manner like hobbies, reading, writing etc.

LEPROLOGY : Branch of dermatology concerned with the dreaded disease known as leprosy which is widespread in many countries and causes ugly disfigurement of body parts. This is caused by the bacterium known as *Mycobacterium leprae* for which multiple drug therapy is now being successfully used.

LEXICOGRAPHY : The act or art or occupation of compiling a lexicon or dictionary.

LEXICOLOGY : The science of words, their derivation and signification.

LIBRAMETRY : Quantitative study of library science.

LIBRARY AUTOMATION : Computerization of the different departments of a library and reducing the need for manual work.

LIBRARY NET WORKING : Connecting different libraries by networking them through computers to facilitate exchange of books and journals.

LIBRARY RESOURCE SHARING : Sharing of the resources of various libraries either by mutual lending of books or by net working. The use of internet has opened up the scope of online sharing of library resources on a world wide basis.

LIBRARY SCIENCE : A branch of science concerned with the classification, cataloguing, indexing, lending, acquiring and preserving books in a library.

LIBRARY TECHNOLOGY : Use of technologies like microfilms, computer disks, computer networking, information technology and modern methods of preserving books in libraries.

LICHENOLOGY : Branch of Botany concerned with the study of lichens which are a distinct group of plants formed as a result of symbiotic association between an alga and a fungus. There are several genera and species of lichens which differ in the algal and fungal species constituents.

LIFE SCIENCES : Group of sciences consisting of botany, zoology physiology, anatomy, biochemistry, genetics, microbiology, molecular biology, biotechnology etc, also known as biological sciences.

LIGHTING ENGINEERING AND TECHNOLOGY : Study of lighting sources, home lighting, decorative and architectural lighting for industrial applications, energy saving lighting, non-conventional energy sources relating to lighting, raw-materials for lighting industry, emergency lighting etc.

LIMNOLOGY : Science concerned with the study of lakes, pools, ponds, marshes and the life forms associated with them and ecological factors obtaining in them.

LINEAR PROGRAMMING : A technique for the formalization and analysis of contained optimization problems in which the objective function is a linear function and is to be maximized subject to a number of linear inequality constraints. The method is very useful in such problems as the determination of the optimal allocation of scarce resources.

LINGUISTIC ANTHROPOLOGY : Study of languages and dialects used by tribals and their characteristics.

LINGUISTIC GEOGRAPHY : 1. Study of geographic distribution and characteristics of the dialects of a language. 2. Geographical distribution of the languages of the world.

LINGUISTICS : The science of language or of the origin, significations, affinities and applications of words; comparative philology.

LIPOSUCTION : The medical treatment of removing excess fat in parts of the body by means of a process known as suction.

LITERACY EDUCATION : Teaching of reading, writing and social skills.

LITERARY CRITICISM : Critical study of literature. Literary criticism is that body of literature which analyses the ideas and methods in a work of literature and delivers judgement. Sometimes a critic analyses the work from a linguistic point of view, and withholds his judgement. Criticism is not just a catalogue of deficiencies or drawbacks as perceived by a critic. A great critic is a creative writer. He is also a promoter and propagator of lofty aesthetic standards.

LITERATURE : 1. The class of writings in which beauty of style is a characteristic feature. 2. The literary productions upon a given subject or a particular branch of knowledge. 3. The collective writings of a country or period.

LITHOGLYPHICS : The art of engraving on precious stones etc.

LITHOGRAPHY : The art of writing or drawing with special pigments on a peculiar kind of stone and of producing impressions from it on paper.

LITHOLOGY : The description of the physical characters of a rock based on colour, structure, mineralogical composition and grain size.

LITHOTRYPSY : The medical technique of breaking stones in the kidney and bladder into small pieces by means of a special device.

LITHOTYPE COMPOSING : A peculiar process of stereotyping by pressing into a mould taken from a form of type, a composition which hardens into a stony substances, used in printing technology.

LIVESTOCK PRODUCTION AND MANAGEMENT : Rearing and breeding cattle and their management.

LIVESTOCK PRODUCTS TECHNOLOGY : Manufacture and utilization of products derived from cattle such as meat, leather etc.

LOCAL ECONOMIC DEVELOPMENT : Branch of economics concerned with the study of economic development in a particular area.

LOCAL ENVIRONMENTAL MANAGEMENT : Study of environmental issues and their management in a given area.

LOCAL GOVERNMENTS : Branch of public administration concerned with the study of administrative set ups at the local level like village panchayats, municipalities etc.

LOCOMOTIVE ENGINEERING : Branch of engineering concerned with the manufacture and maintenance of rail engines.

LOGIC : Branch of science which investigates the principles of reasoning.

LOGISTICS : Technical organization of the flow of goods and services in general as well as the co-ordination of the flow of goods and services from the supplier to the consumer. Formely known as materials management.

LOGISTICS ENGINEERING AND MANAGEMENT : Branch of defence science concerned with the engineering works involved in the flow of goods and services to the armed forces as well as their management.

LOGOGRAPHY : A method of printing in which a type forms a word instead of forming a letter.

LONGEVITY MEDICINE : A fairly new branch of medicine which examines why and how human cells undergo damage and become worn out and dysfunctional, in an attempt to find methods of prolonging longevity.

LONG REFERENCE SERVICE : Branch of library science concerned with the issue of books desired by readers after obtaining them on loan from other libraries.

LOTUS NOTES : Major focus area for businesses and companies world wide; programming used in computers.

LOW ENERGY PHYSICS : That part of physics that studies microscopic phenomena involving energies of several million electron volts or less such as the arrangement of electrons in an atom or solid and the arrangement of protons and neutrons within the atomic nucleus and the nature of forces between these particles.

LOW TEMPERATURE PHYSICS : Branch of physics concerned with the study of characteristics and behaviour of materials at very low temperatures.

LYPOLYSIS : Technique of body contouring by removing excess fat.

M

MACHINE DESIGN : Branch of engineering concerned with design of machines of various kinds meant for carrying out different tasks.

MACHINE INTELLIGENCE : Includes pattern recognition, machine learning, image processing using soft computing approaches.

MACHINE TOOL DESIGN : Branch of mechanical engineering concerned with designing tools for use in machines for carrying out various tasks.

MACHINE TRANSLATION : Converting material in one language to another by the use of computer.

MACHINING : To prepare a job in the required form or to give finishing to a job by means of a machine.

MACHINING TECHNOLOGY : Method of doing some tasks like turning and drilling with the help of a machine.

MACROECONOMICS : Branch of economics which is concerned with the study of relationships between broad economic aggregates the most important of which are national income, savings, investment, employment, money supply etc.

MACROMETEOROLOGY : Study of the largest scale aspects of the atmosphere such as general circulation and weather types.

MACROMOLECULAR CRYSTALLOGRAPHY : Study of the characteristics of the crystalline structure of macromolecules like proteins, nucleic acids etc.

MACRORHEOLOGY : A branch of rheology in which materials are treated as homogeneous or quasi-homogeneous and processes are treated as isothermal.

MACROSONICS : Technology of sound at signal amplitudes which are very large.

MACROSOCIOLOGY : Analysis of either large collectivities (like cities) or more abstractly of social systems and social structures.

MAGIC : The art of applying natural causes whose operation is secret, to produce surprising effects.

MAGNETICS : Study of magnetic phenomena comprising magnetostatics and electromagnetism. Also known as magnetism.

MAGNETIC STRATIGRAPHY : See Palaeomagnetic stratigraphy.

MAGENTISM : See magnetics.

MAGNETOACOUSTICS : Study of the effects of magnetic fields on acoustic phenomena such as various oscillations in the attenuation of ultrasonic sound waves by a crystal placed in a magnetic field at a very low temperature as the magnetic field strength or sound frequency is varied.

MAGNETOAERODYNAMICS : Study of properties and characteristics of highly ionised air and other gases applied principally to study of reentering ballistic missiles and spacecraft.

MAGNETOBIOLOGY : Study of the effects of pulsed magnetic field on living things including man.

MAGNETOBOTANY : Study of the effects of magnetic fields on plants.

MAGNETOCHEMISTRY : The branch of physical chemistry concerned with measuring and investigating the magnetic properties of chemical compounds.

MAGNETOELECTRICITY : Magnetic techniques for generating voltages such as in the ordinary generator.

MAGNETOFLUID DYNAMICS : The study of the motion of an electrically conducting metal, such as mercury in the presence of electric and magnetic fields.

MAGNETO GAS DYNAMICS : Science of motion in a plasma under the influence of mechanical, electrical and magnetic forces.

MAGNETOHYDRODYNAMICS : The study of dynamics or motion of an electrically conducting fluid such as ionised gas or liquid metal interacting with a magnetic field. Also known as hydromagnetics.

MAGNETOMECHANICS : Study of the effects which the magnetization of a material and its strain have on each other.

MAGNETOOPTICS : The study of the effect of a magnetic field on light passing through a substance in the field.

MAGNETOPLASMO DYNAMICS : The generation of electric current by shooting a beam of ionized gas through a magnetic field, to give the same effect as moving copper bars near a magnet.

MAGNETOSTATICS : Study of magnetic fields that remain constant with time. Also known as static Magnetism.

MAGNETOTHERAPY : Treatment of diseases by the application of magnets at specific points on the body and also by drinking magnetised water.

MAINFRANE TECHNOLOGY : Originally implied the main frame work of a central processing unit but now used colloquially to refer to the central processor itself and used to distinguish large computers from minicomputers and micro-computers.

MAINTENANCE MANAGEMENT : Maintenance of industrial machinery and equipment including pridictive maintenance, condition monitoring etc.,

MAINTENANCE TECHNOLOGY : Technical methods employed in maintenance of industrial machinery and equipment.

MALACOLOGY : The branch of Zoology that treats of the mollusca or soft bodied animals.

MALARIALOGY : Branch of medicine concerned with the prevention and treatment of malaria.

MAMMOGRAPHY : Radiography of mammary glands used for the diagnosis of breast cancer.

MAMMOLOGY : Branch of zoology concerned with the study of mammals, a group of animals in which the female suckles the young.

MANAGEMENT ACCOUNTANCY : Business accounting practice concerned with the provision of information to management for policy making purposes.

MANAGEMENT AUDIT : Auditing the accounts of a company's different departments like marketing, costing etc., for the purpose of management.

MANAGEMENT ECONOMICS : See managerial economics.

MANAGEMENT EDUCATION : Instruction in the principles and techniques of management; also known as management training.

MANAGEMENT IN FOOTWEAR TECHNOLOGY : Study of the role of management in the use of technological methods for footwear manufacture.

MANAGEMENT INFORMATION SYSTEMS : Study and use of information systems in management.

MANAGEMENT OF BUSINESS FINANCE : Study of management methods used in securing finance for business.

MANAGEMENT OF FINANCIAL INSTITUTIONS : Principles and methods of management of financial institutions like banks, non-banking financial institutions like chit funds, mutual funds etc.

MANAGEMENT OF HERITAGE AND CULTURE : Application of modern management to sites and structures of heritage value and institutions and organizations engaged in cultural activities.

MANAGEMENT OF EVENTS : Management of large scale events like launching new brands of products, new corporations, sports events and the like as also marriage receptions and other social and official functions.

MANAGEMENT OF MULTINATIONAL CORPORATIONS : Management of corporations which involves the participation as share holders of people belonging to more than one country.

MANAGEMENT SCIENCE : In the context of the study of firms this discipline applies scientific principles to aid pursuit of operational efficiency. Importance is attached to deducing the principles underlying rational co-ordination of the units which comprise firms.

MANAGEMENT TRAINING : See management education.

MANAGERIAL ECONOMICS : A course of study of economics which is applicable to management. Also known as management economics.

MANPOWER STUDIES : Studies of manpower supply and demand.

MANUFACTURING ENGINEERING : Application of engineering in the manufacturing industries.

MANUFACTURING MANAGEMENT : Management of various departments and activities in a manufacturing industry.

MANUFACTURING TECHNOLOGY : Process of manufacturing goods from raw materials.

MARICULTURE : Culturing marine organisms like fish, shrimp etc in artificially created pounds.

MARINE ARCHAEOLOGY : Branch of archaeology concerned with the study of ancient remains found in the sea.

MARINE BIOLOGY : Branch of biology concerned with the study of marine organisms including plants and animals and their ecology and life forms.

MARINE BIOTECHNOLOGY : Processing of marine organisms to obtain useful products and substances.

MARINE CHEMISTRY : Study of the chemical composition of sea water and sediments.

MARINE ENGINEERING : See navigational engineering.

MARINE GEOLOGY : Study of the geological features of the sea bed, sea coast, islands, estuaries and other marine formations.

MARINE GEOPHYSICS : Application of geophysical principles and methods to the study of mineral resources of the sea.

MARINE LIVING RESOURCES : Study of the useful plants and animals found growing in the sea. Several sea weeds and fish and shrimps provide food and industrial raw materials.

MAIRNE METEOROLOGY : That part of meteorology which is concerned with study of oceanic areas including island and coastal regions. It serves the practical needs of surface and air navigation over the oceans.

MARINE MICROBIOLOGY : Study of the micro organisms living in the sea.

MARINE PHARAMACOLOGY : Study of the medicines obtained from marine organisms.

MARINE SCIENCES : Sciences concerned with the study of oceans, like Oceanography, marine biotechnology, marine biology, marine chemistry, marine geology, marine geophysics, marine meteorology etc.

MARINE SURVEYING : Determining the forms of coasts, the positions and distances of islands, rocks shoals, the depth of water, nature of the bottom etc.

MARIOLOGY : Study of the life and teachings of virgin Mary.

MARITAL STUDIES : Study of marriage as a social institution and problems connected with it.

MARITIME LAW : Law pertaining to harbourships and seamen.

MARITIME STUDIES : Studies relating or pertaining to navigation or commerce by sea or connected or belonging to shipping; maritime refers more especially to the sea as a field of human activity; to some use of sea by man.

MARITIME TRANSPORTATION : Refers to management of transport of people and goods by the sea route.

MARKET BEHAVIOUR ANALYSIS : Marketing decision making based on understanding the economic environment.

MARKET ECOLOGY : Marketing ecofriendly goods and articles.

MARKET ECONOMY : An economic system in which decisions about the allocation of resources and production are made on the basis of prices generated by voluntary exchanges between producers, consumers, workers and owners of factors of production.

MARKETING : Broadly the functions of sales, distribution, advertising and sales promotion, product planning, market research, pricing strategies, dealer development planning, developing operation standards for dealers.

MARKETING MANAGEMENT : Management and co-ordination of various departments of marketing.

MARKETING RESEARCH : Investigation and innovation to develop new methods and techniques in various departments of marketing.

MARKET RESEARCH : Research conducted by companies to assess the demand for their products, and the needs and preference of consumers by conducting market surveys in order to determine their manufacturing policies.

MARKET SOCIALISM : A socialist economic system which leaves the day to day running of the economy to the market mechanism. It is based on the notion that the means of production can be socially owned and basic decisions and direction of development may be centrally planned but otherwise the operation of the economy may be left to market forces . It is opposed by influential economists who advocate the use of planometrics and computer aided central planning.

MARTIAL ARTS : Oriental combat arts widely practiced today as sports for example Judo, Kungfu, Karate etc.

MARXIST DIELECTICS : Philosophy of dialectical materialism developed by Marx and Engels.

MARXIST ECONOMICS : A type of economics which seeks to analyse the social and economic development of the capitalist economic system. The revival of Marxist analysis in the 1960's and 1970's was largely due to the partial integration of Marxist economic thought into mainstream economic theory.

MARXIST SOCIOLOGY : Application of Marxist ideas to sociology.

MASS COMMUNICATION : Synthesizing the print and electronic media, advertising and public relations.

MASS COMMUNICATION TECHNOLOGY : Use of technology like radio, T.V, Telephone, internet, etc for Mass communication.

MASSOTHERAPY : Use of massage for the treatment of diseases.

MATERIA MEDICA : A branch of medical science concerned with the preparation and presenting of medications and drugs.

MATERIALS ENGINEERING : Evaluation and selection of materials used in industries.

MATERIALS MANAGEMENT : Procurement, storage and distribution and supply to the concerned department of materials used in industries and other spheres of work.

MATERIALS SCIENCE : Study of the physico-chemical properties and other features of materials used in industries and other spheres of work and assessing their suitability for the purpose for which they are to be used.

MATERIALS TECHNOLOGY : Finding new uses to known materials and finding and developing new materials for specific purposes.

MATERNAL AND CHILD HEALTH : Branch of medicine concerned with the health of the mother and child soon after delivery and in subsequent days. Also forms part of public health programme.

MATERNITY NURSING : Branch of nursing concerned with the care of the mother soon after delivery and in subsequent days.

MATHEMATICAL ANALYSIS : Branch of mathematics which employs methods of algebra and calculus as different from analytical geometry, group theory etc.

MATHEMATICAL BIOLOGY : A discipline that encompasses all applications of mathematics, computer technology and quantitative theorizing to biological systems and the underlying processes within the systems.

MATHEMATICAL BIOPHYSICS : A discipline which attempts to utilize mathematics to explain biophysical processes.

MATHEMATICAL ECONOMICS : Application of mathematical and statistical methods to economics

MATHEMATICAL GEOGRAPHY : Branch of geography concerned with the features and processes of the earth and their representation on maps and charts.

MATHEMATICAL PHYSICS : The study of the mathematical systems which represent physical phenomena; particular areas are, for example, quantum and statistical mechanics and field theory.

MATHEMATICAL PSYCHOLOGY : Psychology presented in mathematical language.

MATHEMATICAL SCIENCES : A group of sciences related to mathematics including mathematics, statistics, mathematical physics, mathematical biology, mathematical geography etc.

MATHEMATICS : Logical study of shape, arrangement, quantity and many related concepts, often divided into three fields algebra, analysis and geometry.

MATRIX ALGEBRA : It defines rules by which matrices may be added, subtracted, multiplied and divided.

MATRIX MECHANICS : The theory of quantum mechanics developed by using the Heisenberg picture and representing operators by their matrix elements between eigen functions of the Hamiltonian operator; Heisenberg's original formulation of quantum mechanics.

MAXILLOFACIAL SURGERY : Branch of dentistry that relates to the surgical correction of deformities pertaining to mouth, jaws or face besides aesthetic improvement.

MAYAN ART : Refers to art of Mayan culture.

MEAT SCIENCE : Science concerned with the production, processing, storage, transport, and consumption of meat.

MECHNICAL ASSEMBLY : To fit together different parts of a machine or of a mechanism.

MECHNICAL ENGINEERING : The art of constructing and using engines or machines.

MECHANICAL ENGINEERING TECHNOLOGY : Application and use of mechanical engineering techniques in industry and other fields.

MECHANICAL METALLURGY : Branch of metallurgy concerned with the use of mechanical methods, in contrast to chemical methods, in the extraction of metals.

MECHANICAL SCIENCES : The following sciences are grouped as mechanical sciences, mechanical engineering, production engineering, metallurgical engineering etc.

MECHANICAL WOOD INDUSTRIES TECHNOLOGY : Manufacture of plywood and other products from wood.

MECHANICS : 1. That branch of physics which seeks to formulate general rules for predicting the behaviour of a physical system under the influence of any type of interaction with its environment. 2. The study of the interactions between matter and the forces acting on it.

MECHANOCHEMISTRY : The study of the conversion of mechanical energy into chemical energy in polymers.

MECHANOPHOTOCHEMISTRY : The study of changes in the dimensions of certain photo responsive polymers upon exposure to light.

MECHATRONICS : Low cost automation techniques in industry using electronics, hydraulics, electrical and mechanical engineering.

MEDIA COMMUNICATIONS : Study of the working of print and electronic modes of communication through the media like newspapers, magazines, T.V. etc.

MEDIA LAWS : Laws pertaining to the operation and code of conduct of print and electronic media including media and public policy, media regulatory framework, media advertisement and law.

MEDIA PLANNING AND MARKETING : Planning the print and electronic media like newspapers, magazines, radio, T.V. etc, and marketing through the media.

MEDIA STUDIES -Studies of the methods and role of print and electronic media in building public awareness and opinion. The influence of the media on social change and life style is also a subject of media studies.

MEDIA TECHNOLOGY : Study of the technologies used in print and electronics media.

MEDIA TRANSCRIPTION : Transcribing news, special reports, documentaries, feature stories, publicity interviews etc., broadcast on the radio and telecast on T.V.

MEDICAL AND SOCIAL PSYCHOLOGY : Study of social and individual behaviour in response to incidence of epidemics and other diseases.

MEDICAL ANTHROPOLOGY : Study of the health and diseases of various ethnic groups and native remedies used by them.

MEDICAL AUDIT : Review of the professional standards usually within the hospital by a medical committee.

MEDICAL BACTERIOLOGY : Study of the pathogenic bacteria from the medical point of view for the diagnosis and treatment of diseases

MEDICAL BIOCHEMISTRY : Study of biochemistry primarily for diagnosis of diseases by means of tests on blood, urine, stools etc. to understand the biochemical changes taking place in the body during the progress of the disease.

MEDICAL BIOTECHNOLOGY : Use of biotechnology in the development of new drugs and treatments including culturing of cells and tissues for transplantation and for extraction of drugs.

MEDICAL EDUCATION : Initial and in-service training for medical professions.

MEDICAL ELECTRONICS : Role of electronics in medical equipment used in the diagnosis and treatment of diseases.

MEDICAL ENTOMOLOGY : Study of insects which cause diseases or serve as carriers of diseases.

MEDICAL ETHICS : Ethical values which are to be adhered to by the medical profession.

MEDICAL GENETICS : Study of hereditary diseases and the genetic basis of diseases.

MEDICAL INFORMATICS : Integration of information technology with medicine and use of computers and computerised medical instruments for the diagnosis and treatment of diseases. Telemedicine, artificial intelligence in medicare, web-based applications in medicare and clinical information systems.

MEDICAL JURISPRUDENCE : 1. Law relating to medicine, 2. Use of medical science for legal purposes. See Forensic Medicine.

MEDICAL LABORATORY EQUIPMENT ENGINEERING : Branch of biomedical engineering specialising in laboratory equipment like radiometer, blood, gas and chemistry analysers, blood cell counters etc.

MEDICAL LABOURTORY TECHNOLOGY : Performing laboratory tests for diagnosis of diseases, for example, testing blood, urine, stools, estimation of hormones, identification of pathogens etc.

MEDICAL MICROBIOLOGY : Study of pathogenic microbes from the medical point of view.

MEDICAL MYCOLOGY : Study of the pathogenic fungi causing diseases in man from the medical point of view. Some skin diseases including genital diseases and diseases of the digestive system are caused by pathogenic fungi.

MEDICAL ONCOLOGY : Treatment of cancer by the use of medicines in contrast to chemotherapy and radiation and surgical treatment.

MEDICAL PHYSICS : Application of physics in medicine. Use of x-rays and other types of radiation in diagnosis and treatment.

Study of the effect of radiation on the body. Use of several physical electronic and optical instruments including lasers in medicine.

MEDICAL RADIATION AND NUCLEAR TECHNOLOGY- Use of different types of radiations and radio active isotopes in medicine.

MEDICAL RECORDS SCIENCE : The science of preparing and maintaining records of treatment and procedures in medicine pertaining to individual patients.

MEDICAL SCIENCE AND TECHNOLOGY : Includes telemedicine, bioinformatics, implant materials, prosthesis, genetic engineering, immuno technology, biophysics, biomechanics, nutritional science, biomedical simulation, cryobiology.

MEDICAL SCIENCES : Sciences concerned with the diagnosis and treatment of diseases like, for example, paediatrics, dermatology, gynaecology, urology, cardiology etc.

MEDICAL SCIENCE THEORY : Theories which form the foundation of medicine like theory of infection, theory of immunity, theory of nutrition.

MEDICAL SOCIAL WORK : Helping and guiding the patients in seeking proper medical care, and in rehabilitation, preventive care and assisting patients in other ways.

MEDICAL SOCIOLOGY : 1. Sociology of the healing professions, 2. Sociology of illness, illness behaviour and help seeking behaviour, 3. Medical institutions and health service organizations, 4. Social factors in the etiology of infertility and mortality, 5. Social factors in the study of causes of diseases, 6. Social factors influencing the demand for and use of medical facilities, 7. Social effects of different medical systems, 8. Sociology of doctor patient relationship, 9. International patterns of illness and helath services.

MEDICAL- SURGICAL NURSING : Branch of nursing science concerned with nursing specially surgically operated patients.

MEDICAL TECHNOLOGY : Use of advanced equipment like CAT-Scan, MRI, X-ray etc., in the diagnosis and treatment diseases.

MEDICAL TRANSCRIPTION : Converting medical records into electronic format; digitised audio into electronic form. Doctors in the United States used to dictate prescriptions and instructions into micro casettes (dictaphones) Now they are dicatating patient records and diagnostic reports into computers, hence the need for transcription.

MEDICAL VIROLOGY : Study of virus diseases of man.

MEDICINAL BOTANY : Study of structure, classification, uses and occurrence of medicinal plants used in the treatment of diseases.

MEDICINAL CHEMISTRY : Study of the chemistry of drugs used in medicine.

MEDICINAL PLANTS : Cultivation processing, uses and marketing of medicinal plants.

MEDICINE : 1. Science, art, profession and industry of disease prevention and treatment. 2. Characteristic activities of doctors considered as a whole. 3. Branch of medicine as a whole practiced by specialist physicians. 4. Drug or mixture of drugs.

MEDICO LEGAL SYSTEMS : All aspects of law pertinent to the medical profession.

MEDITATION THERAPY : New research shows that various forms of meditation can reduce the harmful effects of stress, boost immune system and enhance mood and physical well-being.

MEMBRANE BIOCHEMISTRY : Study of the structure, formation and functions of membranes in living organisms.

MEMBRANE BIOLOGY : Study of membranes of living organisms in relation to their biological functions.

MEMBRANE BIOPHYSICS : Study of the role of membranes in biophysical phenomena. For example, permeability of membranes to certain substances and semipermeable nature of some membranes in living systems.

MEMBRANE TECHNOLOGY : 1. Use of membranes for sewage water treatment. 2. Use of membranes for the purification of substances in some industries.

MENDELIAN GENETICS : Scientific study of heredity as related to or in accordance with Mendel's laws.

MENDELISM : Mendel's theory of heredity that forms the basis of classical genetics.

MENSURATION : Branch of mathematics concerned with the measurement of dimensions like length, area, volume etc.

MENTAL HYGIENE : A system of principles or rules designed for the promotion of mental health especially the mental health of households or communities.

MENTOLOGY : The science of the mind *per se*.

MERCANTILE LAW : Law pertaining to trade and commerce.

MERCHANDISING : It deals with the purchase and stocking of materials required for the firm. It involves identifying the right items and suppliers and negotiating profitable deals with them and also pricing products appropriately. Stocking up new and innovative items to attract and retain customers is also part of merchandising, particularly for retail sales.

MERCHANT BANKING : Merchant banking involves a variety of financial services including acceptance of bills of exchange, loans and securities, portfolio and unit trust management and some banking services.

MERCHANT MARINE TRAINING : Presea cadet course, First mate phase-I, Second mate foundation and functional chief mate, near coastal voyage, radar observer's course, elementary first aid, medical first aid, medicare, proficiency in survival craft, personal survival techniques, fire fighting and fire prevention, personal safety and social responsibilities and tanker familiarization.

MERGERS AND ACQUISITIONS : Managing mergers of companies, and acquisition of one company by another.

MESMERISM : According to this doctrine propounded in 1778 by the german physician Mesmer one person can exercise influence over the will and nervous system of another by virtue of a supposed emanation proceeding from him or simply by the domination of his will over that of the person operated on.

MESOCLIMATOLOGY : Study of moderate climate.

MESOPOTOMIAN ART : The related arts of ancient Chaldes, Babylonia and Assyria.

METABOLIC PHARMACOLOGY : Study of the effects of drugs on metabolism.

METALLOGENY : Study of the genesis of metals in geological formations.

METALLOGRAPHY : The microscopic study of the structure of metals and their alloys.

METALLURGICAL ENGINEERING : Application of engineering methods in the process of separating metals from other matter in the ore, smelting, refining etc.

METALLURGY : Branch of chemistry concerned with the production of metals from the ores, the purification of metals manufacture of alloys and the use of metals in engineering.

METAMORPHIC PETROLOGY : Branch of geology concerned with the study of metamorphic rocks as opposed to sedimentary and igneous rocks.

METAPHYSICS : 1. That science which seeks to trace the branches of human knowledge to their first principles in the constitution of our nature or to find what is the nature of the human mind and its relations to the external world. 2. The science that seeks to know the ultimate grounds of being or what is it that really exists embracing both psychology and ontology.

METARHEOLOGY : A branch of rheology whose approach is intermediate between of macrorheology and microrheology; certain processes which are not isothermal are taken into account such as kinetic elasticity, surface tension and rate processes. See rheology.

METEOROLOGICAL OPTICS : A branch of atmosphere physics or physical meteorology in which optical phenomena occurring in atmosphere are studied.

METEOROLOGY : The science which treats of atmospheric phenomena, more especially as connected with or in relation to weather and climate.

METHODICS- See Methodology.

METHODOLOGY : 1. The science of method of doing a work. For example, research methodology. 2. A term often used loosely in economics to describe the way in which economists proceed in their analysis of a problem. It is also used to describe the set of problems which group of economists are prepared to analyse.

METHODS ENGINEERING : Branch of engineering concerned with the methods used in carrying out various engineering tasks.

METOPOSCOPY : See physiognomy.

METROLOGY : Scientific study of measurement especially the definition and standardization of the units of measurement used in science.

METRONOMY : The measuring of musical time by the metronome.

METROTOMY : The operation of cutting into the uterus.

MIASMOLOGY : The science pertaining to the fine particles of any putrefying bodies rising and floating in the atmosphere and considered to be noxions to health.

MICRO ANALYSIS : See Micro analytical chemistry.

MICRO ANALYTICAL CHEMISTRY : Analysis and estimation of chemical substances present in very small quantities so that specialized instruments such as microscope are needed; the material analysed may be on the scale of one microgram. Also known as microanalysis.

MICROANATOMY : Anatomical study of microscopic tissue structures.

MICROBIAL GENE TECHNOLOGY : The technology of utilizing microbial genes for the production of useful substances like insulin etc.

MICROBIAL GENETICS : Study of the genetics of micro organisms offers certain advantages such as, for example, several generations being completed in a relatively short time. Hence many genetic principles were deduced from the study of microbial genetics.

MICROBIAL GENOMICS : Study of the genomes of microorganisms. It is now known that the genomes of higher organisms including man share some elements with those of microorganisms.

MICROBIAL TECHNOLOGY : It includes genetic engineering, molecular biology, membrane biology, fermentation technology, drugs and pharmaceuticals.

MICRO BIOLOGY : Study of the life of micro organisms has proved useful not only for understanding biological phenomena but also for obtaining useful substances produced by them.

MICROECONOMETRICS : It is an interface between economics and statistics. It encompasses methods used to analyse microdata, namely, economic information about individuals, households and firms.

MICROECONOMICS : Microeconomics is concerned with the study of the individual decision units : the consumers, households, firms, the way in which their decisions interrelate with each other.

MICRO ELECTROMECHANICAL ENGINEERING (MEMS) : Design, fabrication, process development and characterization of microstructures for MEMS, BIOMEMS, OPTICAL MEMS FOR sensors, actuators and disposable smart biochips.

MICROELECTRONICS ENGINEERING : Engineering concerned with the production and application of microelectronics.

MICROELECTRONICS : It is the science and art of designing and fabricating micro chips. Microelectronics technology is based mainly on silicon MOS (metal oxide semiconductors) devices. It was invented in 1965.

MICROGEOLOGY : Branch of geology concerned with micro fossils and other microscopic geological structures.

MICROGRAPHY : The description of objects too small to be discerned without the aid of a microscope.

MICROIONTOPHORESIS : Delivery of minute quantities of drugs by passage of electric currents through capillary tubes containing appropriate solutions.

MICROLITHOLIGY : Microscopic study of rocks.

MICROLOGY : That part of science which is dependent on microscopic investigation.

MICROMACHINING TECHNOLOGY : Use of micromachines in industry and research. These machines are a few microns in size.

MICROMANIPULATION : The techniques and practice of microdissection, microvivisection, microisolation and microinfection used in the study of plants and animals and in human beings for medical purposes.

MICROMETEOROLOGY : Study of the smallest scale physical and dynamic occurrences within the atmosphere. Studies are confined to the surface boundary layer of the atmosphere.

MICROMETRY : The art of measuring with a micrometer which is an instrument or appliance fitted to a telescope or microscope for measuring very small distances or the apparent diameters of objects which subtend very small angles.

MICRO PALAEONTOLOGY : Study of microfossils.

MICRO PROCESSOR TECHNOLOGY : Design and manufacture of microprocessors for use in computers and other applications.

MICRORADIOGRAPHY : Technique for the study of surfaces of solids by monochromatic radiation (such as X-ray). Contrast effect shown (via) projection or enlargement of a contact radiograph.

MICRO RHEOLOGY : A branch of rheology in which the heterogenous nature of dispersed systems is taken into account.

MICROSCOPY : Study of very small objects which cannot be seen with the naked eye, under the microscope.

MICROSOCIOLOGY : This level of sociological analysis is concerned with face to face social encounters in every day life and with interpersonal behaviour in small groups.

MICROSURGERY : It is a kind of re-constructive surgery. Because the small and delicate anatomical components need careful handling with fine instruments, often under magnification, it is called microsurgery example : for hand injuries.

MICROTECHNIQUE : The technique employed for preparing plant and animal materials for microscopic study by the use of physico-chemical processes.

MICROTOMY : The technique of making very thin sections or slices of objects for study under the microscope with the aid of an instrument called microtome.

MICROTHERMOGRAPHY : Detection of areas of raised temperature below skin using output of shorter rays than infra-red.

MICROWAVE ACOUSTICS : The production and study of elastic vibrations in materials of microwave frequencies of the order of 10^9 to 10^{11} hertz, such as in single crystal relay lines used in radar systems.

MICROWAVE ENGINEERING : Microwave integrated circuits, antennas for space communication, radar, navigation and satellite applications.

MICROWAVE LINK ENGINEERING : Engineering concerned with the setting up of micro wave links in communication technology.

MICROWAVE OPTICS : Study of those properties of microwaves which are analogous to the properties of light waves in optics.

MICROWAVE TECHNOLOGY : Use of micro waves in communications and other fields. For example; microwave oven.

MIDWIFERY : The practice and profession of assisting in child birth performed by a woman known as midwife. Also known as obstetrics.

MIGRATION AND URBANIZATION : Branch of sociology and demography concerned with the study of migration of rural population to urban areas.

MILITARY AVIONICS : Avionics used in military operations for flight control, engine control, fly by wire and weapon systems.

MILITARY ENGINEERING : That branch of engineering which relates to the construction and maintenance of fortifications and the surveying of a country for the various operations of war.

MILITARY HISTORY : History of the development and evolution of warfare weapons, armament, ammunition, communications, transport and other military subjects over the ages.

MILITARY INTELLIGENCE : Gathering intelligence about enemy installations, army strength and movements and strategies.

MILITARY LAW: The body of regulations which governs the soldier both in peace and in war.

MILITARY SCIENCE : The science of organising and maintaining the discipline and efficiency of defence forces.

MILITARY TECHNOLOGY : Technological applications in warfare.

MILLING TECHNOLOGY : Technology employed in flour mills, rice mills, sugar mills, paper mills etc.

MIMICRY : The art of ludicrous imitation for entertainment.

MINE MANAGEMENT : Management of mines including logistics and general safety.

MINERAL CHEMISTRY : Branch of mineralogy concerned with the study of chemical properties of minerals.

MINERAL ENGINEERING : Application of engineering methods to the extraction of minerals from their ores.

MINERAL EXPLORATION : Search for useful and economic minerals using geological and geophysical methods.

MINERAL INFORMATICS : Use of information technology in exploration, extraction, processing, manufacturing and sales of minerals and mineral products and to add value to the mine-mineral-metal -material -customer chains.

MINERALOGY : The science which treats of the properties of mineral substances and teaches us to characterise, distinguish and classify them according to their properties.

MINERAL PHYSICS : Branch of mineralogy concerned with the study of the physical properties of minerals.

MINERAL PROCESS ENGINEERING : Engineering methods employed in the processing of minerals for obtaining various value added products.

MINE SURVEYING : To examine with reference to condition, situation, determination of boundaries, extent, position and natural features by means of measurements to determine the dimensions and other topographical features.

MINE VENTILATION : Supplying a mine with necessary quantity of pure fresh air. It also includes steps to prevent and control fires, explosions and inundation of a mine.

MINIMAL ACCESS SURGERY : In this surgical procedure the instrument is passed through a small keyhole like incission but the operation is performed in the same way as in conventional surgery resulting in less trauma and damage.

MINING : Techniques and business of mineral discovery and exploration.

MINING ENGINEERING : Engineering concerned with exploration of coal, ores, minerals as well as clearing, sizing and dressing of minerals.

MINING GEOLOGY : Study of the structure and occurrence of mineral deposits and geological aspects of mine planning.

MINING MACHINERY ENGINEERING : Branch of engineering concerned with the design, manufacture and maintenance of machinery used in mining operations.

MIRROR OPTICS : Science and technology of mirrors which by means of reflecting rays of light either revert optical bundles or focus them to form images.

MISSILES ENGINEERING : Study of the engineering aspects involved in designing, developing and deploying missiles.

MISSILES GUIDANCE : Technology of guiding missiles to reach specific targets.

MOBILE COMMUNICATION : Communication technology involving the use of cellular phones and wireless devices.

MOBILE COMPUTING : Use of computers while the person is in motion including those used in moving vehicles etc.

MODELLING ART : Art of modeling for photography or in video films used for advertisements or in live fashion shows etc.

MODELLING ENGINEERING : Creating timing analysis models for components (Processors memory glue -logic) used in board level circuits, creating models based on customer's requirements either by reusing existing models or building new ones.

MODELS OF SOFTWARE SYSTEMS : Preparation and study of software systems for computers.

MODERN BIOLOGY : Study of modern developments in Biology like structure- function studies of regulatory proteins, structure based drug design, use of bioinformatic tools for protein and genomic analysis, proteomics etc.

MODERN ECONOMICS : Science of economics developed in recent times in contrast to classical economics.

MODERN EUROPEAN HISTORY : Study of history of Europe of recent times in contrast to ancient history.

MODERN EUROPEAN POLITICAL THEORY : Study of political theory developed in Europe in recent times.

MODERN PHYSICS : Science of physics developed from the beginning of 20th century.

MOLECULAR BIOLOGY : Study of structure and function of large molecules associated with living organisms, in particular, proteins and nucleic acids.

MOLECULAR BIOPHYSICS : Study of physical properties of large molecules associated with living organisms, in particular, proteins and nucleic acids.

MOLECULAR CYTOGENETICS : Study of cellular genetic components at molecular level.

MOLECULAR DYNAMICS : Method of numerical simulation of the movements of molecules and atoms.

MOLECULAR ELECTRONICS : This technology involves turning single molecules and small chemical slabs into standard semiconductor components. It is based on the discovery that individual molecules could conduct electricity. Research is being actively pursued in this line by several groups. Researchers believe that finally it may result in practical applications.

MOLECULAR ENDOCRINOLOGY : Study of the molecular structure and its relation to function of the hormones secreted by ductless glands.

MOLECULAR EPIDEMIOLOGY : Study of the pathogenic factors at the molecular level.

MOLECULAR GENETICS : Study of the molecular structure and function of nucleic acids including genetic code.

MOLECULAR IMMUNOLOGY : Study of the molecular basis of immunity.

MOLECULAR MEDICINE : Study of the relation between structure and function of medicines and their effects at the molecular level.

MOLECULAR MODELLING : Study of the models of structure of molecules.

MOLECULAR ONCOLOGY : Study of the molecular basis of cancer.

MOLECULAR OPTICS : Study of the propagation of light and associated phenomena such as refraction, absorption and scattering through collections of molecules in gases, liquids and solids.

MOLECULAR PARASITOLOGY : Study of the pathogenic parasitic organisms like viruses, bacteriophages, bacteria, etc., their molecular structure and method of infection.

MOLECULAR PHARAMACOLOGY : Study of the effects of medicines at the molecular level.

MOLECULAR PHYSICS : Study of the structure and behaviour of molecules including the quantum mechanical explanation of several kinds of chemical binding between atoms in a molecule, directed valence, the polarizability of molecules, the quantization of vibrations, rotational and electronic motions and the phenomena arising from inter-molecular forces.

MOLECULAR PHYSIOLOGY : Study of the physiological functions of biologically active molecules.

MOLECULAR PLANT PATHOLOGY : To classify and characterize plant pathogens at molecular and biological levels to generate data on key epidemiological parameters of viruses and sub-molecular plant pathogens.

MOLECULAR REPRODUCTION : Study of the molecular structure and function of reproductive hormones like estrogen, progesteron etc, in various groups of organisms.

MOLECULAR SYSTEMATICS : Determination of relationships among living organisms on the basis of similarities of genetic structure. Relationships among flowering plants have been worked out in this manner recently.

MOLECULAR VIROLOGY : Study of the molecular structure of viruses and their classification.

MONETARISM : A school of economic thought which argues that disturbances within the monetary sector are the principal cause of instability in the economy.

MONETARY ECONOMICS : Branch of economics concerned with the study of money and its role in economic affairs.

MONETARY MANAGEMENT : The term is sometimes used in a very broad sense to embrace the whole range of modern monetary policy. It is also used with an implicit emphasis on the more narrowly technical aspects of day to day management of the money market, the gilt-edged market and the level and structure of interest rates.

MONETARY POLICY : That branch of economic policy which attempts to achieve the broad objects of policy- stability of employment and prices, economic growth and balance in external payments through control of the monetary system and by operating on such monetary magnitudes as the supply of money, the level and structure of money, the level and structure of interest rates and other conditions affecting the availability of credit.

MONETARY THEORY : The term refers to the branch of macroeconomics which studies money in all its aspects; how it affects the national economy, what part it plays; it covers issues such as supply of and demand for money, inflation, central banks, branch banking, credit creation and financial institutions.

MONEY : A branch of economics and banking. Any thing which is widely accepted in exchange for goods or in settling debts not for itself but because it can be similarly passed on, has the character of money since it serves the primary function of money i.e. a means of payment. As a means of payment, money is an entity which is transferred when a payment is made; as such it acts as a medium of exchange; a function essential for any economy.

MONOTYPE COMPOSING : A mechanical method of setting and casting types in single letters in printing technology.

MONSTEROLOGY : Study of monsters such as the Lochner's monster.

MORAL STATISTICS : Moral statistics involves the collection of social data which are regarded as feature of social pathology suicide, divorce, homicide and illegitimacy.

MORBID ANATOMY : Pathology at naked eye level especially as studied at post-mortem.

MORPHOGENESIS : Study of the processes of origin, differentiation and development of tissues and organs in plants and animals.

MORPHOLOGY : The study of form and structure primarily in biology but also in other sciences.

MORPHOLOGY OF LANGUAGE : Study of the construction and interrelationships of words and their parts.

MORPHOMETRY : Quantitative morphology especially as applied to histology includes stereology.

MOTORS ENGINEERING : Branch of engineering concerned with the study of the construction and operation of motors usually either electrical or of the internal combustion type.

MOULD DESIGN : Design of moulds used in casting machine parts and tools in mechanical engineering.

MOULD TECHNOLOGY : The technique of preparing moulds in engineering industry.

MOUNTAINEERING : The practice of climbing mountains.

MOVEMENT AND ACTIVITY : The science and promotion of physical activity as a key means to reducing risks for cancer, heart disease, stroke, obesity and high blood pressure.

MULTIENGINE RATING : It is a term used in aeronautics in relation to aircraft using more than a single engine.

MULTILINGUAL EDUCATION : Teaching through more than one language medium.

MULTIMEDIA : It involves the integration of different media such as text, sound, video, film, photography, 2-dimensional (2-D) and 3-dimensional graphics and animation, usually involving a digital technology, non-linear application navigation and a capacity for user interaction with a multimedia product. The development in technology and the widespread use of compact disks have enhanced the need for multimedia products and other related applications vastly.

MULTIMEDIA AND INTERNET : A course of study which includes design and publishing, graphics and animation, post production, authoring web design etc.

MULTIMEDIA AND WEB ENGINEERING : A course of study which includes, graphics, modeling, animation, virtual reality, special effects etc.

MUSCOLOGY : Branch of botany concerned with the study of mosses. See bryology.

MUSCULOSKELETAL RADIOLOGY : Diagnosis and treatment of diseases of muscles and bones by the use of radiations.

MUSEOLOGY : Science concerned with the study of museums, acquisition of objects for museums, and their proper upkeep. Museums are repositories of interesting objects connected with literature, art, science or natural history.

MUSHROOM TECHNOLOGY : Growing and processing of mushrooms on a large scale as a source of nutritious and health giving food.

MUSICAL ACOUSTICS : That part of acoustic which is relevant to the composition, performance and appreciation of music including the physical characteristics of sounds that can be heard as music, laws governing the action, design and construction of musical instruments and the effects of musical sounds upon listeners.

MUSIC AND ENTERTAINMENT TECHNOLOGY : Technology concerned with the recording and preparation of audio and video casettes, making microphone, headphone and loudspeaker equipment for music performances, tape recorders, walkmans and related equipments.

MUSIC BUSINESS MANGEMENT : Arranging music performance, symphonies, selling music casettes, compact disks, and manufacturing musical instruments and marketing all kinds of equipment connected with music.

MUSIC COMPOSING : Preparing the written or printed score of a composition of music.

MUSIC DIRECTION : The art of directing musicians who sing or perform on musical instruments; directing an orchestra.

MUSICOLOGY- Academic study of music in various contexts such as historical and scientific aspects; the science of hormonical sounds.

MUTUAL FUND MANAGEMNET : Management of mutual funds which are a type of indirect investment in the share market.

MYCOLOGY : That branch of botany which investigates fungi, a group of saprophytic and parasitic organisms lacking chlorophyll. Some of them are useful as sources of antibiotics while others causes diseases of plants; animals and man. This subject is sometimes considered as a separate branch of biology.

MYOLOGY : The scientific study of the structure and physiology of muscles.

MYRMECOLOGY : That branch of zoology which is concerned with the study of structure and life of ants.

MYSTICISM : Views or tendencies in religion which aspire towards a communication between man and god through the inward perception of the mind; a seeking to solve the mysteries of existence through internal illumination.

MYTHOLOGY : The science which investigates with a view to their interpretation and to discover the degree of relationship existing between the myths of different peoples.

N

NANOFABRICATION : Chemically assembled electronic nanotechnology is an emerging technology. This uses self alignment to construct electronic circuits out of nanometer devices that take advantage of quantum mechanical effects.

NANOPHASE MATERIALS : Materials which are used in nanotechnology.

NANOTECHNOLOGY : Technology of making objects like machines, motors etc made up merely of a few atoms, and a few microns in size. This technology is being developed mainly in U.S.A. Japan and some European countries.

NATURAL HISTORY : Originally the study or description of nature in its widest sense; now commonly applied collectively to the sciences of Zoology and botany or sometimes to zoology alone.

NATURAL PHILOSOPHY : Sometimes applied to the science of physics .

NATURAL RESOURCE ECONOMICS : Study of the economics of utilization of natural resources.

NATURAL SCIENCE : Much the same as natural history in its wide sense.

NATURAL SCIENCES : Sometimes applied collectively to botany zoology, geology and related sciences. Sometimes applied to all sciences as distinguished from social sciences.

NATUROPATHY : A philosophy of natural healing that is under going a new resurgence based on herbal treatment and food supplement therapy.

NAUTICAL SCIENCE : The science of managing ships; prepares cadets in navigation upto master/captain of a ship.

NAUTICAL STUDIES : A course of study of nautical science meant for navigators.

NAVAL ARCHITECTURE : Architecture applied to designing and construction of ships.

NAVAL METEOROLOGY : Branch of meteorology concerned with iteration between the ocean and the overlying air mass and atmospheric phenomena over the oceans.

NAVAL SCIENCE : Science pertaining to the naval defence of a country.

NAVIGATION : The science and art of finding the position and directing the course of vessels or craft from one point to the other.

NAVIGATIONAL ELECTRONICS : Electronics applied to navigation with sea and aerial navigation.

NAVIGATIONAL ENGINEERING : Engineering involved in the management of ships.

NEAR EARTH SPACE ENVIRONMENT : Study of the environmental conditions prevailing in the space which is relatively nearer to the earth in contrast to distant space where the celestial bodies are located.

NECROLOGY : A collection of obituary notices.

NECROMANCY : Divination by means of a presumed communication with the dead; the blacart.

NECROPSY : Post-mortem examination especially full pathological dissection of body.

NEMATOLOGY : Branch of zoology concerned with the study of nematodes or round worms some of which cause diseases of animals and man and destroy crop plants.

NEOCLASSICAL ECONOMICS : A body of economic theory which uses the general approach methods and techniques of the original 19th century marginalist economists. The term neoclassical derives from the view that the original or the so-called 'marginalist revolution' was extending and improving on the basic foundation of classical economists. The founders of the neoclassical systems used marginal analysis to analyse the pricing of foods, services and factors of production in competitive markets.

NEONATALOGY : Branch of medical science concerned with the development of newly born child upto one month.

NEOPALYNOLOGY : A field of palynology concerned with extant microorganisms and dissociated microscopic parts of megaorganisms.

NEOTECIONICS : Study of the most recent structure and structural history of the earth's crust after the Miocene.

NEPHELOMETERY : Quantitative analysis by measurement of the scattered light from a precipitate.

NEPHROLOGY : Branch of medicine concerned with the study of the kidney. See Urology.

NETWORK ENGINEERING: Designing and managing networks, LAN and WAN set up and maintenance ports, add-on cards, thernet cards, routes, modems and cables are the domain expertise of a network specialist.

NETWORKING AND NETWORK MANAGEMENT : Networking computers and managing computer networks.

NETWORKING TECHNOLOGY : Involves connecting all the computers internally in the office or establishment or externally. Networking allows users to retrieve data and information from a mainframe computer or a server and use it on their machine.

NETWORK MANAGEMENT : The set of policies functions and procedures used to control a communication network and to maintain its efficiency and integrity.

NETWORK SECURITY MANAGEMENT : The subject covers various aspects of security of computer networks including network layers and their vulnerables, security through encryption, network threats and vulnerabilities, network security controls etc.,

NEURAL TECHNOLOGY : Branch of computer science involving application of neural networking of brain in computers to create artificial intelligence.

NEUROANATOMY : Study of the structure and arrangement of nerves in the body.

NEURO AND VASCULAR RADIOLOGY : Application of radiology to nervous system and blood vessels.

NEUROBIOCHEMISTRY : Study of the biochemical processes taking place in the nerves, particularly of the neurotransmitters.

NEUROBIOLOGY : Study of the biological role of the nervous systems. It forms an important part of medicine, psychology and biology.

NEUROCHEMISTRY : Study of the chemical nature and function of neurotransmitters which play a part in carrying nervous stimuli.

NEUROENDOCRINOLOGY : Study of the interactions between the nervous and endocrine systems.

NEUROIMMUNOLOGY : Role of the nervous system in immunity development.

NEUROINFORMATICS : An emerging science that combines and aims at understanding electrical and chemical signals in the brain to process information.

NEUROLINGUISTIC PROGRAMME : The programme not only manages stress, it improves confidence levels, builds up communication skills, eliminates mental blocks and helps change personal, social and professional life for the better.

NEUROLINGUISTIC PSYCHOLOGY : Study of the mental processes involve in the interaction between the nervous system and linguistic ability.

NEUROLOGICAL ANAESTHESIOLOGY : Branch of anesthesiology concerned with the study of the effects of anaesthetics on the nervous systems.

NEUROLOGY : Science dealing with the structure and function of the nervous systems. Also known as neuroscience.

NERURONURSING : Branch of nursing science concerned with nursing of patients suffering from neurological disorders.

NEUROPATHOLOGY : Branch of pathology concerned with the study of the diseases of the nervous system.

NEUROPHYSIOLOGY : Branch of physiology and neurology concerned with the study of the functions of the nervous systems.

NEUROPSYCHIATRY : Branch of medicine dealing with the treatment of nervous and mental disorders particularly those of a structural rather than functional character.

NEUROPSYCHOLOGY : Studies the relation between brain and behaviour.

NEURORADIOLOGY : Branch of radiology concerned with the use of radiations for diagnosis and treatment of diseases of the nervous systems

NEUROVIROLOGY : Branch of virology and neurology concerned with the virus diseases of the nervous system.

NEURO SCIENCE : See Neurology.

NEUROSCIENCES : All those sciences concerned with the study of the nervous system like neuroanatomy, neurobiology, neurochemistry, neurobiochemistry, neuropathology, neuropsychiatry, neurophysiology etc.

NEUROSURGERY : Branch of medicine concerned with surgical treatment of nervous disorders.

NEURO SURGICAL ANAESTHESIOLOGY : Branch of anaesthesiology concerned with the surgery of the nervous system.

NEUROTHEOLOGY : An emerging science which explores the links between spirituality and the brain.

NEUROTOXICOLOGY : Branch of science which studies the effects of poisons on the nervous system.

NEUTRON ACTIVATION ANALYSIS : Activation analysis in which the specimen is bombarded with neutrons; identification is made by measuring the resulting radioisotopes.

NEUTRONOPTICS : Study of certain phenomena in which the work character of neutrons dominates and leads to behaviour similar to that of light.

NEUTRON SPECTROSCOPY : A method of observing excited states of matter in which neutrons are used to bombard a target causing nuclei to be transmitted into excited states of various nuclear reactions.

NEW CLASSICAL MACROECONOMICS : Essentially a restatement in a more vigorous form of orthodox classical economics. It rests on the notion of rational expectations combined with a natural rate of unemployment which emerges as a result of efficient market clearing. Accordingly the economy will settle at the natural rate and attempts to disturb this equilibrium will be neutralised by economic agents.

NEW MATHEMATICS : An approach to mathematics based on set theory, especially when taught at the school level.

NEW MICROECONOMICS : The name given to a body of economic literature which has sought to identify the microeconomics of macroeconomics specifically to provide a firm microeconomic rational of the mechanisms underlying the aggregate relationship between price changes and unemployment.

NEW-NEW MICROECONOMICS : The name given to model building exercises which attempt to explain wage and price contracts in terms of microeconomics optimizing behaviour. The existence of wage and price contracts means that prices will react sluggishly to underlying changes in aggregate demand and that the latter will predominantly induce quantity changes in the short run.

NEWSPAPER BUSINESS MANAGEMENT : Management of newspaper production, advertisements, circulation, subscriptions, receipts and payments and other business matters.

NEWSPAPER EDITING : To prepare and publish the newspaper for the public eye by writing, correcting and selecting the matter for publication. Branch of journalism.

NEWSPAPER REPORTING : To give an account of the proceedings of public meetings and entertainments, collect information respecting interesting or important events and the like for publication in a newspaper. Branch of journalism.

NEWSPAPER TECHNOLOGY : Technology used in collecting news and information and in printing and distribution of newspapers.

NEWTONIAN MECHANICS : The system of mechanics based upon Newton's law of motion in which mass and energy are considered as separate, conservative mechanical properties in contrast to their treatment in relativistic mechanics.

NOMENCLATURE : 1. Systematic naming of things. 2. The vocabulary of names or technical terms which are appropriate to any branch of science. As distinguished from terminology it is applied to the names of individual things while the latter is generally applied to the technical terms describing the characteristics of things.

NOMOLOGY : 1. Branch of science which investigates general principles and formulates laws. 2. The science of knowledge of law, legislation, and government.

NON-CONVENTIONAL ENERGY STUDIES : Study of energy sources other than the conventional sources like petroleum, gas and coal. Some of the non-conventional energy sources are petroleum like products obtained from some plants, biogas, hydrogen obtained through some chemical reactions, alcohol derived from some plants, solar energy, wind energy, geothermal energy, energy from ocean tides etc.

NON-DESTRUCTURE TESTING : Testing machinery and installations without causing harm to them. It is carried out by ultrasonic testing, electromagnetic methods, thermography and "eddy" current testing. Raw materials and components fitted into plant and machinery could be scrutinised for the detection of flaws which might have escaped conventional methods to ensure that they are corrected prior to the commencement of commercial production. This is achieved without their being dissected or requiring refabrication.

NON-EQUILIBRIUM THERMODYNAMICS : A quantitative treatment of irreversible processes and of rates at which they occur. Also known as irreversible thermodynamics.

NON-EUCLIDIAN GEOMETRY : A type of geometry that does not comply with the basic postulates of ecluidan geometry.

NON FORMAL EDUCATION : Imparting education not according to regular or conventional method.

NON-QUANTUM MECHANICS : The classical mechanics of Newton and Einstein as opposed to the quantum mechanics of Heisenberg, Schroedinger and Dirac; particles have definite position and velocity and they move according to Newton's laws.

NON-RELATIVISTIC KINEMATICS : The study of motions of systems of objects at speeds which are small compared to the speed of light without reference to the forces which act on the system.

NON-RELATIVISTIC MECHANICS : The study of the dynamics of systems in which all speeds are small compared to the speed of light.

NON RELATIVISTIC QUANTUM MECHANICS : The modern theory of matter and its interaction with radiation, applicable to systems of material particles which move slowly compared to the speed of light, which are neither created or destroyed, and whose internal structure (except for spin) either does not change or is irrelevant to the description of the system.

NORMATIVE ECONOMICS : Economic analysis which provides prescriptions or statements about 'what should be' rather than 'what is'. Normative economics gives rise to statements such as 'monopolies should be regulated' or 'profits should be fixed'. This type of economics may be contrasted with positive economics which is concerned with describing and analysing the economy as it is.

NOSOCOMICAL INFECTIONS : These are hospital acquired infections which occur worldwide. The science of prevention and treatment of these infections is a subspeciality in medicine.

NOSOLOGY : That branch of medical science which treats of the classification of diseases.

NUCLEAR AGRICULTURE : Production of new varieties of seeds using radiation-induced mutations, micropropagation of plants and recombinant DNA technology.

NUCLEAR CARDIOLOGY : Use of radioactive materials in the study of heart diseases and their treatment. The important tests are myocardial perfusion scintigraphy, Stress thallium myocardial perfusion study.

NUCLEAR CHEMISTRY : Study of the atomic nucleus and its reactions.

NUCLEAR ELECTRIC POWER GENERATION : Large scale generation of electric power in which the source of energy in nuclear fission, generally in a nuclear reactor or nuclear fusion.

NUCLEAR ENGINEERING : Branch of technology concerned with design and construction of nuclear reactors and auxillary facilities and development and fabrication of special materials and the handling of reactor products.

NUCLEAR EXPERIMENTAL PHYSICS : Experimental study of nuclear physics.

NUCLEAR FUEL TECHNOLOGY : Design, construction and operation of plants for production of nuclear fuels production and fabrication of special materials and seamless tubes of various alloys with a wide range of nuclear and other industrial applications.

NUCLEAR GENETICS : 1. Study of heredity transmitted through the nucleus in the cell. 2. Use of radioactive materials, radioisotopes and ionizing radiations in the study of heredity.

NUCLEAR MAGNETISM : The phenomenon associated with the magnetic dipole, octapole and higher moments of a nucleus including the field generated by the nucleus the force on the nucleus in an inhomogeneous magnetic field and the splitting of nuclear energy levels in a magnetic field.

NUCLEAR MEDICINE : Use of raidoactive materials, radioisotopes and ionizing radiations in the diagnosis and treatment of diseases.

NUCLEAR MINERAL ENGINEERING : Engineering methods employed in the exploration and study of radioactive minerals.

NUCLEAR MINERAL SCIENCE : Study of the properties of radioactive minerals.

NUCLEAR MINIERAL TECHNOLOGY : Study of the utilization of radioactive minerals in science, medicine and industry.

NUCLEAR PHYSICS : Study of the characteristic behaviour and internal structure of the atomic nucleus.

NUCLEAR REACTOR TECHNOLOGY : Use of nuclear reactors for various purpose like scientific study, production of radio isotopes, power generation etc.

NUCLEAR THEORY : Study of theoretical nuclear physics.

NUCLEAR WASTE DISPOSAL : Disposal of waste material emanating from cyclotrons, nuclear power plants etc., in order to prevent environmental pollution.

NUCLEONICS : Technology based on phenomena of the atomic nucleus such as radioactivity, fission, fusion, etc., includes nuclear reactors, various applications of radioisotopes and radiation particle accelerators and radiation.

NUMBER THEORY : Study of the integers and relations between them.

NUMERICAL TAXONOMY : Uses mathematical procedures to assess similarities and differences and establish taxonomic units and the ordering of these units into taxa on the basis of their affinities.

NUMERICAL WEATHER PREDICTION : Massive amount of data received from diverse sources is suitably ingested and appropriate hydrodynamic equations are integrated to the required time scale to produce the requisite weather forecast.

NUMEROLOGY : Predicting the future on the basis of numbers like date and time of birth etc.

NUMISMATICS : The science of coins and medals.

NUMISMATOGRAPHY : The science which treats of coins and medals in their relation to history.

NURSERY EDUCATION -Education imparted to children below the age of three years through play method without reading and writing.

NURSERY TECHNOLOGY : Comprises irrigation systems, seeds, green house and accessories, pesticides, biofertilizers, garden tools and accessories used in raising plant nurseries.

NURSING : The profession of attending to the patients in a hospital and assisting the doctor in extending medical aid.

NURSING ADMINISTRATION : Administration of nursing services in a hospital including allocation of work to nurses, supervising their work, enforcing discipline and looking after their needs.

NUTRACEAUTICALS : Application of nutritional substances to various health challenges; for example, the finding that vitamin E is helpful in preventing LDL cholesterol from plaquing in arteries or that carotenoids in red and orange vegetables may have a protective effect on cancer.

NUTRITION : The science of nourishment including the study of nutrients that each organism must obtain from the environment in order to maintain life and reproduction.

NUTRITIONAL BIOCHEMISTRY : Study of the biochemical role of nutrients in the body.

NUTRITION AND HEALTH EDUCATION : Branch of education and public health concerned with imparting knowledge about nutrition and health and their importance to the individual and to society.

NUTRITION SCIENCE : Study of the nutritive values of food substances, preservation of nutritive value in processing and packing and the role of nutrients in health.

O

OBSERVATIONAL ASTRONOMY : Branch of Astronomy concerned with the study of stars and other celestial bodies by observing them with the help of various types of telescopes from the surface of the earth or from satellites.

OBSTETRICS : The art of assisting women in child birth and treating their diseases during pregnancy and after delivery.

OCCULOPLASTIC SURGERY : Plastic surgery to treat eyes, baggy eyes, and drooping eyes related to ageing, causing loss of elasticity decreasing subcutaneous fat and resulting in wrinkles. These changes hinder vision.

OCCULTISM : A system of occult or mysterious doctrines; the belief of the theosophists.

OCCULT SCIENCES : Certain so-called sciences of the middle ages as alchemy, necromancy or magic, astrology etc.

OCCUPATIONAL HEALTH : Study of the safety and precautionary measures to be taken to protect the health of industrial workers. Its main objective is to ensure a safe and comfortable work environment. Towards this end, research into causes, prevention, and treatment of occupational diseases and providing guidance to industry on prevention of such diseases by modern scientific methods is encouraged.

OCCUPATIONAL MEDICINE : Branch of medicine concerned with the treatment of diseases of industrial workers caused by factors peculiar to their work and environment.

OCCUPATIONAL PHYSIOLOGY : Physiological changes occurring in response to the nature of work and work environment in people engaged in various occupations.

OCCUPATIONAL PSYCHOLOGY : Psychology of behaviour in the work situation.

OCCUPATIONAL THERAPY : Rehabilitation of the chronically mentally ill along with chronic physical disabilities and illness by engaging them in suitable work.

OCEAN ENGINEERING : Branch of engineering concerned with the development of new equipment and the improvement of techniques to permit humans to operate beneath the ocean surface to exploit resources.

OCEANIC SCIENCES : Sciences concerned with the study of the physical and chemical characteristics, ocean microbiology, biological and mineral resources of oceans, meteorological phenomena related to oceans and other features of oceans.

OCEAN INFORMATION SERVICES : Supply of upto date information concerning ocean to all those interested in the study and exploitation of oceans.

OCEANOGRAPHY : The department of knowledge that deals with oceanic phenomena.

OCEANOLOGY : Same as oceanography. Also see ocean sciences.

OCEAN SURVEY TECHNOLOGY : Development of technologies for the survey of oceans.

OCEAN TECHNOLOGY : Different topics related to ocean engineering and ocean resources exploitation namely. (1) Ocean energy, (2) Deep sea, (3) Coastal and environmental engineering, 4) marine instrumentation.

ODONTOLOGY : That branch of anatomical science which treats of the structure and growth of teeth and their abnormalities.

OENOLOGY : The study of the production, quality and effects of wine.

OESOPHAGEAL SURGERY : Surgical treatment of oesophageal diseases including cancer.

OFFICE AUTOMATION : Automation of office management based on computer software technology like i-leap standardized software.

OFFICE MANAGEMENT : Study of organizing an office in the most effective way.

OFF SET PRINTING : A method of printing which makes use of the offset machine in contrast to letter press printing.

OILS, FATS AND WAXES : Science which deals with the physicochemical properties and uses of oils, fats and waxes obtained mainly from plants.

OIL SEEDS : Branch of agriculture concerned with the cultivation of oil yielding plants.

OIL TECHNOLOGY : Extraction and utilization of edible and industrial oils from natural sources, more particularly plants.

OLERICULTURE : Branch of horticulture concerned with the culturing of vegetables.

ONCOLOGY : Branch of medicine concerned with the study of cancer.

ONCOPATHOLOGY : Study of the pathology of cancer.

ONCOSURGERY : Surgical treatment of cancer.

ONEIROLOGY : Study of dreams.

ONEIROSCOPY : The art of interpreting dreams.

ONOMASIOLOGY- Study of the connotations of names.

ONOMATOLOGY : Study of the genesis of names and their meanings.

ONTOGENY : The history of the individual development of an organism.

ONTOLOGY : Study of nature of things rather than appearances.

OOLOGY : The branch of knowledge that deals with eggs of birds.

OPEN HEART SURGERY : Surgical treatment of heart disease in which heart is opened up after exclusion from circulation maintained by bypass pump.

OPERANT CONDITIONING : Treatment of mental diseases or handicap by teaching skills and behaviour using appropriate stimuli and rewards.

OPERATIONS RESEARCH : To quantify a problem in statistical or mathematical terms and to use these methods to find a solution. Widely used in commerce and industry.

OPERATION MANAGEMENT : Management of the activities and works in an industry.

OPERATION THEATER TECHNOLOGY : Technology involved in the construction and arrangements required in the theater meant for conducting surgical operations.

OPERATIVE DENTISTRY : Surgical treatment of dental disorders.

OPHIOLOGY : That branch of zoology which treats of serpents.

OPHTHALMIC TECHNOLOGY : Technology pertaining to the instruments and other devices used by ophthalmologists in the treatment of eye disorders.

OPHTHALMOLOGY : Branch of medicine concerned with the medical and surgical treatment of eye disorders.

OPTICAL COMMUNICATION : Transmission of information through optical fibres.

OPTICAL COMPUTING : In optical computers electrons are replaced by photons. Thus it is possible to fabricate closely packed nanostructures. Researchers are using new conducting polymers to make transistor like switches smaller and 1000 times faster than silicon transistors.

OPTICAL OCEANOGRAPHY : That aspect of physical oceanography which deals with optical properties of sea water and natural light in sea water.

OPTICS : 1. The study of phenomena associated with the generation, transmission and detection of electromagnetic radiation in the spectral range extending from the long wave edge of the x-ray region to the short- wave edge of the radio region and the science of light. 2. That branch of physical science which treats of the nature and properties of light and vision, optical instruments etc.

OPTO ELECTRONIC INSTRUMENTATION : Manufacture and use of optic instruments fitted with electronic components.

OPTO ELECTRONICS : Branch of electronics concerned with the study optical devices controlled electronically.

OPTOMETRY : Determining the focal lengths of lenses necessary to correct imperfections of the eye with the use of an instrument known as optometer.

ORACLE : A teletext system provided by independent television in the United kingdom.

ORACLE FINANCIALS : Computer course covering account concepts, general ledger, accounts receivable, SGL loader, accounts payable, order entry system, administration, purchasing etc.

ORAL AND DENTAL PATHOLOGY : Branch of medicine concerned with diseases of the mouth, gums, teeth, jaws etc.

ORAL AND MAXILLOFACIAL SURGERY : Surgical treatment of disorders of the mouth, gums, teeth, jaws and face.

ORAL BIOLOGY : Study of the structure and physiology of the mouth and associated structures like gums, teeth jaws etc.

ORAL HYGIENE : Removing tartar and plaque from teeth, oral scaling, polishing of teeth and gum massaging.

ORAL IMPLANTOLOGY : See Implant dentistry.

ORAL MEDICINE : Branch of medicine concerned with the disorders of the mouth.

ORAL MEDICINE AND RADIOLOGY : Radiological treatment of diseases of the mouth including cancer.

ORAL PATHOLOGY : Branch of medicine concerned with the nature, causes and symptoms of oral diseases.

ORAL SURGERY : Extraction of teeth and related operations.

ORBITAL DYNAMICS : A branch of space science with various types of orbits- namely geo stationery, transit, near earth and non synchronous polar.

ORE DRESSING : Cleaning of ore by the removal of certain valueless portions.

ORE GEOLOGY : Branch of geology concerned with the occurrence, abundance and properties of mineral ores.

ORGANIC ARCHITECTURE : It is a kind of architecture which involves the nature of material used like concrete, wood or stone, the environment and the function.

ORGANIC CHEMISTRY : Branch of chemistry concerned with the study of carbon compounds. Many useful substances like hydrocarbons, petroleum, drugs and other industrial products come under this category.

ORGANIC EVOLUTION : The processes of change in organisms by which descendants come to differ form their ancestors and a history of the sequence of such changes.

ORGANIC FARMING : Cultivation of crops using compost, biofertilizers and biopesticides in order to reduce water, food and soil pollution.

ORGANIC GEOCHEMISTRY : That branch of geochemistry concerned with naturally occurring carbonaceous and biologically derived substances which are of geological interest.

ORGANIC METALLICS : Branch of organic chemistry concerned with the study of metal containing organic compounds like haemoglobins, chlorophylls, cytochromes, certain enzymes etc., which are of biological importance.

ORGANIZATIONAL INFORMATION SYSTEMS : Study of information systems pertaining to and of interest to organizations and institutions.

ORGANIZATIONAL PSYCHOLOGY : Branch of psychology concerned with the study of psychological characters and behaviour of members of organizations and institutions.

ORGANOGENY : Study of the development of an organ or of organs in plants or animals.

ORGANOGRAPHY : A description of organs of plants or animals.

ORGANOLOGY : Physiology of different organs of animals or plants.

ORGANO- METALLIC CHEMISTRY : Branch of chemistry concerned with the study of organic compounds having a metal as a prosthetic group. Such compounds serve primarily as catalysts.

ORGANO : THERAPY : Use of animal extracts for curative and other purposes.

ORGAN PROCUREMENT : Overall subject of donor side of organ transplantation for medical purposes.

ORNITHOLOGY : The branch of zoology which treats of the form, structure, classification and habits of birds.

OROGRAPHY : Branch of geography dealing with mountains.

OROHYDROGRAPHY : Branch of hydrogeography dealing with the relations of mountains to drainage.

ORTHOCHRONOLOGY : Geochronology based on faunas and floras or on irreversible evolutionary processes.

ORTHODONTICS : Management of dento : facial and skeletal abnormalities.

ORTHOEPY : Art of uttering words with propriety.

ORTHOGRAPHY : The part of grammar which treats of letters and spelling.

ORTHOKERATOLOGY : Temporary correction of refractive errors in the eye by moulding cornea with hard contact lenses.

ORTHOMETRY : The art of correct versification.

ORTHOPAEDICS : The art of curing deformaties.

ORTHOPTICS : 1. Non- surgical techniques for correction of squint and related eye defects. 2. Corresponding paramedical speciality.

ORTHOPSYCHIATRY : Treatment of slight personality trait abnormalities primarily in adults.

ORTHOSURGERY : Surgical treatment of deformities.

ORTHOTICS : Technology and crafts of making splints and other orthoses.

ORYCTOLOGY : Study of fossils or whatever is dug from the earth except archaeological material.

OSTEOLOGY : That branch of anatomy that treats of bones and bone tissue.

OSTEOMETRY : The study of the size and proportions of the osseous system.

OSTEOPATHIC MEDICINE : A system of treatment mainly involving manipulation of the bones and joints and massage of the muscles.

OTOLARYNGOLOGY : Branch of medicine concerned with the diseases of the ear and larynx.

OTOLOGY : Branch of medicine concerned with the diseases of the ear.

OTORHYNOLARYNGOLOGY : Branch of medicine concerned with the diseases of the ear, nose and throat.

OUTBOUND MANAGEMENT DEVELOPMENT TRAINING : These courses generally concentrate on the following areas; team dynamics, communication, problem solving, decision making and managing change. Such training uses outdoor activities to generate fresh ideas, emotional responses and attitudes. Also known as wilderness training.

P

PACKAGING TECHNOLOGY : Study of packaging materials and methods also includes bulk packaging, bar coding, packaging impact on environment, special packaging for food, drugs, delicate instruments, equipment etc.

PAEDIATRIC ALLERGY AND IMMUNOLOGY : Study of allergies and immunological reactions in children.

PAEDIATRIC ANAESTHESIOLOGY : Branch of medicine concerned with administering anaesthesia to children for surgical operations.

PAEDIATRIC CARDIAC SURGERY : Surgical treatment of children's heart diseases.

PAEDIATRIC DENTISTRY : Branch of dentistry concerned with the treatment of children's dental problems.

PAEDIATRIC ENDOCRINOLOGY : Branch of endocrinology concerned with diseases of the endocrine system and hormonal problems of children.

PAEDIATRIC EPILEPTOLOGY : Branch of medicine concerned with the treatment of children's epileptic fits.

PAEDIATRIC GASTROENTEROLOGY : Branch of medicine concerned with the diseases of the gastrointestinal system in children.

PAEDIATRIC INTENSIVE CARE : Branch of medicine concerned with the intensive care of children after surgery and in all other serious cases requiring close monitoring and treatment.

PAEDIATRIC NEUROLOGY : Branch of medicine concerned with the disorders of the nervous system in children.

PAEDIATRIC NUTRITION : Branch of nutrition science concerned with the nutritional requirements and deficiencies of children.

PAEDIATRIC RADIOLOGY : Branch of medicine concerned with the use of radiation in the diagnosis and treatment of children's diseases.

PAEDIATRICS : Branch of medicine concerned with the diseases of children.

PAEDIATRIC SURGERY : Surgical treatment of children's diseases and disabilities.

PAINTING : 1. The art of reproducing objects by means of figures and colours on a plane surface so as to produce the appearance of relief. 2. The art of laying colour or colours on, with brush or otherwise.

PAINT TECHNOLOGY : Manufacture of paints for various painting purposes.

PALEOAGROSTOLOGY : The study of fossil grasses.

PALAEOAKTOLOGY : Study of ancient sea shore and shallow water environs

PALAEOALGOLOGY : The study of fossil algae. Also known as palaeophycology.

PALAEOANTHROPOLOGY : Study of the early types of man.

PALAEOBIOCHEMISTRY : Study of chemical processes used by organisms that lived in the geological past.

PALAEOBIOCLIMATOLOGY : Study of the climatological events affecting living organisms for millenia or longer.

PALAEOBIOGEOCHEMISTRY : A branch of geochemistry that is concerned with biological materials and their relation to earth chemicals in the ancient past based on the study of fossils.

PALAEOBIOLOGY : Study of the life of ancient plants and animals based on fossils.

PALAEOBOTANY : Branch of botany concerned with the study of fossil plants and their evolutionary significance.

PALAEOCLIMATOLOGY : Study of climates in the geological past.

PALAEOECOLOGY : Ecology of the geological past.

PALAEOENVIRONMENT : Study of the environmental conditions which prevailed in the geological past.

PALAEOETHNOLOGY : Study of ancient human races.

PALAEOETIOLOGY : The mode of investigation which explains past conditions by reasoning for present conditions.

PALAEOFLUMINOLOGY : Study of ancient stream systems.

PALAEOGEOGRAPHY : Geography of the geological past.

PALAEOGEOLOGY : Geology of the ancient earth.

PALAEOGEOMORPHOLOGY : Branch of geomorphology concerned with recognition of ancient erosion surfaces etc.

PALAEOGRAPHY : 1. The art of deciphering ancient writings. 2. Tracing the origin of languages from the writings of the historical past.

PALAEOHERPETOLOGY : Study of fossil reptiles.

PALAEOHYDROLOGY : Study of ancient hydrologic features preserved in rocks.

PALAEOICHNOLOGY : Study of traces of fossils in the fossil state. Also known as palichnology.

PALAEOICHTHYOLOGY : Science of fossil fishes.

PALAEOLIMNOLOGY : Study of ancient lakes.

PALAEOLOGY : Science of ancient things.

PALAEOMAGNETICS : Study of the direction and intensity of the earth's magnetic field throughout geological time.

PALAEOMAGNETIC STRATIGRAPHY : Use of natural remanant magnetization in the identification of stratigraphic units. Also known as magnetic stratigraphy.

PALAEOMAGNETISM : Study of magnetism in rocks, which provides information on variations in direction and intensity of the earth's magnetic field with time.

PALAEOMETEORITICS : Study of variations of extraterrestrial debris over extended periods of geological record.

PALAEOMORPHOLOGY : Study of the form and structure of fossil remains in order to describe the original anatomy of an organism.

PALAEOMYCOLOGY : Study of the fossil fungi.

PALAEONTOLOGY : Study of plants and animal fossils.

PALAEOOCEANOGRAPHY : Study of the history of circulation, chemistry biogeography, fertility and sedimentation of the oceans.

PALAEOPALYNOLOGY : Palynology concerned with fossils of microorganisms and of dissociated microscopic parts of mega organisms.

PALAEOPATHOLOGY : Study of the pathologies in early men or animals.

PALAEOPEDOLOGY : Study of soils of past geological ages including determination of their ages.

PALAEOPHYCOLOGY : See Palaeoalgology.

PALAEOPHYTOLOGY : See Palaeobotany.

PALAEOSEISMOLOGY : Science of identification and dating of palaeoearthquakes.

PALAEOZOOLOGY : Study of animal fossils.

PALICHNOLOGY : See Palaeoichnology.

PALLIATIVE MEDICINE : Branch of medicine concerned with mitigating the disease.

PALMISTRY : The art of telling fortunes by the lines and marks in the palm of the hand.

PALYNOLOGY : Study of pollen grains and spores of plants.

PALYNOSTRATIGRAPHY : Stratigraphic application of palynologic methods

PANCHAYAT RAJ SYSTEM : A system of administration at the village level in India. Branch of local self government under public administration.

PANTOLOGY : A systematic view of all branches of human knowledge.

PAPER TECHNOLOGY : Study of the processes of manufacturing paper from various raw materials.

PARAMEDICAL STUDIES : Concerned with supporting and aiding the work of qualified medical personnel.

PARAMETRIC HYDROLOGY : That branch of hydrology dealing with the development and analysis of relationships among the physical parameters involved in hydrological events.

PARAPSYCHOLOGY : The scientific study of supernormal phenomena by experimental or other systematic means.

PARASITE BIOCHEMISTRY : Study of biochemical action of parasites on their hosts.

PARASITOLOGY : Study of parasitic organisms and the diseases caused by them. Branch of medical and veterinary sciences.

PARENIOLOGY : Study of proverbs.

PARTICIPATORY IRRIGATION MANAGEMENT : Management of irrigation water supply in an equitable manner with the active co-operation and participation of the concerned beneficiary farmers.

PARTICLE DYNAMICS : The study of the dependence of the motion of a single material particle on the external forces acting upon it particularly electromagnetic and gravitational forces.

PARTICLE PHYSICS : Branch of physics concerned with the study of elementary particles like electron, proton etc. especially through study of collisions or decays involving energies of hundreds of MeV (Megaelectrovolts) or more. Also known as high energy physics.

PASIMOLOGY : Art of communicating by means of sign language.

PATENT LAWS : Study of law pertaining to the grant and scope of patents on new ideas, discoveries, inventions etc. to those who report them first.

PATHOBIOLOGY : Biological study of the effects of pathogenic organisms on the host organisms.

PATHOLOGY : That part of medicine which explains the nature of diseases, their causes and symptoms.

PATTERN CUTTING MASTERS COURSE : A Part of garment making involving a study of cutting the cloth or other material for making garments.

PEACE AND CONFLICT STUDIES : Study of the causes of conflicts between various groups of peoples and restoring peace. It also forms a branch of foreign relations.

PEDAGOGY : Art of teaching children.

PEDODONTICS : Branch of dentistry concerned with dental problems of children.

PEDOGEOGRAPHY : Study of geographical distribution of soils.

PEDOLOGY : Science of soils also known as soil science.

PENOLOGY : Scientific study of the treatment and punishment of criminals. Penology is conventionally regarded as a branch of criminology and associated with the movement away from retribution to correction in 19th century penal reform.

PEPTIDE CHEMISTRY : Chemistry of a class of chemical compounds known as peptides which are made up of one or more amino acids but less complex than proteins.

PERFORMANCE REPORTING AND ANALYSIS : Financial accounting, management accounting and decision : making tools.

PERFORMING ARTS : Acting, dancing, singing and allied arts which involve performing on the stage.

PERFUME TECHNOLOGY : The processes of manufacturing perfumes like scents both natural and synthetic.

PERFUSION TECHNOLOGY : A part of medical labouratory technology consisting of the method of pumping of a fluid through a tissue or organ by way of an artery, myocardial scientigraphy, stress thallium study etc.

PERINATAL PSYCHIATRY : A branch of psychiatry concerned with pregnant women before and after delivery.

PERIODONTICS : Management of the diseases of the supporting and associated structures of the teeth.

PERITONEAL DIALYSIS : A method of dialysis employed for kidney failure patients.

PERSONAL BANKING : Deals with loans, credits, mortgages, insurance policies, investment, schedules and pension funds.

PERSONAL LAW : Law relating to individual rights and obligations, relationships, property matters etc.

PERSONALITY DEVELOPMENT : Study of the factors involved in the development of an individual as a distinct person.

PERSONNEL MANAGEMENT : Branch of management concerned with personnel matters such as interviewing, selection of workers, application of wage agreements, health and welfare services.

PERSONNEL MANAGEMENT IN PUBLIC ENTERPRISES : Management of personnel in public sector undertakings as distinct from private enterprises.

PERSONNEL POLICIES AND PATTERNS : Study of the policies to be adopted with regard to personnel and their patterns with regard to recruitment, wages, welfare measure etc.

PERSONOLOGY : Sometimes employed to cover the various aspects of personality as a distinct branch of psychology.

PESTICIDE CHEMISTRY : Study of the structure and properties of various inorganic chemicals and chemical compounds and certain organic compounds which are used to kill crop and domestic pests.

PESTICIDE TECHNOLOGY : Technology concerned with the manufacture of insecticides, fungicides, herbicides etc, primarily for use to control agricultural and domestic pests.

PEST MANAGEMENT : Management of crop and domestic pests and other pests harmful to public health by the use of pesticides, biological control methods and biotechnology.

PETROCHEMICAL TECHNOLOGY : Manufacture of materials derived from petroleum, natural gas etc., and their utilization for various purposes.

PETROCHEMISTRY : 1. Chemical composition of rocks. 2. The chemistry and reactions of materials, derived from petroleum natural gas or asphalt deposits.

PETROGEOMETRY : See structural petrology.

PETROGRAPHY : Description and classification of rocks.

PETROLEUM CHEMSTRY : Study of the chemical constituents and properties of petroleum and its products.

PETROLEUM ENGINEERING : Application of almost all types of engineering to the drilling for production of oil, gas and liquefiable hydrocarbons.

PETROLEUM EXPLORATION : Locating probable petroleum rich sites and drilling.

PETROLEUM GEOLOGY : Branch of economic geology dealing with origin, occurrence, movement, accumulation and exploration of hydrocarbon fuels.

PETROLEUM MANAGEMENT : A course for managers in the petroleum industry including petro-economics and fiscal systems, petroleum project management, strategic management, leadership and negotiation skills, crises management.

PETROLEUM MICROBIOLOGY : Those aspects of microbiological science and engineering of interest to the petroleum industry including the role of microbes in petroleum formation and the exploration, production, manufacturing, storage and food synthesis from petroleum.

PETROLEUM REFINING : The recovery and processing of various usable fractions from the complex crude oils; usable fractions include gasoline, kerosine, diesel oil, fuel oil and asphalt.

PETROLOGY : That branch of geology which determines the constitution of rocks by investigating the chemical composition of the separate mineral ingredients of which they consist.

PETROMORPHOLOGY : See structural petrology.

PHARMACEUTICAL ANALYSIS : Physico-chemical analysis of substances used as medicines.

PHARMACEUTICAL BIOCHEMISTRY : Study of the biochemical changes induced by medicines.

PHARAMACEUTICAL BIOTECHNOLOGY : Production of medicines by employing biotechnological methods.

PHARMACEUTICAL BOTANY : Botanical study of the identification, occurrence, morphology and other features of medicinal plants.

PHARMACEUTICAL CHEMISTRY : Chemistry of drugs and of medicinal and pharmaceutical products.

PHARAMACEUTICAL EDUCATION : Imparting theoretical and practical education and training to students and prospective pharmacists and pharmaceutical scientists.

PHARMACEUTICAL ENGINEERING : Branches of engineering employed in the plant and machinery for manufacturing drugs.

PHARMACEUTICAL HERITAGE : The ancient literature and lore pertaining to medicinal plants and drugs.

PHARMACEUTICAL MANAGEMENT : Production, quality control, sales and marketing management of medicines.

PHARMACEUTICAL MARKETING : Principles and methods employed in marketing medicines, offered as a course of study.

PHAMACEUTICA SCIENCES : Sciences concerned with the study of the chemistry, properties and manufacture of medicines. See Pharmaceutical analysis, Pharmaceutical biochemistry, Pharmaceutical Biotechnology, Pharmaceutics, Pharmacognosy, Pharmacology etc.

PHARMACEUTICAL TECHNOLOGY : Study of the equipment employed in the manufacture of medicines.

PHARMCEUTICS : The science of preparing medicines including product design and development.

PHARMACODYNAMICS : Study of the mode of action of drugs in the body.

PHARMACOECONOMICS : Study of the economic aspects of manufacturing medicines and their marketing and sale including sourcing the raw materials used in the manufacture of medicines.

PHARMACOGENETICS : Study of the genetically determined variations that are revealed solely by the effects of drugs.

PHARMACOGENOMICS : Designing drugs for specific diseases and conditions on the basis of the genomic study of the organism. Also includes study of effects of drugs on specific sites of the genome.

PHARMACOGNOSY : Branch of pharmaceutics concerned with the study of medicinal properties of natural products derived primarily from plants and from animals to some extent.

PHARMACOKINETICS : Study of the effects of drug concentrations on metabolites.

PHARMACOLOGICAL SCREENING : Screening of natural inorganic and organic substances and synthetic compounds for their medicinal properties and effects and usefulness as drugs for the treatment of specific diseases.

PHARMACOLOGY : Science dealing with the nature and properties of drugs, particularly their actions.

PHAMACOTHERAPEUTICS : Study of the use of medicines in the treatment of diseases.

PHARMACY : The art of preparing and compounding medicines and of dispensing them according to the prescription of medical practitioners.

PHELLOPLASTICS : The art of modelling in cork

PHENOGENETICS : The study of the phenotypic effects of the genetic material. Also known as Physiological genetics.

PHENOLOGY : The science which treats of periodic biological phenomena in relation to climate, especially seasonal changes, from a climatologic point of view.

PHENOMENOLOGICAL SOCIOLOGY : Analysis and description of everyday life.

PHENOMENOLOGY : Psychological approach dealing with behaviour from the view point of the individual.

PHILATELY : The practice of collecting all types of postage stamps and the study of their historical and sociological significance .

PHILOLOGY : The science of language.

PHILOSOPHICAL ANTHROPOLOGY : Study of the concepts beliefs and faiths of the human race from early times in the evolution of man.

PHILOSOPHY : Attempts critically to examine concepts and to construct theory in various branches of the subject, namely ethics, logic and metaphysis.

PHILOSOPHY OF EDUCATION : Branch of educational studies which elaborates educational objectives and values. It discharges mainly the speculative, normative and critical functions.

PHLEBOLOGY : That branch of anatomy that treats of the veins.

PHONETICS : The science concerned with the sounds of human voice and the art of representing them by writing.

PHONEMICS : Study of the phonemes of a language.

PHONOLOGY : 1. The science of elementary sounds uttered by the human voice. See phonetics. 2. Study and classification of phonemes on a functional basis. 3. Theory and history of speech sounds.

PHONOSURGERY AND VOICE DISORDERS : Treatment of voice problems arising due to vocal cord disorders which may be by birth or due to trauma, injury, accident or misuse of voice. About 70% of voice problems can be corrected through Physiotherapy with a set of voice hygiene techniques and voice muscle exercises and only the rest need surgery. Information about voice hygiene would be helpful to professionals like singers, lawyers, teachers and presenters in radio and television. Constant use of voice without intermittent breaks would be a misuse of voice and needs to be corrected to maintain the personality.

PHOTOBIOLOGY : Study of the effects of quality, intensity and duration of light on living beings.

PHOTOCHEMISTRY : Study of the effects of light on chemical reactions.

PHOTOCHEMOTHERAPY : Treatment of diseases with both light and chemicals.

PHOTOCOMPOSING : Branch of printing technology concerned with composing letters by means of a photoprocess.

PHOTODYNAMIC THERAPY : A new non-invasive treatment for age-related macular degeneration a disease of the eye affecting vision of people over 50 years of age.

PHOTOFINISHING AND PHOTOLAB MANAGEMENT : Film processing, printer set up, printing practice process monitoring and quality control.

PHOTOGEOLOGY : The geologic interpretation of land forms by means of aerial photographs.

PHOTOGLYPHY : The art of engraving by which photographs and other transparent designs can be etched into steel, copper or zinc plates by the action of light and certain chemicals.

PHOTOGRAMMETRIC TECHNOLOGY : A method of surveying by means of Photography.

PHOTOLITHOGRAPHY : A technique used in the manufacture of semi conductor components, integrated circuits use.

PHOTOLOGY : Scientific study of light.

PHOTOMECHANOCHEMISTRY : A branch of polymer science that deals with chemical conversion of chemical energy into mechanical energy.

PHOTOMETRY : 1. Study of visual radiation especially the calculations of measurements of luminous intensity etc., 2. The calculation and measurement of quantities describing light such as luminous intensity, luminous flux, density of light distribution, colour, absorption factor, spectral distribution and the reflectance and transmittance of light sometimes taken to include measurement of near infra-red and near ultraviolet radiation as well as visible light.

PHOTOMICROGRAPHY : The art of photographing minute objects when magnified by means of a microscope.

PHOTONICS : Scientific study of photons.

PHRENOLOGY : Study of the human mind on the basis of presumed knowledge of the function of different parts of the brain.

PHTHISIOLOGY : Branch of science which deals with the study of tuberculosis of lungs.

PHYCOLOGY : Branch of Botany concerned with the study of algae. Also known as algology.

PHYSICAL ACOUSTICS : Study of the Physics of sound.

PHYSICAL ANTHROPOLOGY : Study of the anatomical features of human races.

PHYSICAL CHEMISTRY : Branch of chemistry concerned with the interpretation of chemical phenomena and properties in terms of underlying physical processes with the development of techniques for their investigation.

PHYSICAL CLIMATOLOGY : Major branch of climatology which deals with the exploration of climate rather than with presentation of it.

PHYSICAL EDUCATION : Branch of education concerned with athletics and sports.

PHYSICAL GEOGRAPHY : Description, analysis, classification and genetic interpretation of natural features and phenomena of earth's surface.

PHYSICAL GEOLOGY : Composition of earth and physical changes occurring in it based on the study of rocks, minerals sediments, their structure and formations and their processes of origin and alteration.

PHYSICAL MEDICINE : Branch of medicine concerned with the treatment of athlets and sports persons. See sports medicine.

PHYSICAL METALLURGY : Heat treatment, experimental metallography etc.

PHYSICAL METEOROLOGY -Optical, electrical, acoustical and thermodynamic phenomena of the atmosphere, its chemical composition; the laws of radiation and explanation of clouds and precipitation. Also known as atmospheric physics.

PHYSICAL OCEANOGRAPHY : Study of the physical aspects of the ocean, movements of the sea etc.

PHYSICAL OPTICS : The study of interaction of electromagnetic waves in the optical frequency range with material systems.

PHYSICAL ORGANIC CHEMISTRY : Study of the Physical properties of carbon compounds.

PHYSICAL SCIENCE : Also known as physics.

PHYSICAL SCIENCES : Physics, chemistry, Mathematics, Meterology, Geophysics and related sciences are grouped under physical sciences. See Natural Sciences.

PHYSICAL STRATIGRAPHY : Stratigraphy based on the physical aspects of the rocks.

PHYSICS : 1. Study of the laws that determine the structure of the universe with reference to the matter and energy of which it consists. 2. The science concerned with those aspects of nature which can be understood in terms of elementary principles and laws.

PHYSIOGNOMY : The art of discerning the character of the mind from the features of the face.

PHYSIOGRAPHY : Science concerned with earth's physical features and the causes by which they have been modified. See physical geography.

PHYSIOLOGICAL BIOPHYSICS : An area of biophysics concerned with the use of physical mechanism to explain the behaviour and functioning of living organisms or parts thereof and with response of living organisms to physical forces.

PHYSIOLOGICAL ECOLOGY : The study of the ecological processes and growth under natural or simulated environments.

PHYSIOLOGICAL GENETICS : Study of the effects of genes on physiological processes. For example, study of the physiological changes occurring due to defective genes etc. See Biochemical genetics and phenogenetics.

PHYSIOLOGICAL PSYCHOLOGY : Study of the effects of Psychological changes on physiological processes.

PHYSIOLOGY : The study of the basic activities that occur in cells and tissues of living oranisms by using physical and chemical methods. See plant physiology, animal physiology, cell physiology etc.

PHYSIOLOGY OF INSECTS : Study of the special features of insect physiology. Due to the economic importance and evolutionary significance of insects, insect physiology received considerable attention.

PHYSIOLOGY OF PROTOZOA : Study of the special features of protozoan physiology has attracted considerable attention of zoologists and allied scientists due to the importance of protozoa as pathogenic organisms causing diseases of man and animals.

PHYSIOTHERAPY : Study and treatment of muscular and bone problems by a system of massages, sometimes involving use of electrical equipment.

PHYTOCHEMISTRY : Branch of science which deals with the chemical compounds occurring in plants primarily for their medicinal value.

PHYTOCHOROLOGY : See Plant geography.

PHYTOCLIMATOLOGY : Study of the microclimate in the air space occupied by plant communities on the surfaces of plants themselves and in some eases in the air spaces within the plants.

PHYTOGENY : Study of the origin and development of plants.

PHYTOGEOGRAPHY : Study of the geographical distribution of plants and demarcation of phytogeographical zones.

PHYTOLOGY : Synonymous to botany.

PHYTOMORPHOLOGY : Branch of botany concerned with the study of morphology of plants including in a broad sense anatomy and embryology.

PHYTOPATHOLOGY : Study of plant diseases.

PHYTOREMEDIATION : It is the direct use of living plants for *in situ* recovery of contaminated soils, sludge sediments and ground water through contaminant removal or degradation. By this method both organic and in organic (metal) contaminants can be cleansed.

PHYTOSOCIOLOGY : Study of the interrelations and mutual effects of plants in a community.

PHYTOTHERAPY : Treatment of diseases using plants and their parts as drugs.

PIEZOCHEMISTRY : The study of chemical reactions under high pressures.

PILOT TRAINING : A course of study and practical training in aircraft flying given to prospective pilots.

PIPING ENGINEERING : Branch of engineering concerned with the construction of pipe lines for the transportation of water, gases and oil.

PISCICULTURE : The breeding, rearing, preservation, feeding and fattening of fish by artificial means.

PLANE ANALYTICAL GEOMETRY : Analytical geometry in the plane (in two dimensions) devoted primarily to the graphing of equations in two variables.

PLANE GEOMETRY : Geometry that treats of the properties and relations of plane figures such as angles, triangles, polygons, circles etc.

PLANETARY GEOLOGY : A science that applies geologic principles and techniques to the study of planets and their satellites. Also known as planetary geosciences.

PLANETARY GEOSCIENCE : See planetary geology.

PLANETARY SCIENCE : Scientific study of the planets. Branch of astronomy.

PLANE TRIGONOMETRY : Branch of mathematics concerned with the solution of plane triangles. See trigonometry.

PLANNED ECONOMY : An economy where crucial economic processes are determined to a large extent not by market forces but by an economic planning body which implements society's major economic goals.

PLANOMETRICS : A branch of economics specifically concerned with the construction of optimal macroeconomic plans.

PLANT ANATOMY : Branch of botany concerned with the study of the internal structure of the plant body comprising root, stem, leaf etc See wood anatomy.

PLANTATION CROPS : Study of commercial crops like tea, coffee cocoa, coconut, rubber, topioca etc., which are grown as plantations; considered as a branch of economic botany, agriculture and horticulture.

PLANTATION MANAGEMENT : Technical and commercial aspects of management of plantations and computer applications.

PLANT BEHAVIOUR : Study of behaviour of plants in response to external factors as well as towards one another.

PLANT BIOCHEMISTRY : Study of biochemical pathways of plant metabolic processes like respiration, photosynthesis, hormone synthesis etc.

PLANT BIOTECHNOLOGY : Production of transgenic crops by introducing desired genes for the synthesis of drugs and vaccines and disease and pest resistance and improvement of crop yield and quality.

PLANT BIOLOGY : Branch of biology concerned with the study of plant life. Also known as botany, plant sciences, phytology.

PLANT BREEDING : Breeding new varieties of crop plants by means of selection, hybridization, mutation breeding, radiations etc, to obtain higher yields, better quality disease and pest resistance and other desirable qualities.

PLANT CHEMISTRY : See phytochemistry.

PLANT DESIGN : Design of engineering plants for the manufacture of sugar, cement, paper, electric power, drugs etc.

PLANT ECOLOGY : Study of the ecological factors, ecosystem etc, with particular reference to plants.

PLANT EMBRYOLOGY : Branch of botany concerned with the formation and development of the embryo in plants.

PLANT ENGINEERING : Branch of engineering concerned with the manufacture and maintenance of production and processing plants for use in industry.

PLANT GENETIC RESOURCES : Study of plant genetic resources involves extensive collections of wild and cultivated species of plants and the preservation of their germplasm for their future application in plant breeding and evolutionary studies on the geographical distribution and on primary centres of origin of plant species.

PLANT GENETICS : Study of inheritance, variation, mutation and other genetic phenomena in plants. This plays an important role in plant breeding and plant biotechnology.

PLANT GENETIC TRANSFORMATION : Plant genetic transformation can be brought about by the use of mutagenic chemicals, x-rays and other types of radiations for use in plant breeding. Certain amount of genetic transformation occurs in nature also due to the influence of various factors and due to natural hybridization.

PLANT GENOMICS : Study of the complete nucleotide sequences of the genomes of plants. Such studies are very useful in biotechnology.

PLANT GEOGRAPHY : A major division of botany concerned with all aspects of the spatial distribution of plants. Also known as geographical botany, phytochorology, and phytogeography.

PLANT GROWTH REGULATORS : Auxins, cytokinins, gibberellins, various growth inhibitors etc., are examples of natural plant regulators. Also known as plant hormones, they influence various aspects plant growth and development like seed germination, flowering, fruiting etc.

PLANT HORMONE PHYSIOLOGY : Physiological study of the mode of action and regulation of plant hormones in plant life.

PLANT MAINTENANCE : Branch of engineering concerned with the maintenance and repair of plant and machinery.

PLANT MOLECULAR BIOLOGY : Study of nucleic acids, protein synthesis and gene mutation in plants.

PLANT NEMATOLOGY : Study of nematode parasites of plants, which cause crop losses. Branch of plant pathology. Application in agriculture.

PLANT NUTRITION : Study of the mineral nutrition of plants including essentiality of elements, deficiency symptoms, effects and dosage requirements. Knowledge of plant nutrition is essential for proper fertilizer application to agricultural crops.

PLANT PATHOLOGY : Study of plant diseases and their control methods. Essential for the control of diseases of agricultural crops.

PLANT PHYSIOLOGY : Study of physiological processes of plants like respiration, photosynthesis, water uptake and transpiration, mineral nutrition, nitrogen metabolism, flowering, seed germination etc. Application in agriculture.

PLANT PROTECTION : Branch of agriculture concerned with protection of crops from diseases and pests caused by viruses, bacteria, fungi, insects, rodents birds etc.

PLANT REPRODUCTIVE ECOLOGY : Study of the ecological factors governing plant reproductive processes like flowering, pollination, fertilization, seed formation, dispersal, germination, growth of seedlings and vegetative reproduction.

PLANT SCIENCES : Plant morphology and anatomy, plant physiology, plant taxonomy, plant ecology, plant genetics, economic botany, plant biotechnology, plant biochemistry, economic botany etc are known as plant sciences.

PLANT SYSTEMATICS : The science of classification of plants. See systematic botany.

PLANT TAXOMONY : A study aimed at producing a hierarchical system of classification of plants which best reflects the totality of similarities and differences. See Taxonomic botany.

PLANT TERATOLOGY : That branch of botany that deals with monsters and malformations of plants.

PLANT TISSUE CULTURE : Culturing plant cells, tissues and organs in nutrient media under sterile conditions.

PLANT VIROLOGY : That branch of plant pathology that deals with plant diseases caused by viruses example : tobacco mosaic virus.

PLASMA DIAGNOSTIC TECHNIQUES : Use of plasma characteristics and their changes in diagnosis of disease.

PLASMA KINETIC SURGERY : Using radio frequency delivered technology to remove and modify the excess body tissues that have accumulated in the prostate and other areas, using minimal access techniques. See plasma kinetic technology.

PLASMA KINETIC TECHNOLOGY : It uses the conductive property of fluids to distend the operative site during medical procedure of plasma kinetic surgery. It also provides the surgeon the ability to control and adjust the power being used in microseconds. The technology also seals the blood vessels as it cuts thus preventing bleeding. See plasmakinetic surgery.

PLASMA PHYSICS : Study of highly ionised gas in which the number of free ions is approximately equal to the number of positive ions. The term plasma refers to the ionised state of matter at high temperatures of about one million degrees and finds applications in many technological and commercial fields.

PLASTIC ENGINEERING : Engineering concerned with the manufacture of plastic and plastic goods like mould making mould design, testing, plastic product design etc.

PLASTIC MOULDS DESIGN : Design of moulds used in the manufacture of plastic goods.

PLASTICS PROCESSING : Processing used to manufacture different types of plastic and plastic foods and machining.

PLASTIC SURGERY : It is a specialized branch of medicine that deals with the restoration of the form and function of the body to make life more wholesome. This includes restoring normalcy to an abnormal body part, correcting deformities and disfigurements, recreating missing body parts and resurfacing and covering wounds of varying depths.

PLASTICS TECHNOLOGY : Technology of manufacturing various goods from plastics including plastic processing etc, use of computer software like CAD, CAM etc in plastics technology.

PLATE TECTONICS : Branch of geology dealing with the movement of the earth's crust in the form of plates. It is now a widely accepted view of the structure of the earth.

PLAY THERAPY : Use of specially designed toys and materials for the diagnosis and treatment of handicapped children specially in case of maladjustments.

PLUMBING : Branch of engineering concerned with laying pipelines for water supply and sewage drainage in buildings.

PLUTOLOGY : Study of the interior of the earth.

PNEUMATICS : Study of the behavious of a gas in a closed systems.

PODIATRICS : Branch of medicine concerned with the treatment of foot disorders.

POETICS : That branch of literary criticism which treats of the nature and laws of poetry.

POLARIMETRY : The art of measuring or analysing the polarization of light.

POLAR METEOROLOGY : Meteorology of polar regions.

POLAROGRAPHY : Measurement of the concentration in solution from current generated by appropriate electrodes immersed in it.

POLAR SCIENCE : Scientific study of the polar regions of the earth.

POLICE PERSONNEL MANAGEMENT : Management of the personnel of the police force.

POLICE STUDIES : Study of the working of the police force in maintaining law and order, liberty, property and individual security and in investigating crimes and nabbing criminals. Study of the methods of maintaining fitness and discipline among police personnel and use of latest weapons and armament and carrying out specialized tasks assigned to them from time to time.

POLISHING AND GRINDING : Processes used in the engineering and optical industries.

POLITICAL AND ECONOMIC JOURNALISM : Branch of journalism specializing in political and economic affairs.

POLITICAL ECONOMY : The term has connotations of the interrelationship between the practical aspects of political action and the pure theory of economic. It is the science of the laws which regulate the production, distribution and consumption of products necessary, useful or agreeable to man which it requires some portion of voluntary labour to produce, procure or preserve.

POLITICAL EDUCATION : Education in the problems, affairs and methods of government.

POLITICAL GEOGRAPHY : Treats of the states and peoples of the earth and their political and social characteristics.

POLITICAL HISTORY : History of political changes and developments which took place in the world in the past.

POLITICAL SCIENCE : The science which relates to the regulation and government of a nation or state for the preservation of its safety, peace and prosperity.

POLITICAL SOCIOLOGY : The social structure and relations of people from the political point of view can be studied at 5 levels ; 1. Sociology of international relations. 2. Nature and role of state within societies, 3. Political movements and parties, 4. Participation of individuals in politics. 5. The relationships of people living out of the countries of their origin with one another and with the parent country.

POLYMER CHEMISTRY : Synthesis and characterization of polymers like plastics.

POLYMER ENGINEERING : Engineering used in the development and production of synthetic polymers like plastic and fibers.

POLYMER SCIENCE : Study of structure and characterization of natural polymers like proteins, nucleic acids, cellulose and synthetic polymers like plastics and fibres.

POLYMER TECHNOLOGY : Utilization of polymers like plastics and various synthetic fibres for the production of products useful to man.

POLYTRAUMA MANAGEMENT : Branch of medicine concerned with the treatment of multiple injuries.

POMOLOGY : Branch of horticulture concerned with the cultivation of fruit trees and fruit production and preservation.

POPULATION DYNAMICS : Study of the fluctuations that occur in the numbers of individuals in animal and plant populations and factors controlling these fluctuations.

POPULATION EDUCATION : Education regarding the consequences of uncontrolled population growth and methods of containing population explosion.

POPULATION GENETICS : 1. Study of distribution of inherited variation among a group of organisms of the same species, 2. The study of both experimental and theoretical consequences of mendelian heredity on the population level, including studies of gene sequences, genotypes, phenotypes and mating system.

POPULATION SCIENCE : Scientific study of increase and decrease of population and factors governing population growth on a global scale.

POPULATION STUDIES : Study of the trends of population growth, consequences, problems and remedies.

PORTFOLIO MANAGEMENT : Study of investment avenues, variations in share prices, business trends and taking appropriate decisions regarding investments.

PORT MANAGEMENT : Management of a port or harbour where ships are anchored and where loading and unloading operations are carried out. It includes traffic management, information management, financial administration, personnel management, medical and health care, environment, pollution and crisis; civil, materials and maintenance engineering.

PORTS AND HARBOUR ENGINEERING : Branch of engineering concerned with the construction, maintenance and operation of ports and harbours.

POSITIONAL ASTRONOMY : The science which studies the relative positions of the stars and planets from day to day as viewed from various places on the earth.

POSITIVE ECONOMICS : That part of economic science which is concerned with statements that can be verified by reference to the facts. In principle, all positive statements should be reducible to some form which is testable by reference to empirical evidence.

POSOLOGY : Study of dosage of medicines.

POST-HARVEST TECHNOLOGY : Methods of processing, preserving and storing agricultural produce after harvest, building godowns, cold-storage facilities etc., to minimise post-harvest crop losses.

POTAMOLOGY : The science of rivers.

POTENTIOMETRY : Use of Potentiometer to measure electromotive forces and the application of such measurements.

POTTERY : The art of making earthenware articles including glazing, and baking. Ornamental articles and vessels are made by this method.

POULTARY BREEDING : Methods of breeding better varieties of poultry.

POULTRY FEEDING : Branch of poultry science concerned with preparing nutritious, balanced feeds to poultry birds.

POULTRY GENETICS : Study of the inheritance of especially economically desirable characters of poultry.

POULTRY HEALTHCARE : Branch of poultry science concerned with the study of poultry diseases and their treatment and taking care of their health and well-being.

POULTRY MARKETING : Study of methods of wholesale and retail marketing of eggs, chicken and other poultry products including popularising their use in the population.

POULTRY SCIENCE : Study of domestic fouls which are reared for their flesh as an article of food, for their eggs, feathers etc such as cocks, hen, turkeys ducks and gees, methods of rearing them, their nutritional requirements and diseases.

POWDER METALLURGY : A process in which powdered metals or alloys are pressed into a variety of shapes at high temperatures.

POWER DEVICES : Branch of electric engineering concerned with devices employed for power generation.

POWER ELECTRONICS : 1. Study of electronics used in electric equipment. It has applications in industry. 2. Design and development of AC/DC converters and switch over power supplies, selection of optimum power conversion topology, design of high frequency magnets for use in power converters. High frequency power conversion techniques such as soft switching, resonant power conversion using CAE tools such as saber, metlab, and mathcad to simulate and analyse power circuits; motor/inverter control algorithms. Design of power electronic circuitary.

POWER PLANT CHEMISTRY : Study of corrosion and erosion in thermal power plants and methods of curbing them.

POWER PLANT ENGINEERING : Branch of electrical engineering concerned with electricity generating plants, their manufacture and maintenance.

POWER SYSTEMS : Study of hydro, thermal, nuclear and other types of power systems.

PRANIC HEALING : A method of healing in which energy is taken form the air, sun and the earth. After removing the diseased energy from the patient's body, the treatment is started. After the first sitting/counseling session the patient need not be present in front of the healer. The patient may be thousands of miles away and still the treatment can be given.

PRAWN AND CRAB FARMING : Methods of rearing prawns and crabs on a commercial scale for utilization as food.

PRAXIOLOGY : Practice or discipline to be followed for a specific purpose such as to acquire a specific art.

PRECIPITATION PHYSICS : Study of formation and precipitation of solid and liquid hydrometeors from clouds; a branch of cloud physics.

PREDICTIVE MEDICINE : Branch of medicine in which carriers for genetic disorders are identified and forewarned well in advance of the clinical eventualities. This could result in these individuals avoiding certain risk factors. It is a form of additional medical surveillance. It is an emerging field.

PREHISTORIC ARCHAEOLOGY : Study of those cultures which did not have written records. It is often used to refer to the study of neolithic and palaeolithic deposits.

PREHISTORY : Study of history from the beginning of hominid existence to early food gathering cultures some of which dated to around 1400 B.C.

PRESEA TRAINING : A course for cadets on the deck of a ship as a preparation for a career in the navy.

PRE-SCHOOL EDUCATION : Branch of education concerned with educating children before the school-going age.

PRESS TOOL DESIGN : Designing tools for use in a machine called press by which any body is squeezed, crushed or forced into a more compact form. Example : hydraulic press.

PREVENTIVE AND PROMOTIVE HEALTH CARE : Life style is the major killer today and manifests itself in heart disease, cancer, AIDS, accidents etc., which account for 80 per cent mortality world wide. The subject covers topics such as cardiac care, cancer risk management, disease management, health management, health Psychology, stress management, exercise and fitness, nutrition and diet, life style management etc, in populations and communities.

PREVENTIVE CARDIOLOGY : Branch of cardiology concerned with measures to be taken to prevent heart diseases.

PREVENTIVE DENTISTRY : Branch of dentistry concerned with the care of the teeth with a view to prevent dental diseases and problems.

PREVENTIVE MEDICINE : Deals with measures for reduction of disease and disability in populations and communities. Nearly equal to public health.

PREVENTIVE ONCOLOGY : Branch of oncology concerned with measures and precautions to be taken to prevent cancer.

PRICE THEORY : One of the main branches of economics concerned with price fluctuations and factors affecting them and their effect on the economy.

PRIMATE PALAENTOLOGY : Branch of paleontology concerned with the study of the fossils of primates and the evolution of primates based on fossil studies.

PRIMATOLOGY : Branch of zoology concerned with the study of primates, generally non-human primates like apes, monkeys chimpanzees, gorillas etc.

PRINTING ENGINEERING : Branch of engineering concerned with the manufacture and maintenance of printing machines.

PRINTING TECHNOLOGY : By the term printing what is called letter press printing was commonly understood, that is the method of taking impressions from letters and other characters cast or cut in relief whether directly from the type surface or stereotype plates. But in modern times many advanced technologies of printing have come into use like offset printing, desk top printing, laser printing etc.

PRINT JOURNALISM : Branch of journalism concerned with printed newspapers and magazines as contrasted with radio and T.V. journalism.

PRINT MAKING : A form of art.

PRISON ADMINISTRATION : A branch of criminology meant to train prison staff in management of prisoners and their rehabilitation by training them in vocational or job oriented trades like gardening, carpentory.

PROCESS CONTROL AND INSTRUMENTATION : Branch of chemical engineering and control engineering including modern control theory transducers and sophisticated instrumentation, neural networks, fuzzy, logic etc.

PROCESS ENGINEERING : Branch of engineering concerned with industrial processes.

PROCESS EQUIPMENT DESIGN : Design and valuation of process equipments relating to plating, printing etc.

PROCESSING AND PRESERVATION OF FRUITS AND VEGETABLES : Post-Harvest technology concerned with the processing of fruits and vegetables and food products prepared from them.

PROCESSING OF POULTARY PRODUCTS : Branch of poultry science concerned with the processing and preparation of poultry products like eggs, meat etc., for food and other uses.

PROCESS METALLURGY : Concerned with the extraction and production of metals.

PROCTOLOGY : Branch of medicine concerned with disorders of the rectum and excretion of faeces, for example, haemarroids, fissures etc.

PRODUCT DESIGN : Design of industrial products for maximum utility and convencience.

PRODUCTION ENGINEERING : Planning of production and control of processes to be carried out.

PRODUCTION MANAGEMENT : Management of various departments involved in production industry.

PRODUCTIVITY MANAGEMENT : Management techniques to increase productivity in industries involving shop floor personnel management, manufacturing maintenance, industrial engineering and applied engineering.

PRODUCTIVITY SCIENCES : See productivity management.

PROFESSIONAL MARKETING : Taking up marketing of goods and services as a profession.

PROFESSIONAL ACCOUNTING : Practice of accounting as a profession, as for example, the profession of chartered accountants.

PROFESSIONAL AND ORGANIZATIONAL ETHICS AND VALUES : Theoretical aspects of moral philosophy pertaining to professional and organizational ethics apart from application aspects of ethics in business, medical area and media.

PROGRAMMING : The task of programming is coding, testing and debugging. A programmer writes instructions in the form of a code using computer languages. Programming helps in developing software.

PROJECT ENGINEERING MANAGEMENT : Branch of engineering concerned with management of projects.

PROJECT EVALUATION AND ANALYSIS : Branch of engineering concerned with the evaluation and analysis of projects.

PROJECT FINANCING AND APPRAISAL : Evaluation of market, assessment of managerial capabilities, technical and financial aspects, financial institutions, capital, software projects etc.

PROJECT MANAGEMENT : Branch of management science concerned with the management of specific projects particularly in the field of information technology.

PROPERTY LAW : Law pertaining to various aspects of property like inheritance, ownership, sale, lease, purchase, mortgage etc., of both movable and immovable property.

PROPOSAL ENGINEERING : Preparing proposals for engineering projects and works.

PROSODY : Study of versification in all its aspects like meter, rhythm, rhyme etc.

PROSPECTING SEISMOLOGY : Application of seismology or the study of earthquakes to the exploration of natural resources especially gas and petroleum.

PROSTHETICS : Technology of devices for replacing organs or parts of body.

PROSTHODONTICS : Branch of dentistry concerned with partial and complete restorations of fixed and removable dentures.

PROSTHOTIC AND ORTHOTIC ENGINEERING : Engineering applied to the manufacture of artificial limbs.

PROSTRATIGRAPHY : Preliminary stratigraphy including lithologic and palaeontologic studies.

PROTEIN AND ENZYME ENGINEERING : Altering chemical structure and physical properties of proteins and enzymes in specific ways to bring about desired changes in their biological properties.

PROTEIN CHEMISTRY : Physical and chemical structure and properties of proteins as a class of chemical substances.

PROTEIN MODELLING AND DRUG DESIGN : Preparing models of proteins and designing drugs to be compatible to each other in an attempt to discover new drugs for specific diseases.

PROTEIN SCIENCE AND ENGINEERING : Covers structure-function relationships, protein design; expression and characterization of novel proteins, protein folding, X-rays, crystallography.

PROTEOMICS : Determination of amino acid sequences in proteins.

PROTOHISTORIC ARCHAEOLOGY : Study of cultures which date from the dawn of history.

PROTOZOOLOGY : Branch of zoology concerned with the primitive phylum protozoa.

PSEPHOLOGY : Study of elections particularly of voting behaviour.

PSYCHIATRIC GENETICS : Study of inheritance and genetic basis of psychiatric behaviour and disorders.

PSYCHIATRIC GERIATRICS : Branch of psychiatry concerned with the treatment of psychiatric disorders and behaviour problems of old people.

PSYCHIATRIC NURSING : Branch of nursing concerned with the nursing of psychiatric patients.

PSYCHIATRIC SOCIAL WORK : Branch of social work concerned with the welfare and care of psychiatric patients in the community.

PSYCHIATRY : Medical treatment of the diseases of the mind.

PSYCHOANALYSIS : A system of psychology and a method of treatment of mental and nervous disorders developed by Sigmund Freud.

PSYCHOBIOLOGY : The investigation of psychological problems in the field of general biology.

PSYCHODYNAMICS : The study of mental and developmental processes from a dynamic point of view as a branch of psychology.

PSYCHODYNAMIC THEORY : Active psychotherapy designed to produce substantial personality changes.

PSYCHOENDOCRINOLOGY : Branch of endocrinology concerned with the study of the effect of endocrine hormones on psychology.

PSYCHOGERIATRICS : Study of psychological problems of elderly people.

PSYCHOKINESIS : Study of psychological changes as reflected by body movements.

PSYCHOLOGICAL COUNSELLING : Professional and technical guidance by experts in solving psychological and relationships problems.

PSYCHOLOGICAL MEDICINE : See psychiatry.

PSYCHOLOGY : Science of the mind derived from a careful examination of the facts of consciousness and from the study of the functioning of the brain.

PSYCHOLOGY AND PUBLIC RELATIONS : Role of psychological studies in public relations.

PSYCHOLOGY OF INDIVIDUAL DIFFERENCES : Study of psychological difference between individuals.

PSYCHOMETRICS : Mathematical or measurement aspects of psychological experiments. More recently applied to statistical treatment of mental tests.

PSYCHONOMICS : 1. Branch of psychology which studies the relation of the individual particularly in his development to his environment, physical and social. 2. The maximization of one's ability to evaluate fundamental and weightless factors of an investment while minimising any tendency to make systematic errors.

PSYCHONOSOLOGY : That branch of medical science which treats of the nature and classification of mental diseases.

PSYCHOPATHOLOGY : Study of all mental factors which are related to personality disturbances and mental abnormalities.

PSYCHOPHARMACOLOGY : Study of mental effects of drugs.

PSYCHOPHYSICS : Branch of experimental psychology which investigates the functional and quantitative relations between physical stimuli and sensory events.

PSYCHOSOMATIC MEDICINE : A method of treatment according to which the main causes of bodily disease symptoms of an individual are mental and emotional factors.

PSYCHOSOMATICS : Correlation of psychological phenomena, normal, abnormal or pathological with somatic or bodily conditions.

PSYCHOSURGERY : Operative treatment designed to correct psychological disease.

PSYCHOTECHNOLOGY : Application of psychology to practical problems.

PSYCHOTHERAPY : Treatment of neuroses and personality disorders by dialogue with therapist designed to improve insights and modify emotional responses.

PTERIDOLOGY : Branch of botany concerned with the study of pteridophytes including lycopods, horsetails and ferms : living and extinct.

PTERILOGRAPHY : Description of the feathers of birds and the manner in which they are arranged on their bodies.

PUBLIC ADMINISTRATION : Study of the working of the government departments, their duties, responsibilities and rules and regulations governing the conduct of administration.

PUBLIC EXPENDITURE MANAGEMENT : Study of the management of government expenditure at the state, central and international level.

PUBLIC FINANCE : A branch of economics concerned with identification and appraisal of effects of government financial policies. There are at least 3 functions of public finance ; 1. Allocation function; 2. Distribution function; 3. Stabilization function.

PUBLIC HEALTH : Branch of health science concerned with safe guarding the health of the people by taking precautionary and preventive measures to check the spread of infectious diseases like cholera, malaria, plague etc.

PUBLIC HEALTH ADMINISTRATION : Administration of public health measures like vaccination, sanitation etc.

PUBLIC HEALTH ENGINEERING : Branch of engineering concerned with public health measures like laying sewage lines waste disposal, control of environmental pollution, supply of safe drinking water etc.

PUBLIC INTEREST LAW : Law pertaining to issues of public interest as opposed to individual interest.

PUBLIC PERSONNEL MANAGEMENT : Formulation and implementation of service conditions and regulations of government employees.

PUBLIC RELATIONS : Study of the methods employed to ensure that the public is given the most favourable impression of the company, or government's or institution's aims, policy and performance.

PUBLIC SPEAKING AND COMMUNICATION SKILLS : A course of instruction and training in public speaking and the skill of communicating with others.

PULMONARY MEDICINE : Branch of medicine concerned with the treatment of diseases of lungs like tuberculosis, asthma, bronchitis etc.

PULMONARY PHYSIOLOGY : Physiology of lung function and how it is affected by various factors.

PULMONARY RADIOLOGY : Use of radiological techniques in the diagnosis and treatment of pulmonary diseases.

PULMONARY TOXICOLOGY : Study of the effects of toxic substances on lungs and their functioning.

PULMONOLOGY : Branch of medicine concerned with the structure and functioning of lungs and prevention and treatment of lung disorders. See Pulmonary medicine.

PULP AND PAPER TECHNOLOGY : Technology of manufacture of pulp from various raw materials and of a variety of papers like writing paper, printing paper, newsprint etc.

PULSE DIGITAL CIRCUIT- Branch of electronics and communication engineering.

PULSES : Branch of agriculture concerned with the cultivation and breeding of pulse crops like black gram, green gram, bengal gram, red gram etc.

PUMP ENGINEERING : Branch of engineering concerned with the manufacture, operation and maintenance of pumps like water pumps, petrol pumps, gas pumps etc.

PURCHASE MANAGEMENT : Procurement of components as per design and specifications, ensure deliveries on just-in-time basis, involvement in cost reduction and value engineering proposals, materials planning, procurement and inventory systems including raw material, chemicals, machinery etc., for manufacturing plants.

PURE MATHEMATICS : Study of the principles of mathematics, for their own sake and future usefulness rather than for immediate usefulness in other fields of knowledge.

PYROLOGY : The science of heat.

PYROMETALLURGY : Chemical metallurgy depending on heat action

PYROMETRY : The science and technology of measuring high temperatures.

PYROTECHNICS : 1. The art of making fireworks. 2. The use of artificial pyrotechnics. 3. The management and application of fire in various operations.

Q

QUADRATICS : A branch of algebra concerned with equations.

QUALITY CONTROL : To check that the desired quality of the product is being maintained. It involves the use of various physical, chemical, biological, engineering and other methods for this purpose.

QUALITY MANAGEMENT : Procuring quality materials and other inputs and ensuring high standards of quality of products in industry, manufacturing process or agribusiness.

QUANTITATIVE BUSINESS ANALYSIS : Analysis of various business sectors like investment, expenditure, sales, purchases, profit, loss etc., in quantitative terms.

QUANTITATIVE ECONOMICS : Application of mathematical and statistical principles to economic analysis.

QUANTITATIVE GEOMORPHOLOGY : The assignment of dimensions of mass, length and time to all descriptive parameters of land form, geometry and geomorphic processes.

QUANTITATIVE TECHNIQUES IN MANAGEMENT : Application of mathematical and statistical principles and methods to management.

QUANTUM CHEMISTRY : 1. Study of wave- particle duality, uncertainty principle and angular momentum, 2. A branch of physical chemistry concerned with the explanation of chemical phenomena by means of the laws of quantum mechanics.

QUANTUM CHROMODYNAMICS : Describes what goes on inside protons and neutrons, the building blocks of the nucleus.

QUANTUM ELECTRODYNAMICS : The study of the properties of electromagnetic radiation and the way of which it interacts with charged matter in terms of quantum mechanics.

QUANTUM MECHANICS : The modern theory of matter, electromagnetic radiation and of the interaction between matter and radiation; it differs from classical physics which it generalizes and supersedes, mainly in the realm of atomic and subatomic phenomena.

QUANTUM OPTICS : The study of the properties of light like wave particle duality based on quantum theory.

QUANTUM PHYSICS : Study of wave particle duality, Heisenberg uncertainty principle etc.

QUANTUM THEORY : The theory devised by Max Plank in 1900 to account for the emission of the black body radiation from hot bodies. See quantum mechanics.

R

RADAR : Short form for Radio detection and ranging. Radar allows pilots and navigators to see through a fog or through darkness. It is also used to map weather systems and storms.

RADAR ASTRONOMY : Astronomy that deals with investigations of the celestial bodies of the solar system by comparing characteristics of reflected radar waves with characteristics of those transmitted from earth.

RADAR METEOROLOGY : Study of the scattering of radar waves by all types of atmospheric phenomena and the use of radar for making weather observations and forecasts.

RADIATION AND ISOTOPE TECHNOLOGY : Design and fabrication of radiation technology equipment like radiography cameras, gamma chambers, sealed radiation sources for teletherapy and brachy theraphy, blood irradiation, setting up plants for sterilization of medical products, preservation of foods and spices, radiation processing services, processing and supply of diagnostic and the therapeutic radio pharmaceuticals and radio immuno and immuno radiometric assay kits.

RADIATION BIOCHEMISTRY : The study of the responses of constituents of living matter to radiation.

RADIATION BIOLOGY : Study of the effects of radiations on living beings.

RADIATION BIOPHYSICS : The study of the response of organisms to ionizing radiations and to ultraviolet lights.

RADIATION CHEMISTRY : The branch of chemistry that is concerned with the chemical effects, including decomposition, of energetic radiation or particles on matter.

RADIATION CYTOLOGY : An aspect of biology that deals with the effects of radiations on living cells.

RADIATION GENETICS : Study of the effects of radiations on genes and genetically controlled characters of organisms; also known as radio genetics.

RADIATION MICRO BIOLOGY : A field of basic and applied radiobiology concerned chiefly with the damaging effects of radiation on micro organisms.

RADIATION ONCOLOGY : Study of the effects of radiation on cancer cells and tumors.

RADIATION PHYSICS : Study of the nature and characteristics of radiations of different wave lengths and their effects on matter.

RADIATION THERAPHY : Study of therapeutic properties of radations of different wave lengths for the treatment of cancer and other diseases.

RADICAL ECONOMICS : The generic name for writing in a socialist or marxist tradition relating in the main to marxism but adopting and using other sources of ideas such as anarchism and libertarianism.

RADIO : 1. The technique of communicating by radio waves, 2. The business of broadcasting programmed material to the public via radio waves.

RADIO ACTIVE WASTE MANGEMENT : An active field of study concerned with the management and disposal of radio active waste materials arising from various sources like nuclear reactors, nuclear power plants, radioisotope using laboratories, hospitals etc.

RADIO ASTRONOMY : The study of the radio frequency radiation emitted by celestial bodies.

RADIO BIOLOGY : 1. Branch of biology concerned with the effects of radioactive substances on living organisms and the use of radio active tracers to study metabolic processes. 2. Study of the scientific principles, mechanisms and effects of the interaction of ionizing radiation with living matter. Also known as radiation biology.

RADIO CHEMISTRY : Branch of chemistry concerned with radio active compounds and with ionization.

RADIOCLIMATOLOGY : Study of regional and seasonal variations in the manner of propagation of radio energy through the atmosphere.

RADIO DIAGNOSIS : The science of diagnosing diseases by making use of radiations like X-rays and radio-active isotopes.

RADIO ECOLOGY : The interdisciplinary study of organisms, radio nucleides, ionizing radiation and the environment.

RADIO ENGINEERING : Branch of engineering concerned with the manufacture of radios, their maintenance and repairs.

RADIO FREQUENCY THERMOTHERAPHY : Treatment (especially cancer) by local induction heating to about 45°C

RADIOGENETICS : See radiation genetics.

RADIOGEOLOGY : Study of distribution patterns of radioactive elements in the earth's crust and the role of radio active processes in geological phenomena.

RADIOGRAPHIC AND IMAGING ENGINEERING : Branch of biomedical engineering specializing in X-ray and ultra sound equipment.

RADIOGRAPHY : The process of producing images of an opaque object on photographic film or on a fluorescent screen by means of radiation such as X-rays and gamma rays.

RADIOHYDROLOGY : The study of hydrologic relationships of extraction, processing and use (including use in hydrologic investigations) of radioactive materials and the disposal of associated waste products.

RADIO IMMUNOTHERAPY : Treatment of immunological disorders with the use of radiations and radio active substances.

RADIO JOURNALISM : Branch of journalism concerned with the preparation of reports, features, discussions, talks etc., for broadcast on the radio.

RADIOLOGICAL PHYSICS : Branch of physics concerned with the study of radiations like x-rays, gamma rays etc., and of radio activity.

RADIOLOGY : The study and use of X-rays, radioactive materials and other ionizing radiations for medical purposes especially for diagnosis and treatment of cancer and allied diseases.

RADIO MECHANISM : A course for technicians in radio repairing.

RADIO METEOROLOGY : That branch of meterology which embraces the propagation of radio-energy through the atmosphere and the use of radio and radar equipment in meteorology.

RADIOMETERY : The detection and measurement of radiant electromagnetic energy, especially that associated with infrared radiation.

RADIO PHARMACEUTICALS : Manufacture of medicines containing radio active substances for the treatment of cancer and allied diseases.

RADIO TELEMETRY : Monitoring ambulant patients using radio transmission of signals.

RADIO THERAPY : Treatment of diseases by using ionizing radiations and radioactive substances.

RADIO THERAPY TECHNOLOGY : The technology of delivering ionizing radiations and administering radio active substances for radiotherapy.

RAIL TRANSPORT MANAGEMENT : Management of transportation of goods and people by railways.

RAILWAY ENGINEERING : Branch of engineering concerned with the construction of railway track.

RAILWAY SIGNALLING : The system of signals to regulate rail traffic.

RAMAN SPECTROSCOPY : 1. Light from a laser is passed though a substance and the scattering is analysed spectroscopically. It is used as a means of determining molecular structure and as a tool in chemical analysis, 2. Analysis of the intensity of Raman scattering of monochromatic light as a function of the frequency of the scattered light.

RAPID PRODUCT DEVELOPMENT : It covers the entire cycle of product development and management. It adopts multidisciplinary approach to the innovative and/or processes from a systems perspective.

REACTION KINETICS : Branch of chemistry concerned with rates of chemical reactions and the factors affecting them. See chemical kinetics.

REACTOR PHYSICS : The science of the interaction of the elementary particles and radiations characteristics of nuclear reactors with matter in bulk.

READY REFERENCE : Branch of library science concerned with preparing an index of books so as to facilitate supplying books and journals to readers for reference at short notice.

REAL ESTATE DEVELOPMENT AND MANAGEMENT : The business of developing land by creating infrastructure facilities like roads etc, and selling plots and sites and buildings.

RECOMBINANT DNA TECHNOLOGY : The technology of production of genetic strains in which elements of DNA of one line of discent are replaced by those of another line or additional elements.

RECONSTRUCTIVE SURGERY : It is a kind of plastic surgery which includes all procedures adopted in plastic surgery done to restore form and function by correcting deformities and disfigurements. Examples; cleft lip repair, reconstruction of a thumb.

RECORD MANAGEMENT AND ARCHIVES ADMINISTRATION : Maintenance and preservation of old records and archives and making them available for reference for research purposes.

REFERENCE SERVICE : Branch of library science concerned with the supply of dictionaries, encyclopaedias and other reference books to readers.

REFERENCE TOOLS : Branch of library science concerned with reference books, microfilms, computer discs etc.

REFINING TECHNOLOGY : Technology of refining crude oils, especially petroleum refining.

REFLEXOLOGY : A system of treatment based on the belief that every part of the body is reflected in the hands and feet. By applying pressure at specific points at these two places diseases are supposed to be treated.

REFRACTOMETRY : The measurement of the index of refraction of a substance; it is an important tool in analytical chemistry.

REFRACTORIES TECHNOLOGY : Substances which resist ordinary treatment such as metals that are difficult of fusion are known as refractories. Methods of utilizing such materials for useful purposes come under this technology.

REFRIGERATION ENGINEERING : Engineering concerned with the manufacture of machines like refrigerators for a supply of ice, to keep provisions cool in warm weather.

REGIONAL ANATOMY : The detailed study of a part or region of the body of an animal.

REGIONAL ECONOMICS : It is that branch of economic analysis which is concerned with the spatial distribution of economic activity and spatial variations in levels of economic performance. The subject can be split in the usual way into macroeconomic and micro economic topics. In regional macro economics the analysis is usually carried out in terms of the comparative economic performance of a number of regions within a national economy. Regional microeconomics is concerned with the location and interaction of particular economic activities.

REGIONAL GEOLOGY : Geology of a large region of the earth.

REGIONAL PLANNING : Preparation of a plan for the development of a large region within a country or a group of small countries.

REHABILITATION : Study of the methods of rehabilitation of displaced and physically and mentally handicapped persons.

REHABILITATION PSYCHOLOGY : Study of the psychology of people who are in need of rehabilitation and who are being rehabilitated.

REHABILITATION SOCIAL WORK : Social work concerned with rehabilitation of persons who are in need of rehabilitation and who are being rehabilitated.

REHABILITATION THERAPY : Treatment of physically and mentally handicapped persons aimed at making their lives better.

REHABILITATIVE MEDICINE : Exercise solutions for preventing, delaying and in some cases reversing the onset of major diseases and disabilities.

REIKI : Japanese word meaning universal life energy defined as that power which acts and lives in all created matter. The transfer of universal and all pervading life energy and its use for healing the body and harmonise the soul is the principle involved in the practice of Reiki.

RELATIVE CHRONOLOGY : The practice of dating archaeological finds relatively to each other even though the age in terms of years is not correctly known.

RELATIVISTIC THERMODYNAMICS : The study of the interaction between charged particles and electronic and magnetic fields when the velocities of the particles are comparable with that of light.

RELATIVISTIC MECHANICS : 1. Any form of mechanics compatible with either the special or general theory of relativity, 2. The non quantum mechanics of a system of particles or of a fluid inter acting with an electromagnetic field in the case when some of the velocities are comparable with the speed of light.

RELATIVITY : 1. One of several theories concerning motion designed to account for departures from newtonian mechanics that occur with very high speed relative motion. 2. The study of physics theory which recognises the universal character of the propagation speed of light and the consequent dependence of space, time and other mechanical measurement on the motion of the observer performing the measurements. The two main divisions are special theory and general theory.

RELIABILITY AND FAILURE ANALYSIS OF ELECTRONIC COMPONENTS : Reliability testing and reliability stress screening of components, failure analysis techniques and physics of failure mechanisms. Application of scanning electronic microscope in failure analysis, electrostatic discharge and effects on components.

RELIABILITY ENGINEERING : Engineering methods to test the reliability of materials, structures etc, reliability assessment of mechanical systems. Failure modes and effects. Analysis using risk priority assessment number technique to design and process reliability of telecommunication and electronic systems, spares and costs optimization. Reliability of electronic and electromechanical systems.

REMOTE SENSING : Gathering and recording information concerning the earth's surface by techniques that do not involve actual contact with the object or area under study.

RENAL TRANSPLANT SURGERY : Surgery to transplant kidneys from live persons or from cadavers in the body of patients whose kidneys have become dysfunctional.

REPRODUCTIVE BEHAVIOUR : The behaviour pattern in different kinds of animals by means of which the sperm is brought to the egg and the parental care of the resulting young insured.

REPRODUCTIVE BIOLOGY : Branch of biology concerned with the study of the reproductive system and its functioning, more particularly in humans.

REPRODUCTIVE ENDOCRINOLOGY : Branch of endocrinology concerned with the study of the role of the endocrine hormones in the reproductive processes.

REPRODUCTIVE GENETICS : Functional and comparative genomics, DNA sequencing, statistical analysis of genetic variations, genotype-phenotype correlations are included in this subject.

REPRODUCTIVE HEALTH : Study of prevention and treatment of disorders concerned with the reproductive system and processes, particularly in women at the time of pregnancy and child birth.

REPRODUCTIVE MEDICINE : Branch of medicine concerned with disorders of the reproductive system and processes in men and women.

REPRODUCTIVE PHYSIOLOGY : Branch of physiology concerned with reproductive processes, particularly the role of hormones

REPRODUCTIVE TECHNOLOGY : The study of the technological developments in the field of artificial induction of fertility like artificial insemination, *in vitro* fertilization etc. and most recently the method of cloning.

RESEARCH IN EDUCATION : Research concerned with the curriculum, syllabus teaching methods, evaluation methods etc.

RESEARCH METHODOLOGY : General methods of research applicable to all subjects and special methods applicable to individual subjects.

RESOURCE MANAGEMENT : Management and leadership in manufacturing and service operations and financial resources management.

RESPIRATORY ALLERGY AND APPLIED IMMUNOLOGY : Study of the relationship between respiratory allergies like asthma and the immunological reaction.

RESPIRAORY MEDICINE : Branch of medicine concerned with respiratory disorders like bronchitis, asthma, tuberculosis etc.

RESPIRATORY THERAPY : Treatment of certain diseases with the help of respiratory exercises like yogasanas etc.

RESTORATIVE DENTISTRY : Providing dentures and conduct operations in the case of loss of teeth due to accidents or decay.

RETAIL BANKING : Deals with routine transactions like deposits and with drawls, money transfer, foreign currency exchange and issue of travellers' cheques.

RETAILING MANAGEMENT : Management of retail marketing including customer care.

RHEOLOGY : 1. Study of the deformation and flow of matter, that is, flow stress relationship. It is a subject of increasing technological importance in several industries.

RHETORIC : 1. The art or branch of knowledge which treats of the rules or principles underlying all effective composition in prose or verse, 2. Art of using a language for persuasion both in speech and writing.

RHEUMATOLOGY : Branch of medicine concerned with the study of rheumatic diseases.

RHINOLOGY : Branch of medicine concerned with the study of diseases of the nose see Rhinolaryngology, otorhinolaryngology.

RISK MANAGEMENT : It can be defined as the systematic identification and analysis of the various loss exposures faced by a firm or individual and the best methods of treating the identified loss exposures consistent with the firms/individuals objectives.

ROBOTICS : Study of automatic devices used in industries usually comprising a mechanical arm controlled by a computer.

ROCKET ENGINEERING : Branch of engineering concerned with building and launching rockets used in space exploration.

ROMANCE LANGUAGES : A term applied to the languages which arose in the south and west of Europe based on the Latin as spoken in the provinces and including Italian, French, Spanish, Portugese and Romanian which are therefore known as the Romance languages.

ROMAN HISTORY : Study of the ancient Roman empire and its history which once played important part in world history.

RUBBER TECHNOLOGY : Study of the manufacture of rubber from natural sources like plant latex and of artificial rubber and of various products of rubber.

RURAL BANKING : Deals with credit needs of people in the rural sector.

RURAL DEVELOPMENT : Study of the economic development of rural areas particularly agriculture and industry

RURAL INDUSTRIES : Cottage industries and agri- based industries making agricultural implements, milling industry, handloom, textile industries etc.,

RURAL MANAGEMENT : Management of sustainable institutions for ecofriendly and equitable socio-economic development of rural people including management of co-operatives, agricultural rural marketing rural economics and natural resource management, development management and water and irrigation management.

RURAL MARKETING : Marketing of consumer goods in rural areas and of products of agri-based industries and of agricultural implements and inputs.

RURAL PLANNING : Planning for economic development of villages.

RURAL RECONSTRUCTION : Eradication of illiteracy, improving health and medical facilities, creating employment avenues by developing rural industries and uplifting the quality of life of village people.

RURAL SOCIOLOGY : Study of the family, caste system, social customs and traditions etc., in villages.

RURAL ENERGY TECHNOLOGY : Technology pertaining to the utilization of rural energy resources like gobar gas plants, solar energy converters, wind mills etc.

RURAL TECHNOLOGY : Development of useful products making use of natural resources available locally by means of agro-based and forest-based industries.

S

SAFETY EDUCATION : Educating the workers about safety in industries and explaining about how accidents occur.

SAFETY ENGINEERING : Engineering methods concerned with the maintenance of safety in industry.

SAIVA SIDDHANTA : Branch of Hinduism concerned with the theory of saivism.

SALARY ADMINISTRATION : Branch of personnel administration concerning fixation and payment of salaries to the personnel.

SALES MANAGEMENT : Establishing effective dealer network leading to a highly satisfied customer base. Sales forecasting, target setting and monitoring market trends, competitors' activities etc.

SALES PROMOTION : Developing and implementing sales promotion activity in close coordination with sales and marketing. Liason with advertising agencies for product and corporate advertisements, media planning, market research and event management, formulate internal and external communication and public relations strategy.

SAMPLE SURVEY DESIGN : Methods of designing sample surveys conducted in social sciences.

SAND BLASTING : A method of cleaning ships, factories, buildings, machinery etc.

SANITARY ENGINEERING : Engineering concerned with the construction of sanitary facilities like toilets, drainage etc.,

SANITARY SCIENCE : Study of the methods of removal and disposal of garbage and sewage and measures to maintain environmental cleanliness, and prevent the spread of infectious diseases in urban and rural areas and promote health and hygiene.

SAP : Short form for Systems Analysis and Programme. Development of applications, provide the capability to manage financial assistance and cost accounting, production operations and materials, personnel, plant and archived documents.

SATELLITE COMMUNICATIONS : Communication technology through the use of satellites operating from space as for example world wide transmission of T.V. Programmes.

SATELLITE METEOROLOGY : Study and prediction of atmospheric conditions on a global scale through the use of meteorological satellites.

SATELLITE OCEANOGRAPHY : Study of the oceans on global scale through the use of remote sensing satellites.

SATELLITE TECHNOLOGY : Construction and operation of artificial space satellites like communication satellites, meteorological satellites remote sensing satellites etc.

SCANNING ELECTRONIC MICROSCOPY : Study of the gross structural features of an object by the use of an electron microscope.

SCHOOL ADMINISTRATION : Branch of education concerned with the administration of primary, upper primary and secondary schools.

SCHOOL PSYCHOLOGY : Involves resolving students' learning and behavioural problems, collaborating with teachers, parents and school personnel to improve classroom management and working with students with disabilities or gifted and talented students with improved teaching and learning strategies. Also evaluating effectiveness of academic programmes, behaviour management procedures and other services provided in the school.

SCIENCE : Study of systematised knowledge produced by careful observation, measurement and experiment.

SCIENCE EDUCATION : Theory and method of science teaching in the curriculum.

SCIENCE FICTION : Fictitious literatures consisting of stories novels, dramas etc., based on existing scientific knowledge and making projections of future probabilities and conjectures.

SCIENCE JOURNALISM : Branch of journalism concerned with reporting and commenting on science news and discoveries, events, science personalities, conferences etc., and writing science features for news papers, weeklies, monthlies and other journals.

SCIENCE POLICY STUDIES : Study of science policies of governments and of institutions and organisations like UNESCO, WHO, UNICEF, FAO, WMO and other national and international scientific associations, congresses etc.

SCIENCE WRITING : A specialised branch of writing concerned with writing scientific reports, communications, textbooks, monographs, popular books etc.

SCIENTIFIC MANAGEMENT : The development of a set of principles of management based on a systematic study of the operations of production.

SCIENTOMETRICS : Quantitative study of the progresses of science.

SCLEROTHERAPY : A mode of treatment by giving injections to thrombose varicose veins.

SCREEN PRINTING : A method of printing used for printing visiting cards, greeting cards, letter heads etc.

SCULPTURE : The art of carving, cutting or hewing stone or other materials into images of men, beasts etc.

SECRETARIAL PRACTICE : A course of study concerned with office correspondence arranging meetings, recording minutes, preparing reports etc.

SECURITY ANALYSIS : Analysis of financial securities.

SECURITY TECHNOLOGY STUDIES : Study of the technological devices and methods employed in security operations.

SEDIMENTARY PETROLOGY : Study of composition, characteristics and origin of sediments and sedimentary rocks.

SEDIMENTOLOGY : Science concerned with description, classification, origin and interpretation of sediments and sedimentary rocks.

SEED SCIENCE : Study of seed structure, development classification and physiology.

SEED TECHNOLOGY : Seed testing, grading, storing, production etc.

SEISMOLOGY : Study of earthquakes

SELENOLOGY : Study of nature, origin and movement of moon; branch of astronomy.

SELF DEVELOPMENT : A multidisciplinary study of methods of developing one's own skills and personality traits as a guide to achieve success in life and minimize stress.

SEMANTICS : Systematic study of the meanings of words and the relationships between symbols and signs.

SEMATOLOGY : The study of languages as expressed by signs.

SEMICONDUCTOR DEVICES : Study of semiconductor devices like transistors etc.

SEMICONDUCTOR PHYSICS : Branch of physics concerned with the study of semiconductors which are solid crystalline materials whose electrical conductivity is intermediate between that of a conductor and an insulator ranging from about 10^5 mohs to 10^1 mohs per meter and is usually strongly temperature dependent.

SEMICONDUCTOR TECHNOLOGY : Semiconductor product design and production of integrated semiconductor solutions for the consumer; networking and computing, transportation and wireless communication.

SEMIOLOGY : See semiotics.

SEMIOTICS : Study of signs. It covers the entire range of signals used by man for communication. Also known as semiology.

SENSOR TECHNOLOGY : Utilization of sensors which receive impulses from the environment.

SEROLOGY : The laboratory study of blood serum and its constituents, particularly antibodies.

SERICULTURE : The breeding and treatment of silk worms for the production of silk fibre.

SERVER AND CLIENT TECHNOLOGY : A server is a centralized computer holding information and resources centrally. A client machine is connected to the centralized server and request for information is sent through cables. The server processes the request and sends it back to the client.

SERVICE LAW : Law affecting employees of government, banks, statuatory corporations and institutions.

SERVICES MARKETING AND MANAGEMENT : Marketing and management of services to be rendered to customers of a firm.

SEWING MACHINE MECHANISM : Study and training in the working of a sewing machine and its parts and repairing the same.

SEWING MACHINE TECHNOLOGY : Technology concerned with the development and manufacture of sewing machines.

SEX EDUCATION : Education concerned with the anatomy and physiology of the reproductive system and the reproductive process in humans.

SEXOLOGY : The science which deals with the sexual organs, their functions, diseases and defects, sexual relations between men and women.

SEXUAL MEDICINE : Branch of medical science concerned with the treatment of sexual disorders and defects.

SHIP BUILDING : The art of constructing vessels for navigation.

SHIP DESIGN : The subject concerned with the preparation of designs of ships meant for cargo transport, passenger travel, warfare, aircraft carriers etc.

SHIP HYDRODYNAMICS : Study of the mutual actions of ships and ocean water and hydrodynamic principles involved in the movement of ships in water.

SHIP MAINTENANCE AND REPAIR TECHNOLOGY : The subject concerned with the maintenance of ships in good ocean-going condition and repairing in case of damage due to various factors.

SHIP MANAGEMENT : Management of ocean- going vessels both cargo and passenger ships.

SHIPPING INDUSTRY : The commercial activities connected with shipping of a country or a port.

SHIPPING MANAGEMENT : Management of a fleet of vessels belonging to a government or a private company.

SHIPWRIGHT ENGINEERING : Docking, undocking, block-setting, blasting, painting, scaffolding, tank clearing, carpenting and material handling.

SHORTHAND : A general term for any system of contracted writing; also known as stenography; generally employed by press reporters, personal secretaries etc.

SHRIMP AND FISH PATHOLOGY : Study and treatment of diseases of shrimp and fish which are widely used as food.

SIDDHA MEDICINE : It is an ancient traditional system of Indian medicine which is akin to Ayurveda. Diagnostic methodology is eight fold. It is based on pulse reading, tongue, complexion, speech, eyes, palpatory findings and examination of urine and stools.

SIGNAL AND IMAGE PROCESSING : Branch of optical networks.

SIGNAL ENGINEERING : Mainly concerned with the construction and operation of various kinds of signals to regulate the movement of trains and road traffic.

SIGNALS AND SYSTEMS : Branch of electronics and communications engineering.

SILICON TECHNOLOGY : Making silicon containing alloys; use of silicon in rectifiers and transistors and in making silicon chips for computers.

SILVICULTURE : Branch of forestry concerned with methods of growing trees and protecting them from pests and diseases.

SOCIAL AND ECONOMIC HISTORY : History of social and economic developments of a country or a region or of the world as a whole.

SOCIAL ANTHROPOLOGY : Study of social phenomena in a quantified and comparative manner.

SOCIAL DEMOGRAPHY : Study of social characteristics of a population like age, sex, caste, dress, religion, occupation, education, income and also study of social classes and stratification in a population.

SOCIAL ECOLOGY : Study of ecological factors influencing social characteristics.

SOCIAL ECONOMICS : The branch of applied economics which deals with problems such as population, health, unemployment, education, poverty, housing, national insurance etc.

SOCIAL EDUCATION : Education about social life, values and responsibilities.

SOCIAL ENGIENEERING : Study of the methods of bringing about progressive and purposeful changes in society.

SOCIAL FORESTRY : Study of the participation and involvement of tribals and other villagers in the protection, growth and utilization of forests and forest products.

SOCIAL HEALTH : Study of protective and preventive measures for the maintenance of health like maternity and child health, reproductive health, health of the aged and the handicapped.

SOCIAL HISTORY : Study of the historical changes in society.

SOCIAL MEDICINE : Variously defined; perhaps best as an attempt to identify and modify features of social organization that promote disease.

SOCIAL MORPHOLOGY : Study of the gross form and features of society.

SOCIAL PATHOLOGY : Abnormal social conditions like crime, suicide, homicide etc.

SOCIAL PSYCHIATRY : Study of the mental health and psychological diseases prevalent in society and methods to prevent and alleviate them.

SOCIAL PSYCHOLOGY : 1. Branch of psychology which studies the psychological conditions underlying the development of social groups. 2. Treats of effects on individual's behavious of actual or imagined presence of others. 3. Critically examines human beings' interactions with others and with the social environment. Study of group behaviour, leadership, attitudes and perception.

SOCIAL SCIENCE : The science dealing with all that relates to the social conditions or the relations and institutions which are involved in man's existence and his well : being.

SOCIAL SCIENCES : 1. A general term covering all the sciences dealing with human relations. 2. Scholarly scientific study of human relationships, for examples, economics, Psychology, sociology, social administration etc.

SOCIAL STUDIES : Those aspects of social sciences selected for study in schools.

SOCIAL WELFARE MANAGEMENT : Management of social welfare activities and programmes undertaken by government and non-government organizations.

SOCIAL WORK : Study of the programmes and methods for undertaking work for the welfare of different sections of society.

SOCIOBIOLOGY : Social organization of animals including man by reference to biological characteristics such as genetic constitutions and population constraints.

SOCIOBOTANY : Study of social relations among a group of plants. Some evidence is being adduced in recent years to show that plants too are capable of social relations.

SOCIOCULTURAL ANTHROPOLOGY : Study of the social and cultural life of man through the ages.

SOCIOLINUISTICS : Study of the sociology of languages or the relationships between language, culture and social structure.

SOCIOLOGICAL JURISPRUDENCE : Legal studies pertaining to the sociological relations of man.

SOCIOLOGY : 1. The science which investigates the laws that regulate human society in all its grades. 2. The science which treats of the general structure of society, the laws of its development and the progress of civilization.

SOCIOLOGY OF CULTURE : Social groups engaged in art status, economic status etc.

SOCIOLOGY OF GENDER : Physical differences between man and woman are mediated by culture and social structure.

SOCIOLOGY OF LAW : Study of how social conditions influence the making and enforcement of law.

SOCIOLOGY OF RELIGION : Application of sociological concepts and thinking to the study of man's religious behaviour.

SOCIOMETRY : Form of social psychology which measures preferences in social relationships.

SOCIOTECHNICS : Use of knowledge and methods of social sciences in bringing about social change, solving social problems and designing social institutions.

SOFTWARE APPLICATIONS : Use of computer software in various fields of activities.

SOFTWARE DESIGN AND DEVELOPMENT : Designing and developing computer software for specific purposes.

SOFTWARE ENGINEERING : Includes development processes, software life cycles, software development in large projects, configuration management system, integration and testing, operating systems, networking systems, database concepts, internet concepts, ERP Packages etc.

SOFTWARE ENTERPRISE MANAGEMENT : It covers issues that integrate typical business administration concepts with IT orientation. They include organising and managing people in the software industry, gaining domain expertise in areas of telecom, banking and financial institutions and value chain management, planning and implementing software projects and strengthening technology skills and marketing professional services and products.

SOFTWARE FOR BUSINESS APPLICATIONS : SPSS, TALLY and EXCEL covering marketing, production, finance and accounts functions.

SOFTWARE MARKETING : Marketing of software needed by different users has now become an important international business activity.

SOFTWARE PROJECT MANAGEMENT : Comprises software development models, project planning and scheduling, configuration management, software process matrices, risk analysis, software quality management, architectural management.

SOFTWARE QUALITY MANAGEMENT : The subject covers standards and quality philosophy, metrices, verification and validation, software configuration management, project management etc.

SOFTWARE RELIABILITY ENGINEERING : It is a multifacted discipline covering the entire software product life cycle and addresses both technical and management activities in 3 basic areas; software development and maintenance, measurement and analysis of reliability data and the feed back of reliability information into the software life cycle activity. The essential components are to establish reliability goals, to develop operational profile, to plan and execute tests and to use results to drive decisions.

SOFTWARE TECHNOLOGY : Technology concerned with the preparation of programmes of instruction to the computer to perform specific tasks. Includes courses like computer network and internet applications.

SOFTWARE TESTING : The subject covers testing the life cycle, static testing methods, dynamic testing methods, test management and software testing tools.

SOIL AND CROP ENVIRONMENT SCIENCES : Sciences concerned with soil water relations, soil micro-flora and fauna, soil chemistry, soil structure, crop water relations etc.

SOIL BIOENGINEERING : Methods of improving soil fertility by the use of soil enriching organisms like Rhizobium and other bacteria, blue green algae, earthworms etc.

SOIL CHEMISTRY : Study and analysis of inorganic and organic components and the life cycles within soils.

SOIL CONSERVATION ENGINEERING : Engineering techniques employed in promoting soil conservation.

SOIL MECHANICS : Application of laws of solid and fluid mechanics to soils.

SOIL MECHANICS AND FOUNDATION ENGINEERING : Application of soil mechanics in laying foundations for buildings, dams, water tanks, reservoirs etc.

SOIL MICROBIOLOGY : Study of microorganisms found in the soil and their functions and the effect of their activities on the character of the soil and the growth and health of plant life.

SOIL PHYSICS : Study of physical characteristics of soils; concerned also with the methods and instruments used to determine these characteristics.

SOIL SCIENCE : See Pedology.

SOLAR ENERGY STUDIES : Study of the application of solar energy for useful purposes.

SOLAR PHYSICS : Study of the physical aspects of the sun.

SOLID ANALYTICAL GEOMETRY : Analytical geometry in 3 dimensions.

SOLID GEOMETRY : Branch of geometry which studies figures in space (3 dimensions) such as cubes, spheres etc.

SOLID STATE CHEMISTRY : Chemical properties of solid materials.

SOLID STATE PHYSICS : Branch of physics concerned with the physical properties of solid materials; it is usually concerned with the properties of crystalline materials only but is sometimes extended to include the properties of glasses or polymers.

SOLID WASTE MANAGEMENT : Disposal of solid waste material in such a way that it will cause least pollution and also to produce energy from it.

SOMATIC MEDICINE : Various types of body oriented practices such as therapeutic massage, cranio-sacral pulse detection, Feldon Krais therapy and somatic psychotherapy.

SOMATOLOGY : The branch of science dealing with the constitution and physiology of the body.

SOMATOMETRY : Measurement of the human body with the soft parts intact.

SONOCHEMISTRY : See chemical ultrasonics.

SOUND ENGINEERING : See Acoustic engineering.

SOUND MIXING : Regulating volume and quality of sound during filming of motion picture, phonograph recording or T.V. or radio production.

SOUND RECORDING : The engineering and technology of recording sound like songs, and dialogues in cinema, T.V., audio and video casettes etc.

SOUTH ASIAN STUDIES : Study of civilization, culture, politics etc of south Asian countries.

SPACE AND AVIATION MEDICINE : Branch of medicine concerned with the study of the health, fitness and diseases of space and aircaft travellers.

SPACE BIOLOGY : A term for the various biological sciences and disciplines that are concerned with the study of living things in the space environment.

SPACE ENGINEERING AND ROCKETRY : Engineering aspects concerned with the construction and launching of rockets, space vehicles and satellites.

SPACE GEODESY : Study of geodesy from observations made from space craft.

SPACE MANAGEMENT : Management concerned with the launching of rockets, space vehicles and satellites, allotment of slots for satellites and space Vehicles in space and related subjects.

SPACE PHYSICS : Study of the physical properties of outer space, particularly for the purpose of space exploration and space travel.

SPACE SCIENCE : Study of the physical, chemical, climatological, metereological phenomena concerned with outer space.

SPACE TECHNOLOGY : Various technological developments involved in construction and operation of space craft, space travel, residing in space for long periods, communicating with the ground stations from space craft, launching space craft etc., Benefits derived from these technologies directly and indirectly are world wide communication, information exchange, satellite, T.V. etc.

SPASTICS : Branch of medicine concerned with abnormal muscular contraction and associated pain.

SPATIAL INFORMATION TECHNOLOGY : Information technology derived form space studies.

SPATIAL STUDIES : Scientific investigation of space and related subjects.

SPECIAL EDUCATION : Education provided for children requiring special treatment either because they are gifted students or because they have mental or physical handicap or are backward in studies.

SPECTRAL PHOTOGRAPHY : A technique used in air-borne surveys for mineral deposits; narrow-band-pass filters and special film are used to accentuate minor colour effects caused by mineralization and alteration which would be undetectable by broad-band photography.

SPECTROGRAPHY : The use of photography to record the electromagnetic spectrum displayed in a spectroscope.

SPECTROMETRY : The use of spectrographic techniques for deriving the physical constants of materials.

SPECTROPHOTOMETRY : A procedure to measure photometrically the wave length range of radiant energy absorbed by a sample under analysis; can be by visible light, ultraviolet rays or X-rays.

SPECTROSCOPY : 1. Branch of physics concerned with the production, measurement and interpretation of electromagnetic spectra arising from either emission or absorption of radiant energy of various substances. 2. The study of methods of producing and analysing spectra using spectroscopes, spectrometers, spectrographs and spectrophotometers.

SPEECH AND HEARING : Study of speech and hearing of hearing-impaired persons and persons having speech problems, more especially children and methods of improving their capabilities.

SPEECH AUDIOMETRY : Determination of percentage of spoken words recognised at various soundness levels.

SPEECH PATHOLOGY : Study of anatomical and physiological diseases associated with speech defects.

SPEECH RECOGNITION SOFTWARE : It is a computer software which can listen, understand and respond to the user in his natural speech.

SPEECH THERAPY : Correction work with any individual suffering from disorders of speech.

SPELEOLOGY : Branch of science concerned with the study of caves.

SPHERICAL TRIGONOMETRY : Study of spherical triangles, finding unknown sides, angles and areas by the use of trigonometric functions of plane angles.

SPHRAGISTICS : Study of the seals on coins and medals including old metal and stone signets.

SPHYGMOLOGY : Science of the pulse.

SPICES : Branch of agriculture concerned with the cultivation of spice yielding plants like cloves, cardamom, pepper, nutmeg, cinnamon etc.

SPINE SURGERY : Branch of surgical medicine concerned with the surgical treatment of spine disorders and injuries.

SPINNING TECHNOOGY : Branch of textile technology concerned with spinning of fibres.

SPIRITUAL MEDICINE : Ever since clinical investigators proved beneficial effects of prayer on healing and recovery in a double : bind study, new symposiums on science and spirituality have been sponsored by Harvard university Medical School.

SPORTS JOURNALISM : Branch of journalism concerned with reporting sports events, commenting on sports and writing features on sports for newspapers and magazines.

SPORTS MANAGEMENT : Management of sports activities, events and competitions etc.

SPORTS MEDICINE : Branch of medicine concerned with the treatment of sports persons' health problems and injuries.

SPORTS NUTRITION : Study of the special nutrition requirements of sports persons belonging to various sports disciplines.

SPORTS PHYSIOLOGY : Analysis of athelet's movements, muscle analysis etc. to gain answers to why some are good and some slow.

SPORTS PHYSIOTHERAPY : Special methods of physiotherapy for injuries of sports persons belonging to various sports disciplines.

SPORTS PSYCHOLOGY : Providing psychological assistance to sports persons seeking to excel professionals in various sports focussing on performance enhancement, personal development, well being and adjustment skills.

SPORTS SCIENCE : The entire subject of sports studied as a science.

SPORTS SCIENCES : All those subjects concerned with sports like sports medicine, sports nutrition, sports physiology, sports psychology, sports sociology etc.

SPORTS SOCIOLOGY : The social relations of sports persons among themselves, with the sports officials and with the general public.

SPORTS TECHNOLOGY : Technology involved in the manufacture of sports goods like bats, balls and other materials and in the preparation of sports fields, courts and other facilities. Also may be included sports communication and observation technologies and detection of frauds like use of drugs etc.

SPORTS TRAUMATOLOGY : Injuries suffered by sportspersons and their treatment.

STATHMOKINETICS : Study of rates of cell multiplication.

STATIC ECONOMICS : The theoretical study of an economic situation in static or unchanging conditions as distinct from dynamic economics which takes account of changes.

STATIC MANAGETISM : See Magnetostatics.

STATIC OCEANOGRAPHY : Physical and chemical nature of water in the ocean and shape and composition of ocean bottom.

STATICS : Branch of mechanics concerned with force abstracted from matter and forces which act on bodies in equilibrium.

STATISTICAL COST ANALYSIS : In its specific sense the employment of statistical techniques such as regression analysis to cross section and time series cost data, the objective being to identify the nature and shape of the long-run average cost curve. Statistical cost analysis is also used as a banner heading for a range of techniques employed in cost studies such as the engineering method and the survivor technique.

STATISTICAL MECHANICS : 1. Branch of physics in which statistical methods are applied to the microscopic constituents of a system in order to predict its macroscopic properties. 2. Use of statistical methods to calculate the function of the total number of microstates that have an assigned energy.

STATISTICAL PROCEDURES IN EDUCATIONAL RESEARCH : Statistical methods adopted in educational research.

STATISTICAL PROCESS CONTROL : This software package addresses frequency distribution, scatter diagram, histogram, pareto diagram, run-chart, x-bar and R-chart, X-bar and S-chart, R-bar and R-chart, X and MR-chart, Standard deviation control limits, process capability, process capability index etc. It has all the advanced features like on line acceptance of production process data, graphical display, detailed report generation, exhaustive help utility etc. Benefits of this software include reduced scrap rework, inspection time, better understanding of the process methodology, controlled process, motivated workforce etc. It can be effectively used by any type of industry such as automobile, textile, chemical, mechanical, electronic, telecom software, banking and financial sectors etc.

STATISTICS : 1. Method of planning experiments for obtaining data and drawing conclusions and inferences. 2. Descriptive statistics : characterizing and summarizing a given set of data. 3. Methods of obtaining samples. 4. Study concerned with the inferences that can be drawn from numerical data on the basis of probability.

STATUARY : The art of carving or making statues; a branch of sculpture.

STEEL TECHNOLOGY : Technology of manufacturing various types of steel and their products.

STEGANOGRAPHY : Literally means covered writing in greek. It is meant to hide a message which could contain text, images or maps inside picture, music file or video on a web page or by e-mail or in conventional writing or pictures. It can only be deciphered by some one who knows where to look for criminals terrorists and hostile governments may use stegangraphy.

STEM CELL THERAPY : This technique makes use of the ability of embryonic and other stem cells to develop into diverse cell types and tissues and involves transplanting stem cells into diseased parts of the body.

STENOGRAPHY : A generic term which embraces every system of shorthand.

STEREOCHEMISTRY : Concerned with the structure of molecules and the way the arrangement of atoms and groups affects the chemical properties. See chiral chemistry.

STEREOGRAPHY : The art of delineating solid bodies on a plane.

STEREOLOGY : Techniques (of measurement and calculation) for deriving 3-dimensional quantities from 2-dimensional quantities. Originally used in geology; now applied to histological sections.

STOCK MARKET STUDY : It is a training course which covers secondary markets, trading, clearing and settlement, rolling settlement, mutual funds, tax provisions, dematerialization of shares, surveillance, sensex and other indices, futures and options, inspection of brokers books, ethics and code of conduct of brokers, sub-brokers, primary markets, books building and IPO's listing, investors' grievances, redressal systems.

STOICHIOMETRY : A branch of chemistry concerned with atomic and molecular weights or more generally with the relations of physical properties to composition.

STRATEGIC MANAGEMENT : Management of strategies for competing in global arena.

STRATEGIC STUDIES : Political, diplomatic, military strategies adopted by nations for self defence.

STRATEGIC THINKING : Strategies design; behaviour creation, structuring and managing organizations, competing in global arena.

STRATIGRAPHIC GEOLOGY : See Stratigraphy.

STRATIGRAPHY : Form, arrangement, geographic distribution, chronological succession, classification, correlation and mutual relation ships of rock strata especially sedimentary. Also known as stratigraphic geology.

STRESS ANALYSIS : Branch of engineering concerned with analysis of stress in materials and structures.

STRESS MANAGEMENT : Branch of psychology concerned with the management of mental stress.

STRUCTURAL AND ENGINEERING STUDIES OF MONUMENTS : Covering materials, designs, structural strength, acoustics, water management of monuments.

STRUCTURAL BIOLOGY : Study of structure of plants and animals and other organisms.

STRUCTURAL GEOLOGY : Form, arrangement and internal structure of rocks.

STRUCTURAL INORGANIC CHEMISTRY : Study of molecular structure of inorganic compounds.

STRUCTURAL ORGANIC CHEMISTRY : Molecular structure of organic compounds.

STRUCTURAL PETROLOGY : Internal structure of a rock to determine its deformational history. Also known as Petromorphology, petrogeometry.

STRUCTURAL STEEL DESIGN : Design of steel used in construction work in preference to reinforced concrete. Branch of civil engineering and construction engineering.

STYLISTICS : It is that branch of linguistics which studies the varieties of speech or writing appropriate to different situations and develops in the student awareness and control of these variations.

SUBSURFACE GEOLOGY : Geological features beneath the land or sea floor surface. Also known as underground geology.

SUBSURFACE SCIENCE : physico-chemical characteristics and other features of subsurface structures.

SUGARCANE : Branch of agriculture concerned with the cultivation of sugarcane crop.

SUGAR TECHNOLOGY : Technology of manufacturing sugar from sugarcane, beetroot and other sources.

SUPER COMPUTER EDUCATION AND RESEARCH : Training and research in supercomputers which are several times more efficient than ordinary computers.

SUPERCONDUCTOR PHYSICS : Branch of physics concerned with superconducting materials which conduct electricity without any resistance.

SUPERCONDUCTOR TECHNOLOGY : Technology of utilizing superconductors in industries and for other purposes.

SUPERSONIC AERODYNAMICS : Study of aerodynamics of supersonic speeds.

SUPPLY CHAIN MANAGEMENT : Management of transactions between suppliers and customers. The world wide web allows suppliers to create a web presence for primary product and service information directly to the customer. A customer can go directly to a vendor and download information with no human intervention.

SUPPLY SIDE ECONOMICS : A body of thought which emphasizes that the principal determinant of the rate of growth of natural output in both the short and long run is the allocation and efficient use of the labour and capital in an economy. Accordingly it focusses on impediments to the supply of and efficient use of factors.

SUPRAMOLECULAR CHEMISTRY : Study of chemistry of substances at higher than molecular level.

SURFACE CHEMISTRY : The study and measurement of the forces and processes that act on the surfaces of fluids (gases and liquids) and solids or as an interface separating two phases, for example, surface tension.

SURFACE GEOLOGY : Study of the features of the surface of the earth.

SURFACE PHYSICS : Study of the physical properties of surfaces of fluids and solids or at an interface separating two phases, for example surface tension.

SURFACE SCIENCE AND TECHNOLOGY : Study of surface characteristics and phenomena and their uses.

SURGICAL GASTROENTEROLOGY : Surgical treatment of diseases of the stomach and intestine.

SURGICAL ONCOLOGY : Surgical treatment of certain types of cancer. See medical oncology, radiation oncology.

SURGERY : Surgical treatment of certain diseases and injuries.

SURVEYING : Making a survey of a portion of the earth's surface by means of measurements and calculations.

SUSTAINABLE DEVELOPMENT : Agricultural and industrial development without affecting the natural resources and the environment.

SYMBOLIC COMPUTATION : Developing computer proofs of mathematical identities and computer algebra packages.

SYMBOLOGY : The art of expressing by symbols. Also known as symbolology.

SYMBOLOLOGY : See Symbology.

SYNCHOLOGY : A study which involves the distribution ranges of plant communities, phytosociological zones, vegetation and geographical complexes, dissemination spectra and current migration patterns.

SYNDESMOLOGY : Branch of anatomy that deals with the ligaments.

SYNDYNAMICS : The study of the causes of and trends in successional changes within a plant community.

SYNECOLOGY : Ecological study of a group of organisms of the same species particularly with reference to their mutual influences and the effects of environmental factors.

SYNOPTIC METEOROLOGY : Concerned with those atmospheric processes connected with the weather.

SYNPHYLOGENY : The study of the trends and changes in plant communities through historical and evolutionary perspectives.

SYNPHYSIOLOGY : The study of the metabolic processes of plants or species which constantly compete with each other by investigating water needs, transpiration, assimilation and production of organic matter, physiological effects of light, temperature, root exudates and various other ecological factors.

SYNTHETIC CHEMISTRY : Branch of chemistry concerned with the synthesis of chemical compounds in the laboratory.

SYNTHETIC MEDICINAL CHEMISTRY : Development of new molecules etc., which can be used as drugs through chemical synthesis.

SYNTHETIC ORGANIC CHEMISTRY : Chemical synthesis of organic compounds many of which are used as drugs, pesticides etc.

SYSTEMATIC BOTANY : Branch of botany concerned with the nomencluture, relationships and classification of plants. See taxonomy.

SYSTEMATICS : Study of the diversity of organisms and their natural relationships sometimes used as a synonym of taxonomy.

SYSTEMS ADMINISTRATION : To take care of all the computer systems, installation of software, taking regular backups, virus protection, fire wall implementation and maintenance of heterogeneous multi-user operating systems.

SYSTEMS ANALYSIS : The art of analyzing methods of doing things and designing and implementing new and better methods with particular reference to computers. Software design and optimization of resources and arriving at a solution. Survey and analysis of software infrastructure needs. Systems analysis uses computer technology to meet an organization's specific needs. It plans and develops new computer systems or devises ways to apply existing systems, resources to additional operations. Designing new systems including both hardware and software or adding a new software application is all part of systems analysis.

SYSTEMS ECOLOGY : The combined approaches of systems analysis and the ecology of whole systems and subsystems.

SYSTEMS-EMBEDDED : Combinations of hardware and software mounted on compact electronic circuit boards integrated into the devices for which they are meant. See Embedded systems.

SYSTEMS ENGINEERING : Design and organization of a complex of resources and devices.

SYSTEMS MANAGEMENT : Management of computer software systems.

SYSTEMS SCIENCE : It comprises systems engineering, systems analysis, systems management, systems software and systems administration.

SYSTEMS SOFTWARE : It is any software that supports the development or execution of application programmes but are not ready made for any specific vendor application.

T

TACHYGRAPHY : The art of quick writing. See shorthand, stenography.

TAILORING : The profession and art of cutting cloth and stitching dresses.

TANK BODY AND FRAME MANUFACTURE : Design and manufacture of the body and frame of tanks used in warfare.

TANK TECHNOLOGY : Manufacture of tanks used in warfare including tank electrical systems, optoelectronics and night vision devices, tank control systems etc.

TANTRA- Tantra is regarded as scripture to spread knowledge and as a technical branch of spiritual knowledge. It was practiced by the lower classes to gain worldly knowledge from the vedic tradition. Thus it served as a parallel to vedic tradition. The gradual infusion of vedic elements into the tantrik system paved to the vedic sanction by followers of vedas ultimately leading to the patronization by all classes.

TASTING : Tasting tea, coffee, wine and other beverages is a specialized branch of learning which involves a capacity to distinguish the flavours on the basis of which the quality of the products is determined. Trained tasting professionals are employed in the respective industries.

TAXATION : Compulsory levies on private individuals and organisations made by government to raise revenue to finance expenditure on public goods and services and to control the volume of private expenditure in the economy. Taxes are direct and indirect. Income and wealth tax are examples of direct taxes. Excise duties and value added tax are examples of indirect taxes.

TAXIDERMY : The art of treating the skins of animals so that they retain their natural appearance and also stuffing and mounting them.

TAX LAWS : Study of the union and state laws concerned with all kinds of taxes like income- tax, excise, sales tax, commercial taxes etc.

TAXONOMIC BOTANY : See plant taxonomy.

TAXONOMY : The science of classification of living things on the basis of various morphological and other characters and relationships.

TEACHER EDUCATION : Professional education and training of teachers. Also known as teacher training.

TEACHER TRAINING : See teacher education.

TEA SCIENCE AND TECHNOLOGY : Cultivation, harvesting, plant nutrition and growth, biotechnology, processing, crop protection and effect of tea on human health.

TECHNICAL DRAWING : The art of preparing drawings pertaining to scientific, technical and engineering subjects.

TECHNICAL WRITING : Writing technical and scientific reports, articles, brochures and documents to present technical subjects in an easy to understand language.

TECHNOLOGY : Technology includes all forms of production techniques.

TECTOLOGY : Study of structural units of animal body.

TECTONOPHYSICS- Branch of geophysics dealing with the physical processes involved in forming geological structures.

TELECOMMUNICATION ENGINEERING : Branch of engineering pertaining to communication devices like telegraph and telephone.

TELECOM MANAGEMENT : National long distance and international long distance, the concept of convergence becoming the key factor in this growth of the sector study of major aspects of telecom technology management and information technology management.

TELEMATICS : Communication systems, distributed systems, networking, telematics application in business, design of communication systems, standards of network management, process quality assurance, operations, procedures and service levels.

TELEMEDICINE : Medical information including imaging data and live video footage could be exchanged between different centers and doctors could discuss with one another through videoconference. It connects hospitals in cities, countries and continents. It is an important application of information technology.

TELEMETEOROGRAPHY : Science of the design, construction and operation of various types of telemeteorographs.

TELEMETRY : Transmission of measured data from its source to an observer at a distance from the source by electrical (through wires) or by electromagnetic radiation.

TELEOLOGY : The science of causes.

TELEPATHY : The communication of feelings or impressions between persons at a distance from each other.

TELEPHOTOGRAPHY : Photographing distant objects by means of a specially constructed lens.

TELEPHOTOMETRY : The body of principles and techniques concerned with measuring atmospheric extinction by using various types of telephotometers.

TELERADIOTHERAPY : X-Ray treatment of diseases from a distance.

TELESEISMOLOGY : Aspect of seismology dealing with records made at a distance from the surface of the impulse.

TELETRAINING : Imparting training through T.V, internet etc.

TELEVISION CAMERA TECHNIQUES : Techniques of operating television cameras.

TELEVISION EDITING : Editing of television and video footage.

TELEVISION JOURNALISM : Collecting news and events, conducting interviews and the concerned visuals for telecasting.

TELEVISION MECHANISM : Maintenance and repair of T V Sets.

TELEVISION PRODUCTION AND DIRECTION : Production and direction of TV Programmes including plays and skits.

TELEVISION TECHNOLOGY : Technology of manufacture of television sets.

TEMPLE ARTS : Arts like, sculpture, music, dance and other performing arts associated with temples.

TENDERING : It is concerned with preparing tender documents for engineering works and finalizing tenders submitted by contractors.

TEPHROCHRONOLOGY : Dating of different layers of volcanic ash for the establishment of a sequence of geologic and archaeologic occurrences.

TERATOLOGY : That branch of biology concerned with monsters and malformations in plants and animals.

TERMINOLOGY : 1. The science of technical terms. 2. The collection of technical terms used in a subject.

TEROTECHNOLOGY : Technology of acquisition, installation, commissioning, maintenance, replacement and removal of plant, machinery and equipment.

TERTIARY EDUCATION : That which follows the completion of secondary education or its equivalent; includes higher education and more advanced education.

TEST ENGINEERING : Testing, calibration and maintenance of electronic equipments.

TEXTILE CHEMISTRY : Chemical analysis, dyeing and finishing textile fibres / fabrics; quality testing and yarn spinning.

TEXTILE DESIGN : The art of preparing designs for textile fabrics.

TEXTILE DYEING AND PRINTING : The technology of dying textile fibres and fabrics and printing designs on fabrics.

TEXTILE ENGINEERING : Design, manufacture and maintenance of machinery used in the textile industry.

TEXTILE MICROBIOLOGY : That branch of microbiology concerned with textile materials; deals with microorganisms that are harmful either to the fibres or to the consumers and microorganisms that are useful as in the retting process.

TEXTILE PHYSICS : Study of the physical properties of textile fibres and fabrics like strength, stretching, shrinking , durability etc.

TEXTILE PROCESSING : Study of the processes involved in the manufacture of textile fibres and fabrics.

TEXTILE TECHNOLOGY : The technology of spinning, weaving, dyeing, printing, involved in the manufacture of textile fibres and fabrics.

THANATOLOGY : The science dealing with the study of death has been in existence for centuries and is still being studied and investigated.

THEATER ARTS : Study of the arts involved in staging plays like decoration of stage, arranging the sets, acting, directing, writing script etc.

THEATER TECHNOLOGY : Technology of arranging the stage sets, costumes, ornaments, lighting, sound effects etc. for staging plays.

THEOLOGY : The science of divine things.

THEORETICAL CHEMISTRY : Explaining chemical reactions and processes in mathematical terms.

THEORETICAL COMPUTER SCIENCE : Study of the mathematical and theoretical aspects of computer structure, hardware and software.

THEORETICAL NUCLEAR PHYSICS : Explaining nuclear structure and other phenomena associated therewith in mathematical terms and making predictions on that basis.

THEORETICAL PHYSICS : The description of natural phenomena in mathematical form.

THEOSOPHY : It is a school of philosophy that has been accepted and practiced by people from over 50 countries. The basic teachings of theosophy are based on universal brotherhood.

THERAPEUTIC GASTROINTESTINAL ENDOSCOPY : Use of endoscopy for the treatment of gastrointestinal diseases. Fast developing as a separate discipline.

THERAPEUTIC RADIOLOGY : Use of radiological techniques for the treatment of cancer and other diseases.

THERAPEUTICS : 1. Branch of medicine concerned with composition, application and operation of remedies. 2. Branch of medicine concerned with treatment to cure or alleviate disorders.

THERAPEUTIC GENETICS : Application of genetic principles in the treatment of disorders. An example is gene therapy.

THERMAL ENGINEERING : Branch of mechanical engineering concerned with the generation and utilization of heat.

THERMAL POWER PLANT ENGINEERING : Design, manufacture and maintenance of thermal power plants for the generation of electricity from heat sources like coal.

THERMAL SCIENCE : Sciences like thermodynamics, thermochemistry, fluid dynamics, heat, and heat transfer which are considered as branches of physics and engineering and which are concerned with the study of heat are grouped as thermal sciences.

THERMAL ENGINEERING : Concerned with the generation and utilization of heat.

THERMIONICS : The branch of electronics concerned with the study and design of devices based on the emission of electrons from metal or metal oxide surfaces as a result of high temperatures.

THERMOCHEMISTRY : Branch of chemistry concerned with the heats of chemical reactions, and heats of formation of chemical compounds.

THERMODYNMICS : 1. The branch of physics which seeks to derive from a few basic postulates, relations between properties of substances, especially those which are affected by changes in temperature and a description of the conversion of the energy forms from one form to another. 2. Study of the laws that govern the conversion of energy from one form to another, the direction in which heat will flow and the availability of energy to do work.

THERMOGRAPHY : Production of images showing distribution of skin temperature.

THERMOMAGNETISM : Magnetism resulting from or as affected by heat.

THERMOMETRY : The science and technology of measuring temperature and the establishment of standards of temperature measurement.

THERMOTICS : The science of heat.

THEROLOGY : Branch of zoology concerned with the study of mammals. See mammology.

THESPIAN ART : See acting.

THORACIC MEDICINE : Branch of medicine pertaining to the diseases of the chest region.

THORACIC SURGERY : Surgical treatment of diseases of the chest region.

THREE DIMENSIONAL DESIGN : Includes design of furniture, interiors, product and exhibition design.

THREE DIMENSIONAL GEOMETRY- See solid geometry.

THROMBOSIS : Study of the clotting of blood in blood vessels.

THYROIDOLOGY : Branch of medicine concerned with the diseases caused by abnormal functioning of the thyriod gland as well as diseases of the thyroid gland.

TIBETAN MEDICINE : It is an ancient oriental system which is akin to Ayurveda. Pulse diagnosis and urine analysis are the distinctive features. It is an integrated Buddhist approach to mind body relationship.

TIBETAN STUDIES : Study of the history, geography, language, culture, literature etc, pertaining to Tibet.

TISSUE CULTURE : Technique of culturing plant and animal tissues in synthetic medium containing nutrients, hormones and other growth promoting substances. This technique is being extensively used for the study of physiological and biochemical processes as well as for obtaining useful chemical substances. Plant tissue culture can also be used for plant propagation.

TISSUE ENGINEERING : Growing parts of the human and animal body like heart valves, arteries, skin etc., by culturing living cells and tissues.

TOBACCO CULTIVATION : Branch of agriculture concerned with the methods of cultivation, fertilizers, plant protection, breeding and curing of tobacco varieties.

TOOL DESIGN : Design of tools used for engineering purposes like plastic moulds, press tools, jigs and fixtures and gauges.

TOOL ENGINEERING : Computer aided design of press tools, fixtures and gauges, die casting and manufacture of tryouts.

TOPOGRAPHIC ANATOMY : The use of soft tissue and bony landmarks on the surface of the body to indicate the known locations of deeper structures.

TOPOLOGY : That branch of geometry which deals with the topological properties of figures. 2. That branch of geometry concerned with the properties of solids that are unchanged by continuous deformation such as twisting or stretching.

TOPONOMATOLOGY : Systematic investigation and analysis of the names of the places within a particular geographical area or peculiar to a language. Also known as toponymy.

TOPONYMY : See toponomatology

TOTAL COST MANAGEMENT : Cost computation, cost analysis, identification of cost reduction areas; management techniques like value engineering, waste control and utilization.

TOTAL PRODUCTIVE MAINTENANCE : The process involves autonomous maintenance, quality maintenance, planned maintenance, continuous improvements, employee education and training (all levels), initial control, safety environment, tooling management and TPM in administration.

TOTAL QUALITY MANAGEMENT : Time consciousness, cost, productivity, quality, safety and environment consciousness.

TOURISM ADMINISTRATION : Developing tourist places by developing infrastructure like accommodation, transport, communications etc and improving and maintaining tourist spots and other attractions.

TOURISM MANAGEMENT : Management concerned with the provision of facilities for tourists, helping tourists in planning their itinery, making arrangements for travel, accommodation, food etc.

TOURISM STUDIES : Study of places of tourist interest, their development, impact of tourism on local population and environment, income from tourism industry etc.

TOURIST GUIDE TRAINING : Training given to prospective tourist guides includes study of history, geography and languages relevant to the concerned places of tourist interest.

TOWN PLANNING : Preparation of the layout, demarcating the area for residences, play grounds, recreation, commercial and industrial areas, water supply and drainage lines, roads and other amenities for people living in towns. See Urban planning.

TOXICOLOGY : That branch of science which treats of poisons and their antidotes. Poisons may be of biological or chemical origins. Biological poisons are known as toxins. The study of their effects on man and other organisms also comes under this subject.

TOY MAKING : Art and technology of making toys with a variety of materials including mud, wood, cloth, metal, plastic etc., for children's play and for decoration.

TRADITIONAL FOLK MEDIA : Folk dances, dramas and other forms of entertainment and educative value including music and songs.

TRAFFIC ENGINEERING : Building structures like flyovers, subways, metros, traffic signals etc., for regulating traffic.

TRAFFIC MANAGEMENT : Management of traffic regulation to avoid accidents in towns and cities involving one way movement of vehicles on certain routes, diversion of vehicular traffic from main roads and other similar measures. Collaboration with traffic engineering personnel is essential for traffic management.

TRAINING DEVELOPMENT : Developing training methodologies and strategies to meet specific needs.

TRAINING TECHNOLOGY : Methods of imparting training in various fields to students and employees at all levels. Advanced training may be necessary even to senior personnel.

TRANSFORMER TECHNOLOGY : Branch of electrical engineering concerned with the manufacture of electrical transformers.

TRANSFUSION MEDICINE : Branch of medicine concerned with blood transfusion. It involves determination of blood groups, blood testing for pathogens and other harmful substances before using the blood for transfusion.

TRANSLATION : The process of converting material in one language into another. Literary, scientific, commercial, legal, administrative works require different skills and methods of translation. It is considered as a science.

TRANSPLANTATION : 1. The artificial removal of a part of an organism and its replacement in the body of the same or of a different individual. 2. Removing seedlings from the nursery bed and planting them in the main field.

TRANSPLANT MEDICINE : Branch of medicine concerned with transplanting an organ from a healthy person to another person in whose body the concerned organ is not functioning properly or not at all. It also involves testing for compatibility before transplanting and prevention of rejection of the organ by the body of the recipient after transplanting. Several legal problems are also to be taken into consideration in the case of cadaver transplantation : Also known as transplantology.

TRANSPLANTOLOGY : See transplant medicine.

TRANSPORT : Branch of commerce concerned with the conveyance of men and materials from one place to another by roadway, railway, waterway or airway means.

TRASPORTATION ENGINEERING : Engineering pertaining to various transportation systems.

TRANSPORT ECONIMICS : Travel demand estimation, traffic forecasting, economic, financial and commercial evaluation for major highway projects.

TRANSPORT PLANNING : Planning of transport methods and facilities for various purposes in the public and private sectors.

TRAUMATOLOGY : Treatment of wounds; primarily injuries caused by accidents; branch of medicine.

TRAVEL AND TOURISM : Making travel arrangements and reservations, supplying information about tourist spots and arranging accommodation and other facilities to tourists.

TRAVEL MANAGEMENT : Supplying information about bus, train, ship, boat, steamer, airplane, taxi and other modes of travel, journey timings, rates of charges, making bookings, reservations etc. Employment potential in government, corporations, travel agencies etc.

TRAVEL MEDICINE : Treatment of ailments associated with travel and during travel.

TREASURY MANAGEMENT : Concerned with treasury management, forex management, risk management and portfolio management.

TRIBAL ECONOMICS : Study of economic conditions of tribals including income, expenditure, indebtedness, loan facilities, marketing of forest products etc.

TRIBAL HISTORY : History of tribal populations all over the world.

TRIBAL LANGUAGES : Study of tribal languages, their origins and inter-relationships.

TRIBO- CHEMISTRY : Chemistry of lubricants.

TRIBOLOGY : Study of friction, lubrication and lubricants.

TRICHOLOGY : Branch of dermatology concerned with the study of hair.

TRIGONOMETRY : 1. The science of determining the angles and sides of triangles by means of certain parts which are given, 2. Branch of mathematics concerned with measurement of triangles. It has applications in surveying, navigation, construction work and many branches of science.

TROPICAL MEDICINE : Study of tropical diseases and their treatment.

TROPICAL METEOROLOGY : Branch of meteorology concerned with the study of tropical weather.

TUMOR BIOLOGY : Biological study of the nature and growth of tumors.

TURBO MACHINERY : Branch of mechanical engineering concerned with turbo machines.

TYPE-WRITING : The trade of printing with a type-writer machine.

U

ULTRAFAST PROCESSES : Study of ultrafast chemical reactions and processes

ULTRASONOLOGY : Application of ultrasound in biology and medicine.

ULTRA SONICS : The study and use of sound waves that have a frequency in excess of 2000 Hz and therefore inaudible to the human ear.

ULTRASTRUCTURE STUDIES : Study of fine structure of biological and industrial materials with the use of the electron microscope.

UNANI MEDICINE : It is a system of medicine based on the humoral theory which supposes the presence of 4 humours in the body; blood, phlegm, yellow bile and black bile. The unani system is the result of the fusion of diverse thoughts and experiences of nations and countries with an ancient cultural heritage like arabia, Egypt, India, Iraq, Iran and China. It originated in 4th and 5th centuries before christ.

UNCERTAINTY OF MEASUREMENT : Deals with calibration, testing, quality control, standards and production control.

UNDERGROUND GEOLOGY : See subsurface geology.

UNDERWATER ACOUSTICS : Study of the propagation of soundwaves in water.

UNIVERSOLOGY : Science of the universe.

UNIX : An operating system designed by bell labouratories for use with microcomputers and small business computers and widely adopted by many manufactures.

UPPPER ATMOSPHERIC AND PLANETARY ATMOSPHERIC PHYSICS : Branch of physics dealing with the study of the atmosphere of the planets and the atmosphere above the level of the planets.

URBAN AND RURAL COMMUNITY DEVELOPMENT : Study of the methods of development of urban and rural communities.

URBAN DESIGN : Preparing designs for cities and towns.

URBAN ECOLOGY : Study of environmental factors in urban life.

URBAN ECONOMICS : That branch of economics which applies the tools of economic reasoning to the analysis of economic activity in and the economic problems of cities and towns. Much of urban economics is concerned with analysing the pattern of location of economic activities in and between urban areas. Thus it has strong links with regional economics and with location theory.

URBAN ENGINEERING : Engineering concerned with creation of facilities for cities and towns like water supply, drainage, roads etc.

URBAN FORESTRY : Growing trees in appropriate places in cities and towns.

URBAN GEOGRAPHY : Branch of geography concerned with population, professions and occupations, life styles, urbanization, growth of urban areas, suburbs etc.

URBAN INFRASTRUCTURE : Concerned with development of roads, local trains, metro railway, transport, power etc.

URBAN PLANNING : See town planning.

URBAN WATER MANAGEMENT : Management of water supply lines to homes and industries, regulation of water supply in different localities depending on availability, facilities for purification of drinking water, construction of reservoir, overhead water tanks etc.

UROGYNECOLOGY : A branch of gynecology and urology which deals with the lower urinary tract and continence problems in women.

UROLOGY : Branch of medicine concerned with diseases of the urinary system.

UROSCOPY : The diagnosis of diseases by the inspection of urine.

V

VACCINOLOGY : Branch of science concerned with the design, development and manufacture of vaccines, their preservation, use etc.

VACUUM TECHNOLOGY : Management of devices which involve the use of vacuum like vacuum brake, vacuum guage, vacuum pan, vacuum tube etc.

VALUATION ENGINEERING : Branch of engineering concerned with the valuation of buildings, factories, industries, plant and machinery various types of constructions and other public and private assets, real estate etc.

VALUE ENGINEERING : Philosophy implemented by the use of a set of techniques, a body of knowledge and a group of learned skills for the identification of unnecessary cost.

VALVULAR DISEASES : Study of diseases of heart valves and their treatment.

VALVULOPLASTY : Surgical treatment of diseases of heart valves.

VASCULAR AND INTERVENTIONAL RADIOLOGY : The speciality includes image guided biopsy procedures for obtaining tissue samples for diagnosis, catheter drainage procedures, angiography of brain, kidney, liver and limbs of the body and angiographically assisted treatment procedures. It is highly useful for embolization procedures by blocking blood supply to tissues, tumors and other abnormalities to halt their growth and reducing bleeding on operation table.

VASCULAR SURGERY : Surgical treatment of diseases and defects of blood vessels which might be manifested in various forms.

VECTOR ANALYSIS : Vector is a quantity such as a velocity or a force which has direction as well as magnitude. Vector analysis is a branch of mathematics.

VECTOR BIOLOGY : Biological control of vectors and transmission dynamics of diseases.

VECTOR CONTROL AND ZOONOSIS : Study of methods of control of pathogen carrying insects and other biological agents and diseases transmitted to man through animals.

VECTOROLOGY : Study of disease germ carrying vector insects like mosquitoes.

VEDIC STUDIES : Study of vedas and their significance. Veda is the general name for the body of ancient sanskrit hymns with accompanying commentaries on which the brahmanical system is based.

VEGETABLE CROPS : Branch of horticulture concerned with growing vegetable crops. Also known as olericulture.

VEGETATIONAL PLANT GEOGRAPHY : A field of study concerned with the mapping of vegetation regions and the interpretation of these in terms of environmental or ecological influences.

VEGETATION AND ECOSYSTEM MAPPING : An art and a science concerned with the drawing of maps which locate different kinds of plant cover in a geographical area.

VEGETATION MANAGEMENT : The art or practice of manipulating vegetation such as timber, forage crops and wild life forms to produce a desired part or aspect of that material in higher quantity or quality.

VENDOR DEVELOPMENT : Localizing and development of components by providing technical support to the vendors. Interaction and co-ordination with research and development department on matters related to component development, identification and development of vendors based on quality, cost capacity. Development of alternate vendors etc.

VENEREALOGY : Branch of medicine concerned with sexually transmitted diseases like gonorrhea, syphilis etc.

VENTILLATION ENGINEERING : Branch of engineering concerned with the operation of supplying buildings, mines and other confined places with the necessary fresh air.

VENTRILOQUISM : The art of speaking by employing the vocal organs in such a manner that the voice appears to come not from the person but from some distance.

VERMICULTURE : Preparation of compost from organic waste material with the use of earthworms.

VERTEBRATE ZOOLOGY : Branch of zoology concerned with the study of vertebrate animals like fish, frogs, snakes, birds and mammals.

VETERINARY ANATOMY : Branch of veterinary science concerned with the anatomy of animals.

VETERINARY CLINICAL MEDICINE : Treatment of diseases of animals in a hospital

VETERINARY BIOCHEMISTRY : Branch of veterinary science concerned with the biochemical processes involved in the diagnosis and treatment of diseases of animals.

VETERINARY EPIDEMIOLOGY : Branch of veterinary science concerned with the study of the causes and methods of transmission of diseases of animals.

VETERINARY HISTOLOGY : Branch of veterinary science concerned with the histological study of the diseases of animals.

VETERINARY MICROBIOLOGY : Branch of veterinary science concerned with the study of the microorganisms causing diseases of animals.

VETETINARY PARASITOLOGY : Branch of veterinary science concerned with the study of parasitic organisms associated with animals.

VETERINARY PHARMACOLOGY : Branch of veterinary science concerned with the study of the effects and mode of action of drugs on diseases of animals.

VETERINARY PHYSIOLOGY : Branch of veterinary science concerned with the physiology of animals.

VETERNIARY PREVENTIVE MEDICINE : Branch of veterinary science concerned with the steps to be taken for the prevention of diseases of animals.

VETERINARY PUBLIC HEALTH : Branch of veterinary science concerned with the methods to be adopted for the protection of the wealth of animals like provision of clean drinking water, immunization, isolation of infected animals, keeping the surroundings clean etc.

VETERINARY SCIENCE : Branch of science concerned with the treatment and prevention of diseases, reproduction, artificial insemination etc. of animals.

VETERINARY SURGERY : Surgical treatment for diseases and injuries of animals.

VETERINARY TOXICOLOGY : Branch of veterinary science concerned with the study and treatment of problems caused by poisons and toxins to animals.

VICTIMOLOGY : Science concerned with doing justice for victims of crime and abuse of power; social, psychological, emotional and financial support to victims.

VIDEOGRAPHY : The art and technique of producing video pictures.

VINICULTURE : Branch of horticulture concerned with the technique of growing grape vine, including propagation, fertilizers, protection from pests and diseases pruning, hormone treatment etc. also known as viticulture.

VIROLOGY : Science concerned with the study of viruses.

VISUAL COMMUNICATION : Includes satellite communication, electronic communication, videography, press and T.V. journalism with language skills for creative programming.

VISUAL AND INTERNET PROGRAMMING : Branch of computer science and technology concerned with internet programming.

VITICULTURE : See Viniculture.

VOCAL MUSIC : Music performance involving singing either accompanied by instrumental music or not in contrast to only instrumental music.

VOCATIONAL COUNSELLING : Giving guidance and advice about vocational courses and opportunities available and suitable to individual needs, aptitude and capability.

VOCATIONAL EDUCATION : All activities in or out of school designed to contribute to occupational proficiency

VOCATIONAL TRAINING : The part of technical and commercial education devoted to training students in the skills required in their future occupations.

VOICE PRINT TECHNOLOGY : Identification of human voice on the telephone systems with an advanced speech recognition computer which understands what they say, at the same time analyses their voice print to verify the identity of the speaker.

VOICE TRAINING : Training the voice to give proper modulation and other qualities required for broadcasters, T.V. anchors and all others whose work involves the use of voice in a proper presentable form.

VOLCANOLOGY : Branch of geology concerned with the study of volcanoes.

VULGARIZATION : The art of making understandable to rural folk.

W

WAP : Acronym for wireless applications protocol. It enable us to integrate the internet with mobile telephony. It will move connectivity from conventional desk top P.C.'s to hand held cellular phones creating the foundation for mobile commerce.

WAR STUDIES : Multidisciplinary study of war, historical study, strategic problems, civil-military relations and ethical issues.

WASTE MANAGEMENT : Waste policy legislation and regulation, materials and energy recycling, waste minimization, waste water engineering, waste stablization, incineration and landfill disposal.

WATCH TECHNOLOGY : Technology of designing, developing, manufacturing and repairing watches, clocks and other chronometers.

WATER CHEMISTRY : Study of chemical composition of water, analysis of water to identify chemical and biological impurities and monitoring the quality of drinking water and water used in industries.

WATER ENGINEERING : Engineering pertaining to design and construction of water supply.

WATER MANAGEMENT : Branch of engineering concerned with measures to conserve and make proper use of water sources.

WATER MICROBIOLOGY : An aspect of microbiology that deals with the normal and adventitious microflora of natural and artificial water bodies.

WATER RESOURCES ENGINEERING : Branch of engineering concerned with exploration and utilization of water resources.

WATERSHED MANAGEMENT : Techniques intended to conserve ground water and rain water sources in arid areas.

WATER TREATMENT TECHNOLOGY : Physical, chemical and biological methods of purifying drinking water as well as waste water.

WAVE ACOUSTICS : The study of the propagation of sound based on its wave properties.

WAVEFORM ANALYSIS : The determination of the amplitude and phase of the components of a complex wave form, either mathematically or by means of electronic instruments.

WAVE MECHANICS : The version of non-relativistic quantum mechanics in which a system is characterized by a wave function which is a function of the coordinates of all particles of the system and time and obeys a differential equation, the Schroedinger equation. Physical properties are represented by differential operators which may act on the wave function and expectation values of measurements are equal to integrals involving the corresponding operator and the wave function.

WAX PATTERN MAKING : The art of making models and toys with wax.

WEAVING TECHNOLOGY : The technology of producing cloth or other textile fabrics from cotton, silk, wool or synthetic fibre.

WEB DESIGNING : Creating pages on the net. Basics of web design are HTML, XML, JAVA Script, DHTML, Microsoft, Front page, Macromedia Dream weaver, Adob photoshop etc.

WEB ENGINEERING : Creating web sites and hosting them on the net, internet technologies, Java programming, server technologies.

WEB JOURNALISM : Writing news reports, features, reporting events such as sports etc, for the web sites.

WEB MARKETING : Marketing through the internet customer service and support, advertising on the net and starting an online business venture.

WEB PROGRAMMING : Programming with CGI, JAVA, Visual Basic, Scripting ASP Technology.

WEB TECHNOLOGY : World wide web (WWW) programming, web tools, web administration, web transactions, web integrated data bases and e-commerce, web applications like web reservation systems, web information retrieval systems, web commerce applications and web integrated data base applications.

WEED SCIENCE : Science concerned with the description, distribution, and classification of weed plants and their eradication; it has a role in agriculture, ecology, public health etc.

WELDING ENGINEERING : The technique of joining together into firm union two pieces of metal by hammering or compression when raised to a high temperature. Extensively used in various types of engineering works.

WELFARE ECONOMICS : Branch of economics concerned with defining economic efficiency and analysing the conditions under which economic policies may be said to have improved social welfare.

WILDLIFE BIOLOGY : Study of life of wild animals in their natural habitat with particular reference to their food hunting habits, mating habits, reproduction, care of the young etc.

WILD LIFE FORENSICS : Wildlife identification and detailed documentation to build a case and testify in courts of cases of poaching violations.

WIND ENGINEERING TECHNOLOGY : The technology of producing electric power from high speed wind.

WINDOWS TECHNOLOGY : A form of split screen in computers where different applications can display their information independently on different areas of a visual display.

WIRELESS TECHNOLOGY : It is a general term applied to many technologies like wireless, internet, ultra wide band radio, mobile, wireless internet access etc.

WOMEN'S STUDIES : Such studies which are being usually undertaken with the aim of correcting the imbalance of what is seen as a male dominated society. They deal with the problems faced by women.

WOOD ANATOMY : Study of the internal structure of secondary xylem in dicotyledonous trees. It is of importance economically as a source of timber and biologically from the evolutionary point of view.

WOOD TECHNOLOGY : Seasoning. preservation, determination of quality of wood and its utilization for various purposes. Forms a part of forest science.

WORK DESIGN AND ERGONOMICS : Branch of management discipline concerned with the design of work in a particular area of work aimed at creating optimum conditions for efficient performance.

WORKER EDUCATION : Education and training of workers. Also called labour education.

WORK STUDY : Management discipline covering techniques such as method study and work measurement with the object of examining all aspects of a particular area of work to make it more efficient and economic.

WORK STUDY COURSE : Type of course developed in universities in which credits are given for work done off campus in social service agencies and local government or in industry.

WORLD ECONOMY : Study of the economic conditions, trends in economic and financial developments in different parts of the world and their mutual influences on one another.

WORLD HISTORY : History of world civilization, regions, governments and societies and politics of various countries.

WRITING AS A PROFESSION : Courses are offered in some universities to train prospective writers.

X

XML : Stands for extensible mark up language used in computers. It defines a universal standard for electronically exchanging data. World wide web consortium recommended the XML in February 1998 and is being widely and rapidly adopted as a standard for document and data exchange in a variety of markets. XML documents are self-describing, i.e., each document contains the set of rules to which its data must conform and these sets of rules can be reused to easily create the same class of XML documents.

X-RAY ASTRONOMY : The study of X-ray sources by rockets and balloons, in the earth's atmosphere and by satellites beyond it.

X-RAY CRYSTALLOGRAPHY : The use of X-ray diffraction to determine the structure of crystals or molecules.

XYLOGRAPHY : A process of decorative painting on wood.

Y

YOGA : 1. The Hindu ascetic doctrine of union of the believer's soul with the world-spirit, 2. A body of exercises known as asanas; recommended by more and more physicians as a means for increasing flexibility and energy and enhancing general health.

Z

ZOOGEOGRAPHY : Branch of zoology concerned with the geographical distribution of animals.

ZOOLOGY : The science which treats of the natural history of animals or their structure, physiology, classification, habits and distribution.

ZOO MANAGEMENT : Management of the well-being and needs of animals kept in zoos in contrast to wild life biology.

ZOOTOMY : That branch of anatomy concerned with the structure of lower animals.

ZYGOLOGY : Branch of science concerned with the study of natural and synthetic adhesives.

ZYMOLOGY : Science of fermentation.

ZYMURGY : Chemistry of fermentation processes.